D1529213

Gandhi's Philosophy and the Quest for Harmony

Anthony Parel affords an entirely new perspective on the philosophy of Mahatma Gandhi. He explores how Gandhi connected the spiritual with the temporal. As Parel points out "being more things than one" is a good description of Gandhi, and with these words in mind, he shows how Gandhi, drawing on the time-honored Indian theory of the purusharthas or "the aims of life," fitted his ethical, political, aesthetic and religious ideas together. In this way Gandhi challenged the notion which prevailed in Indian society that a rift existed between the secular and the spiritual, the political and the contemplative life. Parel's revealing and insightful book shows how far-reaching were the effects of Gandhi's practical philosophy on Indian thought generally and how these have survived into the present.

ANTHONY J. PAREL is Emeritus Professor of Political Science at the University of Calgary. His previous publications include *Gandhi: "Hind Swaraj" and Other Writings* (ed., 1997) and *Gandhi, Freedom and Self-Rule* (ed., 2000).

Gandhi's Philosophy and the Quest for Harmony

Anthony J. Parel
University of Calgary

CAMBRIDGE
UNIVERSITY PRESS

CAMBRIDGE UNIVERSITY PRESS
Cambridge, New York, Melbourne, Madrid, Cape Town, Singapore, São Paulo

Cambridge University Press
The Edinburgh Building, Cambridge CB2 8RU, UK

Published in the United States of America by Cambridge University Press, New York

www.cambridge.org
Information on this title: www.cambridge.org/9780521867153

First published 2006
Reprinted 2007

Printed in the United Kingdom at the University Press, Cambridge

A catalogue record for this publication is available from the British Library

ISBN-13 978-0-521-86715-3 hardback

For Tara and Peter, Kamala and Evan, Aidan, Asher, Caleb, Sasha, Aaron and Jacob.

Contents

Preface

As a thinker and a man of action, Mahatma Gandhi had always kept two great aims in view. All that he did for India and for the world are best understood when seen in the light of those two aims. The first was to demonstrate through his life and work that there was a basic harmony underlying all the fundamental human strivings – the strivings for wealth, power, pleasure, ethical goodness, beauty, and spiritual transcendence. In so far as they were grounded in the quest for truth and freedom, there was unity in their diversity. In an age that gives perhaps undue importance to the compartmentalization of life-issues, and to the resulting fragmentation of life-goals, Gandhi's approach was truly exemplary.

His second aim was to forge a moral link between the contemplative life and the modern secular life as it was lived in the fields of economics and politics. He sought to do this at a time in human history when modern economic and political theories, in concert with modern science, were presenting themselves as the master theories of human action, marginalizing spiritual values. Modern secularism seemed to be bent on making the same mistake that ancient spirituality had made. The mistake was to assume that the secular interests and spiritual aspirations could be pursued only at each other's expense.

Modern secularism seemed to him to place its complete faith in the assumed power of science, economics and politics to change people's lives and to move them forward to a better future. It seemed to ignore, perhaps even deny the need for a healthy spiritual life and for the public recognition of the sacred – to complement sound economics, wise legislation, free elections and fair adjudication. Hence its skepticism of, if not outright hostility towards, values that transcend science, economics, and politics. Gandhi's theory of the four purusharthas (the aims of life), with its focus on the need to bring a working harmony between the political, economic, ethical, aesthetic, and spiritual values, was meant to remedy what he saw as the malaise of modern secularism. He sought to end the historic hostility between material interests and spiritual aspirations. In today's world, he insisted, humanity could end this hostility only if people everywhere came to believe that science, politics and economics could solve some, but not all, of its problems.

And he had the right credentials to undertake this daunting task. Apart from the deep understanding that he had of his own traditions, he also had a sound grasp of the radically secular direction of much of modern thought. Rather than reject secularism, however, he sought to maintain a creative dialogue with it in the hope of arriving at a healthy common ground. In his view what the modern world needed most was a working harmony between secular pursuits and spiritual pursuits. Peace within the individual, and peace between states, between religions, and between civilizations depended, ultimately, on this harmony.

Indians, therefore, can and ought to learn from Gandhi the art of absorbing such modern economic and political values as they need without the fear of losing their identity and what is truly valuable in their cultural patrimony. They can also learn that bringing a balance between secularism and spirituality means, at the present time, the removal of the injustices under which the poor, especially the Dalits (the so-called Untouchables) suffer, the gender gap that still handicaps women, and the religious antagonism that still vitiates human relations. Gandhi's philosophy requires nothing short of the transformation of Indian society along these three lines.

The others, especially those from the West (from which Gandhi had absorbed so much) and from the world of Islam can also learn from him how to harmonize the secular and the spiritual in their own respective civilizations. He had little doubt that the gradual stifling of the yearning for the transcendent by modern Western civilization was a worse calamity for humanity than was the stifling of the secular interests by the ancient Eastern civilizations. The harmony that he was seeking to introduce was not only between the different civilizations of today, and between selected elements of the old and the new, but also between the secular and spiritual yearnings within the modern soul. Without seeking to resolve the spiritual crisis which individuals in all civilizations experience today, it was vain to attempt to resolve the outer crisis of "the clash of civilizations."

As this is a work heavily dependent on Indian philosophical vocabulary, I have used the following words without italicizing them: atman, artha, Dalit(s), dharma, kama, moksha, purusha, purushartha, satyagraha and swaraj. I have done this not without hesitation. However, I was greatly encouraged by the fact that the "Indian English Supplement" of the fifth edition of the *Oxford Advanced Learner's Dictionary of Current English* (1996) had recognized all the above-listed words, except purushartha.

How long it will take the last of these terms to be accepted as an English word is anyone's guess. Simon Winchester, the author of the delightful *The Meaning of Everything: The Story of the Oxford English Dictionary* (Oxford University Press, 2003), has described for us the process by which foreign words eventually come to be accepted by the English language. I hope that the way I have used this word in this work will contribute in a humble way to its eventual acceptance by the OED. Should that happen, it would indeed be a fitting tribute to Gandhi.

Acknowledgments

In writing this book I had received over the years very valuable help from friends and colleagues, and it gives me great pleasure to acknowledge it here. It will be obvious to anyone who reads this book carefully how much it owes to other scholars who have cultivated the Gandhi field so fruitfully. I mention with pleasure and gratitude the names of my friends Judith Brown, Margaret Chatterjee, Antony Copley, Dennis Dalton, Ashis Nandy, Thomas Pantham, Bhikhu Parekh, and Ronald Terchek.

This book had its origin in a series of lectures that I gave in Cambridge University in the Lent term of 1995, under the auspices of the Hinduja Institute of Indic Research. I am very grateful to Julius Lipner, the then director of that Institute, for arranging for the lectures and for his interest in my Gandhi research. Its final version was presented as a series of seminars at the Liverpool Hope University College in October 2004. I thank very warmly Gerald Pillay, the Rector, and Terry Phillips, the Dean of that College, for inviting me to their wonderful institution. The Calgary Institute for the Humanities of the University of Calgary was very generous in offering me a Senior Fellowship for the academic year 1995–96. I hereby express my deep appreciation to Jane H. Kelly, its then director. The financial assistance to meet the publication costs given by Douglas Peers, Associate Dean of Social Sciences, and the indexing assistance given by Anita Singh, a political scientist, both of the University of Calgary, are very gratefully acknowledged. During the years 2000–2005, Fred Dallmayr of the University of Notre Dame, Farah Godrej of Georgetown University, and the Comparative Political Philosophy group active in the annual meetings of the American Political Science Association have been very supportive of my ventures into the field of Gandhi interpretation. I take this opportunity to thank each one of these friendly colleagues.

Christopher K. Chapple's doctoral thesis, "The Concept of Will (Paurusa) in *Yogavasishta*," and his additional comments sent in writing were indispensable for my understanding of the philosophy of *Yogavasishta*. I record my gratitude for his help and permission to cite from his dissertation. Antony Copley of the University of Kent, John Sayer Martin of the University of Calgary, and Ronald Terchek of the University of Maryland went out of their way to find time to read an earlier version of this book. Their corrections, criticisms, queries, and suggestions helped greatly in the improvement of the text. The imperfections that remain are due entirely to my own limitations. To each of these friends I express my deep appreciation.

As always, Rolande has been very supportive of my seemingly endless preoccupation with Gandhi, for which I remain very thankful. Now that Gandhi belongs to the future generations, I dedicate this book to Tara and Kamala, my daughters, and their families – the generations nearest and dearest to me.

A rare studio photograph of Gandhi taken in 1931 in London at the request of Lord Irwin, Earl of Halifax, and Viceroy, 1926–1931. Copyright Vitalbhai Jhaveril Gandhi Serve, Berlin.

Part I

The four aims of life

Introduction

"The fact that I have affected the thought and practice of our times does not make me fit to give expression to the philosophy that may lie behind it. To give a philosophical interpretation of the phenomenon must be reserved for men like you."[1]

Harmony is the coming together of the different elements that constitute a coherent whole. Gandhi's philosophy is made up of different elements. That is why it has been interpreted from different angles. Some treat it primarily as a political theory. Others approach it as a religious philosophy of great contemporary relevance. Still others see it as an original theory of conflict resolution and non-violence. There are those who regard it as containing ideas extremely relevant for both economic development and for the maintenance of a sustainable economy. Finally there are those who find in it significant ideas on the relationship of art to society.

There is of course a great deal of truth in what these interpretations have to say. Taken individually, each gives an in-depth, but unavoidably partial understanding of the whole. The fact is that individual themes in Gandhi's philosophy make full sense only when they are seen in their relationship to one another and to the whole. It is the reality of this interaction that needs to be understood. It is not enough to juxtapose a series of different Gandhis – the political, the religious, the ethical, or any other. It is not enough to know that Gandhi teaches non-violence. To know his doctrine of non-violence really well one has to know how it interacts with his position on war or his theory of the state and the relations between states. Likewise it is not enough to know that he put his religious insights into socially and politically beneficial practice. To know his religious philosophy really well we have to know how it comports with secularism that he also professed. And so on with the other major

---

[1] M. K. Gandhi to S. Radhakrishnan, 16 September 1934, cited in S. Gopal, *Radhakrishnan: A Biography* (Delhi: Oxford University Press, 1989), p. 138.

themes of his philosophy. The point is that there is an inner dynamism that brings the diverse elements into a fruitful relationship with one another. And it is necessary to understand the nature of this inner dynamism if we are to understand his philosophy accurately and fully.

While specialists tend to focus on specific elements of Gandhi's thought, it is often the generalist – apart from the historian, of course – who catches a glimpse of the whole. This is the case, for example, with the assessment made by Sir Ernest Barker, a Cambridge political philosopher and a personal friend of the Mahatma. He saw different elements meeting in him and reinforcing one another. There was the St. Francis, "vowed to the simple life of poverty, in harmony with all creation and in love with all created things." There was the St. Thomas Aquinas, "able to sustain high argument and to follow the subtleties of thought in all their windings." And then there was the statesman, "who could come down from mountain tops, to guide with shrewd advice transactions in the valley." Finally there was the bridge that connected the Indian tradition of "devout and philosophic religion" and the Western tradition of "civil and political liberty in the life of the community." "The mixture was the essence." He could mix "the spiritual with the temporal, and could be at the same time true to both." "What he was to the world, and what he could do for the world, depended on his being more things than one."[2]

"Being more things than one" is a label that fits Gandhi well. Any study of his thought that aspires to be comprehensive is bound to expose the student to the comparative perspective that it provides. The ancient and the modern, the Indian and the Western perspectives jointly illumine the substance of his thought. The question is how the different elements come together and constitute a coherent whole. This book attempts to answer this question. It uses a framework of analysis that does justice to the basic unity of his practical philosophy. Gandhi was not a philosopher in the normal sense of that term, much less a system builder. But a philosophy does underlie his thought and actions. He was aware of this, though not willing to expound systematically the underlying philosophy. He wisely left the task of exposition and interpretation to the philosophers themselves. That was the point of his letter to Sarvepalli Radhakrishnan cited at the beginning of this Introduction.

This letter is of great value to every serious interpreter of Gandhi. For it tells us that non-philosophers like Gandhi often work from certain basic philosophic principles. The fact that he was not a philosopher in the

---

[2] Sir Ernest Barker, "Gandhi, as Bridge and Reconciler," in S. Radhakrishnan (ed.), *Mahatma Gandhi: Essays and Reflections on His Life and Work* (Bombay: Jaico, 1995), pp. 41–42.

formal sense need not therefore inhibit his interpreters from looking for the underlying philosophy. By the same token, there is no excuse for not looking for the philosophic underpinnings of his thought. In the history of human thought there have been several non-philosophers who produced important bodies of philosophical ideas. Machiavelli is a well-known example from the West. The crucial issue is whether in interpreting such thinkers we can find the right interpretive key, the key that fits the available data. I believe that in Gandhi's case such a key is available. It is the Indian theory of the purusharthas (the aims of life). Apart from opening the vast storehouse of Gandhian ideas, it also enables us to enter a truly Indian intellectual edifice.)

This theory is of course one of the foundational theories of the entire Indian civilization.[3] It underpins the basic ethics of the *Mahabharata* and the *Ramayana*. Without an understanding of this theory one cannot grasp the ethical nuances of the *Pancatantra*, that celebrated fictional counterpart to the *Arthasastra*.[4]

The concept of purushartha has three related meanings. First, it means any human striving. Secondly, it refers to human striving directed towards overcoming fate and karma. And thirdly, it refers to any one of the four canonically recognized aims of life, viz., dharma (ethics and religion), artha, (wealth and power), kama (pleasure), and moksha (liberation from *samsara*, the cycle of birth, death and rebirth).[5] The bulk of our argument will be taken up with the third meaning, even although the other two meanings also, as we shall see, will receive their due attention.

Etymologically the term purushartha, made up of purusha (spirit) and artha (for the sake of), carries the literal meaning of "that which is pursued for the sake of the spirit or the immortal soul." In Indian philosophical anthropology humans are seen as composites of body and spirit. It is the purusha that provides the spiritual and moral "foundation" (*adhistan*) to the human personality. Accordingly, human values are seen, ultimately, as those that are pursued for the sake of the purusha. Put simply, the pursuit of purushartha is what gives human activities their basic meaning and purpose. Not that the body and its interests do not have their own internal structure and relatively autonomous goals, but

---

[3] For a brief history of the concept of purusharthas see Gavin Flood, "The Meaning and Context of the *Purusharthas*," in J. Lipner (ed.), *The Fruits of Our Desiring: An Enquiry into the Ethics of the Bhagavad Gita for Our Times* (Calgary: Bayeux Arts, 1997), pp. 12–18.

[4] See Patrick Olivelle (trans.), *Pancatantra: The Book of India's Folk Wisdom* (Oxford: Oxford University Press, 1997).

[5] A. Sharma, *The Purusharthas: A Study in Hindu Axiology* (East Lansing, MI: Asian Studies Center, Michigan State University, 1982), p. 1, and Sir Monier Monier-Williams, *A Sanskrit-English Dictionary* (Oxford: Oxford University Press, 1899), p. 637.

that, in moral and philosophic terms, such goals acquire their full *human* significance only when they retain a reference to the immortal purusha. Any human pursuit that deliberately excludes a reference, however remote, to the purusha is considered *pro tanto* not beneficial to human well being.

It is no wonder that those who wish to understand the Indian civilization as a whole find in the theory of the purusharthas a very convenient tool for analysis and communication. For example, William Theodore de Bary's *Sources of Indian Tradition*, a well-known college text, uses "the four ends of man" as its framework of analysis of Indian thought.[6] Heinrich Zimmer's *Philosophies of India* does something similar.[7] He groups Indian philosophical thought under two headings: "philosophies of time" and "philosophies of eternity." Under the first heading he deals with the three "temporal" purusharthas of artha, dharma and kama. The masterworks of these purusharthas are, respectively, the *Arthasastra* of Kautilya, the *Dharmasastra* of Manu, and the *Kamasutra* of Vatsyayana. And under the second heading he deals with moksha, the fourth purushartha. Historically it received canonical recognition later than did the other three. But it soon acquired preeminence over them. As many as six systems of philosophy – Nyaya, Vaisesika, Yoga, Samkya, Mimamsa and Vedanta – were invented to do justice to this one purushartha. And, as if to underline the contemporary relevance of the theory, the Centre d'études de l'Inde et de l'Asie du Sud, Paris, has entitled its annual publication *Collectio Purushartha*.

The mutual relationship of the four aims

The question of the mutual relationship between the four aims has been one of the major methodological questions associated with this theory. Do they interact positively with one another or do they counteract each other? The question was raised in Indian classical thought, and it continues to be raised even today. The *Arthasastra*, for example, advises the good ruler to devote himself or herself equally to dharma, artha and kama, because they are morally "bound up with one another" (*anyonya-anubaddham*). Any one of the three, when indulged in excess, does harm to itself as well as to the rest.[8] If one's duty (*svadharma*) is pursued

---

[6] W. T. de Bary (ed.), *Sources of Indian Tradition* (New York: Columbia University Press, 1958), pp. 203–366.

[7] H. Zimmer, *Philosophies of India* (New York: Meridian Books, 1961), pp. 87–464.

[8] R. P. Kangle (trans.), *The Kautiliya Arthasastra* (2nd edn, Delhi: Motilal Banarsidass, 1997), bk. I, ch. 7, vv. 4–7, p. 14.

within the context of the balance achieved by the three mundane goals of life, it would lead to the transcendent goal of *svarga*, i.e., "endless bliss."[9] The *Dharmasastra* of Manu, in its turn, takes note of the different views held by its contemporaries. Some held that the chief good consisted in dharma and artha, others in kama and artha, and still others in dharma alone or artha alone. But the correct answer, according to Manu, was that it consisted of the aggregate of the three.[10] The aggregate of the three would lead to moksha.[11] Vatsyayana's *Kamasutra* also noted the existence of competing views on the subject. The prescribed procedure was that dharma should have precedence over artha, and artha over kama. However, there were exceptions, as in the case of kings, where artha should have precedence over the other two, just as in the case of courtesans, kama should have precedence over the rest. Vatsyayna's own advice was in favor of a balanced approach: "Undertake any project that might achieve the three aims of life, or two, or even just one; but not one that achieves the one at the cost of the other two."[12]

Adding moksha to the existing canon of three, the so-called triad – dharma, artha, and kama – created a problem of its own. It was that the triad was held by some to be unable to contribute directly to the attainment of moksha. The claims of the *sramanic* or the "renouncer" movements – Brahminical, Buddhist, and Jain – were largely responsible for this. We see the Buddha, the *sramana* (renouncer) par excellence, renouncing his princely status, and even family ties, for the sake of attaining nirvana. As a result, in Buddhism, as in ascetic Brahminism and Jainism, artha and kama came to be marginalized to the point of being treated as negative values. At best artha was conflated with dharma, as in the case of Asoka the Great, the Buddhist emperor. His famous edicts sought to establish the reign of dharma at the expense of artha.

The radical separation of moksha and nirvana from the other purusharthas had had disastrous consequences for Indian civilization taken as a whole. The achievements of Kautilya, for example, were rendered nugatory and, as a result, Indian political philosophy stagnated for nearly two millennia.[13] The great thinkers of India, including Sankara and

---

[9] Ibid., bk. I, ch. 3, v. 14. Kangle interprets the term "endless bliss" as meaning moksha, not just heaven. Ibid., p. 8, n. 14.

[10] W. Doniger and B. K. Smith (trans.), *The Laws of Manu* (London: Penguin, 1991), ch. 2, v. 224.

[11] Ibid., ch. 6, vv. 79, 81, and 85.

[12] W. Doniger and S. Kakar (trans.), *Vatsyayana Kamasutra* (Oxford: Oxford University Press, 2002), bk. I, ch. 2, vv. 14 and 15, and bk. 1, ch. 2, v. 41.

[13] For a brief analysis of the impact of the *sramana* movement on the purusharthas, see Flood, "The Meaning and Context of the Purusharthas," pp. 22–23.

Ramanuja, supported the ascendancy of moksha over all the other purusharthas.

The trend continued even after the nineteenth century, despite Raja Ram Mohan Roy's (1772–1833) effort to reverse it. Swaminarayan (1781–1830) and Ramakrishna Paramahansa (1836–86) lent their support to the world-renouncing and artha-devaluing approach to moksha.[14]

The ascendancy of moksha is so great that even today some of the major discussions on the relationship between the purusharthas often come down to a discussion of the relationship between dharma and moksha, as if the other purusharthas do not matter. For an example we need to look no farther than the debate between D. H. H. Ingalls and J. A. B. van Buitenen on the subject. Van Buitenen held dharma and moksha to be incompatible. Moksha was the release from the entire realm governed by dharma. The idea was that "the world and phenomena," being transitory, could never be an ultimately valid goal, that there was lesser truth in creation than in the principle or person from which creation originated.[15]

Ingalls on the other hand found dharma and moksha "to have been usually harmonized within one single religious path." The two arose in different milieus, and the majority of Hindus attempted "to harmonize" the two. To those who accepted the goal of moksha, it was a goal beyond dharma. The harmonizers regarded the two "as points along a single journey, a journey for which the viaticum was discipline and self-training."[16] The conflict was the exception rather than the rule. It was "the monastic disharmonizers," as Ingalls called them, (among them Nagarjuna, Sankara and Vallabha), who insisted on "the contradiction" between the two.[17]

In the late twentieth century, however, the scope of the discourse broadened to include all four purusharthas. But disagreements still persist on the question of whether the four constitute a system of oppositions or one of relative harmony. Louis Dumont and A. K. Ramanujan, for example, defend a theory of opposition.

Dumont, in his *Homo Hierarchicus*, first of all radically separates moksha from the rest. Even within the rest, i.e., the triad, a hierarchical relationship exists. Dharma, artha, and kama represent a hierarchy of ends – moral universalism, calculating egoism, and immediate satisfaction, respectively. Each is accorded legitimacy. At the same time, each is

---

[14] Sharma, *The Purusharthas: A Study in Hindu Axiology*, pp. 30–32.
[15] J. van Buitenen, "Dharma and Moksha," *Philosophy East and West*, 7 (1957), p. 37.
[16] D. H. H. Ingalls, "Dharma and Moksha," *Philosophy East and West*, 7 (1957), p. 46.
[17] Ibid., p. 48, n. 20.

opposed to the other, though not absolutely. A hierarchical opposition exists when an "inferior" goal is pursued only when a "superior" goal does not intervene. Thus, in case of conflict, kama should yield to artha, and artha to dharma. If this rule were followed, the triad would work as a system of hierarchical opposition. However, between the triad and moksha, no positive relationship is possible, as the latter requires the radical renunciation of the former. In the end, any attempt to bring together the four into a system will only mask the heterogeneity that exists between moksha and the rest.[18]

Dumont appears to be oblivious of Kautilya's principle of mutuality (*anyonya-anubaddham*), which should relate the four to each other. That is why he is forced to posit opposition where mutuality should prevail. This faulty concept of the relationship between the purusharthas forces him to make a faulty analysis of Gandhi's philosophy. He sees two Gandhis – the politician and the *sannyasi* (ascetic) – co-existing without any internal integration. It was as if the two Gandhis were unable to communicate with each other. To the British, Gandhi appeared to be a political representative of Indians, to the Indians he appeared to be a holy man.[19] At the root of this falsification of Gandhi is Dumont's inability to see what Gandhi was really attempting to do, namely to reconstitute the system of values of Indian civilization and to rehabilitate the principle of mutuality especially between artha and moksha.

A. K. Ramanujan, in his turn, favors what he calls a theory of "successive encompassment" to explain the internal relationship of the purusharthas. Dharma, artha and kama form "concentric nests" (*kosas* or sheaths) formed from the center – the individual. In so far as they are concentric nests they are relational in their values. The individual needs to follow them in succession. Moksha, however is not part of the system of nests, for it is "release from all relations." *Sannyasa* (the final stage in life), writes Ramanujan, "cremates" all one's past and present relations.[20] Moksha for him is pure isolation, *kaivalyam*. Once more, disharmony between values is the end result of this particular interpretation of the theory of the purusharthas.

---

[18] L. Dumont, *Homo Hierarchicus: The Caste System and Its Implications*, translated by M. Sainsbury, L. Dumont, and B. Gulati (rev. edn, Chicago: University of Chicago Press, 1980), pp. 271–74.

[19] Ibid., p. 328.

[20] A. K. Ramanujan, "Is There an Indian Way of Thinking?" in M. Marriott (ed.), *India Through Hindu Categories* (New Delhi: Sage, 1990), pp. 51, 54.

From opposition towards harmony

The need to go beyond the negative attitude fostered by these "dishar-monizers" is recognized by many Indian thinkers today. For them it is not enough to *restate* what the last two millennia thought of what the relationship of the triad to nirvana or moksha had been. For them it is necessary to rethink the whole theory of the purusharthas. No one has expressed the need for this with greater conviction and intellectual authority than has Pandurang Vaman Kane, the author of the monumental *History of Dharmasastra*. One of the general conclusions that he has reached is that the radical separation of the spiritual from the political, the economic from the ethical had cost Indian civilization dearly. He lays much of the blame at the feet of the *acharyas* (Indian religious philosopher-saints) for placing "too much emphasis on other worldliness and Vedanta," and for not placing "equal or greater emphasis" on the importance of the active life. He is saddened not to find an Indian Alberuni[21] in the eleventh century who would inquire into the reasons why Indians did not form a permanent state for the whole of India, why they did not develop manu-facturing and industries, and why they were unable to resist successfully external aggression. Indian intellectuals were mostly engaged in "mental gymnastics" about Logic, Vedanta, Poetics and similar subjects, giving little attention to the means of removing the weaknesses and the defects of the country's political and economic systems.[22] The starting point of such rethinking should include a new understanding of the meaning of the theory of the purusharthas.

Several students of Indian thought have contributed to this rethinking. The work of the philosopher R. Sundara Rajan has been quite innovative here. His knowledge of Western phenomenological thought enabled him to see the purusharthas as "modes of being in the world," or "the grounds of the possibility of our humanity." It is the purusharthas in their "simul-taneity" that distinguish us as human. To sunder one from the other is to negate it as a purushartha. Kama, for instance, without the other three would be animal impulse, but with them, it would be a form of being human. What makes kama a human value is its mediation by the other three.[23] And so on with the other three.

---

[21] Abu Rihan Muhammad Alberuni (973–1048), the celebrated Muslim savant who wrote a cultural history of India. For more information see chapter 2, note 12.

[22] P. V. Kane, *History of Dharmasastra*, vol. V (2nd edn, Poona: Bhandarkar Institute, 1977), part 2, pp. 1620–23. For his exposition of the meaning of the *purusharthas* see ibid., pp. 1626–32.

[23] R. Sundara Rajan, "The *Purusharthas* in the Light of Critical Theory," *Indian Philosophical Quarterly*, 7 (1979–80), p. 343.

Rajan also sees a connection between the purusharthas and constitutive reason. They are not apart from reason. They exemplify the fourfold way in which reason constitutes our humanity.[24] While each purushartha has its own "specific autonomy," each is at the same time "oriented" to the others; and it is this relationship to the other that makes each one of them a distinctly human orientation.[25] Each expresses the totality from the point of view of one of the purusharthas. The connection between them is not merely logical and empirical: "they have the kind of necessity which synthetic a priori connections have in the Kantian scheme."[26]

One outcome of this approach to the purusharthas is the rejection of any radical separation between moksha and the rest. Daya Krishna, for example, sees the need for "building a new theory of the purusharthas which would take into account the diverse seekings of man, and do justice to them."[27] In Mircea Eliade's view, the purusharthas are "integrative": an integrated life involves the pursuit of all the four goals.[28] Arvind Sharma recognizes the need of contemporary Hindu culture "to justify itself by the doctrine of the purusharthas; if it is found wanting in the area of artha, for instance, then it is to this area that creative thinkers within Hinduism must turn their attention."[29] Gavin Flood sees the relevance of the theory of the purusharthas not only for modern India but also for the modern world. It lies in "their recognition of pluralism and the tolerance which that recognition entails." The theory can also act as "cultural critique" of modern civilization, which seems to be too preoccupied with wealth, power and pleasure, and too little with art, aesthetics, and the spiritual life.[30] Klaus Klostermaier's comparative study of the ideas of liberation (moksha) in Sankara and emancipation in Jürgen Habermas, has enabled him to weigh the relative merits and defects of each of these thinkers. The defect in Sankara was to argue that liberation always and everywhere would require "uninvolvement" in the social, economic and processes in which the seeker after liberation found himself or herself. The defect in Habermas is to identify emancipation with emancipation from ideology and complete faith in science and modern psychoanalysis. What is needed is a broadening of the socio-economic base of the

---

[24] Ibid., p. 345.
[25] R. Sundara Rajan, "Approaches to the Theory of the *Purusharthas*: Husserl, Heidegger and Ricœur," *Journal of the Indian Council of Philosophical Research*, 6 (1988–89), p. 135.
[26] Ibid., pp. 137–38.
[27] D. Krishna, *Indian Philosophy: A Counter Perspective* (Delhi: Oxford University Press, 1991), p. 205.
[28] M. Eliade (ed.), *Encyclopedia of Religion* (New York: Macmillan, 1987), vol. VI, p. 345.
[29] Sharma, *The Purusharthas: A Study in Hindu Axiology*, p. 40.
[30] Flood, "The Meaning and Context of the *Purusharthas*," p. 26.

Sankarite liberation process and a deepening of the Habermasian emancipation project. As Klostermaier rightly points out, "Sankara seems to be clearer and more definite" on offering a "solution" to the human predicament. The depth which *atma-jnana* (self-knowledge) reaches surpasses that reached by psychoanalysis, referred to by Habermas.[31]

Klostermaier does not directly mention Gandhi in this context, but he does so indirectly in his criticism of Sankara. Whereas the latter isolated the pursuit of moksha from other human pursuits, Gandhi, to his credit, "considered his struggle for political and economic betterment of the masses as the only path to moksha available to him."[32]

But the philosopher who linked the new approach to the purusharthas directly to Gandhi was K. J. Shah.[33] Interestingly, Shah arrived at his new understanding of the working of the four purusharthas from a careful reading of the First Book of the *Arthasastra*. There, Kautilya discusses the nature of the four sciences – philosophy, revelation (the Vedas), economics and political science. These are not four unconnected sciences, for they constitute one science, the science of right living or the science of the human goals or the science of the four purusharthas interacting with one another.[34] To treat them as if they were independent of one another is to treat them incorrectly. Artha by itself would be greed, kama by itself lust, dharma by itself mechanical ritual, and moksha by itself escapism.[35] It is their harmony, achieved through their interaction, that makes them what they were supposed to be.

Shah's reading of Kautilya influenced his reading of Gandhi. Just as the former argued for mutuality between the four goals of life, so the latter actually demonstrated how mutuality could be realized. This explains why he made the bold claim that "the foundation of Gandhi's thought [was] the theory of purushartha."[36] Accordingly, a radical separation of moksha from the rest was not justified. The theory as Gandhi understood it, was applicable to individuals, nations, and civilizations. It was not

[31] K. Klostermaier, "Moksha and Critical Theory," *Philosophy East and West*, 35 (1985), p. 69.

[32] Ibid., p. 71, n. 15.

[33] Kantilal Jethabhai Shah (1922–94), who studied philosophy at Cambridge University under Wittgenstein, was professor of philosophy at Karnataka University, India. *Wittgenstein's Lectures on Philosophical Psychology, 1946–47*, was based on notes taken by him, P. T. Geach and A. C. Jackson.

[34] K. J. Shah, "Of *Artha* and the *Arthasastra*," in A. J. Parel and R. C. Keith (eds.), *Comparative Political Philosophy* (2nd edn, Lanham, MD: Lexington Books, 2003), p. 146.

[35] Ibid.

[36] K. J. Shah, "*Purushartha* and Gandhi," in R. Roy (ed.), *Gandhi and the Present Global Crisis* (Shimla: Indian Institute of Advanced Study, 1996), p. 155.

aligned to any particular theology or metaphysics. If it needed a theological grounding, Christian and Islamic theology could do as easily as could Hindu theology. He went so far as to assert that "it could be a Hindu religious theory but it need not be."[37] He writes: "If this kind of formulation is of any value, I suggest that this formulation would free us from the idea that Gandhi's thought is dominated by Hindu theory or Hindu thought."[38] It was a general theory of life, of human existence as such. That is to say, it could be treated as being free of any sectarian bias. Striving for wealth, power, pleasure, ethics, and transcendence was a universally observable fact in most cultures and in all periods of time. Though historically we find its first articulation in the Hindu culture, it was flexible enough to be transferred to other cultures, including the Western culture. Its potential for universality was in no way compromised by its origin in the Hindu culture.

The only defect that Shah found in Gandhi's approach was his restriction of the value of sexual pleasure to procreation. The original theory of the purusharthas did not place any such restriction. Here he did not follow the original insight of the theory.[39] However, he did recognize the importance of the arts and aesthetics to an integrated pattern of life, which, as Arvind Sharma rightly points out, came under the province of kama.[40]

Shah did not provide a detailed analysis of Gandhi's writings in support of his claim.[41] He was confident, however, that a "careful consideration" of Gandhi's "words" and "way of presenting" would prove him (Shah) to have been right.[42]

To conclude the foregoing discussion, the recent debates help us to place Gandhi in the proper historical and intellectual contexts. He belongs to the group of forward-looking thinkers who want to explore new ways in which the theory of the purusharthas might be made to work. The old ways have been discarded. As a result there is now a new Gandhian paradigm. It has a specific view of the universe and of human nature, as being composed of perishable body and imperishable soul. Above all, it has a new theory of the purusharthas. Whereas the old paradigm saw the purusharthas as working in mutually exclusive terms, the new paradigm shows how they may be made to work in interactive terms. The coordinated pursuit of all the purusharthas constitutes the new Gandhian paradigm.

---

[37] Ibid., p. 156.   [38] Ibid., p. 157.   [39] Ibid., p. 160.
[40] Sharma, *The Purusharthas: A Study in Hindu Axiology*, p. 40.
[41] He passed away not long after he presented the paper mentioned in note 36 above.
[42] Shah, "*Purushartha* and Gandhi," p. 157.

1   Gandhi's reconstitution of the four aims

> "I believe it is our duty to augment the legacy of our ancestors and to change it into current coin and make it acceptable to the present age."[1]

It was by innovating the theory of the purusharthas that Gandhi augmented the legacy of his ancestors and made it relevant to the present age. To innovate is to introduce something new into an existing state of affairs. He introduced several new things into the theory of the purusharthas. First, he removed the perceived gender bias from the concept. Second, he pointed out that the ability to pursue purushartha was unique to human beings, distinguishing them from all other living things. Third, he emphasized its role in overcoming fate and karma. Fourth, he gave the value of artha an unprecedented dignity and importance. And finally, he made the theory of the purusharthas the framework of his philosophy.

However, his approach to the theory was not systematic – not surprising, since he was a man of action, and not a philosopher. His approach was practical, depending on the intellectual needs that he faced from time to time. Our approach to him, however, is systematic. Accordingly, we start with a distinction between his treatment of the four canonical purusharthas on the one hand, and his redefinition of the concept itself, on the other. They address slightly different issues, although in the end they in unison constitute the whole theory.

To take his treatment of the canonical purusharthas first. Here we pass several milestones. In 1894, in an attempt to meet an intellectual crisis that he was experiencing in South Africa, he wrote his famous letter to Rajchandbhai, his spiritual advisor. The letter raised twenty-seven questions regarding such grave matters as the nature of the soul, God, moksha, the universe, avatars, etc.[2] As many as five of these questions were concerned with moksha, the fourth purushartha: what it was and

---

[1] M.K. Gandhi, *The Collected Works of Mahatma Gandhi*, 100 vols. (New Delhi: Publications Division, Ministry of Information and Broadcasting, Government of India, 1958–1994) (hereafter CW), 51: 259.

[2] CW, 32: 593–602.

how it might be attained. Rajchandbhai's answer was that moksha was the release of the soul from the state of ignorance and from its involvement with the affairs of the world. Mystical knowledge and withdrawal from the world were the chief means of attaining it.

Gandhi accepted the first part of the advice, but not the second, the part that required the withdrawal from the world. Instead of withdrawing from it, he sought to engage with it. He decided to plunge into the politics of South Africa – and the rest is history. This did not mean, however, that he had abandoned the pursuit of moksha as a spiritual goal. On the contrary, he deliberately reaffirmed his faith in it as the ultimate goal of life; but in doing so he chose, contrary to the advice, politics as the very means to it. That is to say, already by 1894 he had put the two purusharthas – moksha and artha – into a new dynamic relationship with each other. This was a major turning point in his intellectual life.

Rajchandbhai was disturbed by the fateful turn that Gandhi had taken. He went so far as to warn him – "for the good of his soul" – not to get too involved in the politics of Natal.[3]

At about the same time (late 1890s) Rajchandbhai had also supplied him with an important reading list. Included in it was *Yogavasishta*, a lengthy medieval philosophic poem.[4] It is an account of a fictional conversation between a despondent Prince Rama of Ayodhya and the ancient sage Vasishta. Rama was not sure that he could combine his kingly duties (which belonged to the field of artha) with the pursuit of moksha. Vasishta advised him that he could, provided he exercised his purushartha. The work contains some fifty-five stories, some fictional, others historical, to illustrate the various points made in the argument. The story of King Janaka of Videha, the father of Sita, Rama's wife, was one of them. Janaka successfully pursued the goals of both artha and moskha, without ever having to renounce the world.

More interesting, however, was the story of Queen Chudala of Malva. Her husband, the king, found it impossible to combine the duties of kingship and the pursuit of moksha. He, therefore, thought it best to renounce kingship, which compelled the queen to take over the administration. To everybody's surprise, not only did she rule well, but she also succeeded in pursuing moksha at the same time. The king was so

---

[3] B. R. Nanda, *Gandhi and His Critics* (Delhi: Oxford University Press, 1993), p. 143.
[4] V. L. S. Paniskar (ed.), *The Yogavasishta of Valimiki* (Delhi: Motilal Banarsidass, 1984). It is dated somewhere between the eleventh and the fourteenth centuries AD and consists of six books. Gandhi had definitely read the first book (CW, 32: 12), and the second book (CW, 39: 114). In 1911 we see him recommending the sixth book to his son Harilal (CW, 11: 94), and in 1933, the entire work was recommended for study to S. Gupta, a friend. (CW, 53: 469).

impressed that he felt confident enough to resume his kingly duties without fearing the danger of neglecting the pursuit of moksha. The point of the story was that neither gender difference nor kingship had to be seen as obstacles to the harmonious pursuit of the two purusharthas. There is no question that Gandhi received much encouragement from *Yogavasishta* in his own desire to harmonize the political and the spiritual.

But it was book II of this work, "the Mumukshu Prakarana" (On the Desire for Liberation), that had the strongest and lasting impact on Gandhi.[5] Its central theme was that moksha could be attained by the proper exercise of purushartha.[6] Purushartha was the defining attribute of human beings. One of the major obstacles that stood in the way of its proper exercise was the belief in fate (*daivam*). *Yogavasishta*'s position was that there was no such thing as fate, and that it existed only in the imagination of the weak and the indolent. Those who did not have the will to exercise their purushartha attributed their lack of success in life to an imaginary entity called fate. The fear of this imaginary entity paralyzed them psychologically. It was the aim of "the Mumukshu Prakarana" to free Rama from such fear and to teach him how to exercise his purushartha properly. A few passages give us the flavor of the argument:

Indeed, Rama, everything that is here in this world is obtained as a result of correctly applied effort and will. (II. 4. 8)

The effects of past karma can be erased by right action in the present:

Through exertion [purushartha], the prior will is quickly overcome by the present [will]. (II. 4. 17)

Without doubt, the evil consequences of the past are overcome by the attribute of the present; the aim of this is the destruction of yesterday's fault by today's merit. (II. 5. 12)

Having negated fate by continual reflection on the present, one should strive in one's self for a better life in this existence. (II. 5. 13)

It is sloth and the lack of purushartha that account for the miseries of this life:

It is due to sloth that this ground between oceans is full of poor and beast-like people. (II. 5. 30)

---

[5] For a critical study of the "Mumukshu Prakarana," see Christopher Chapple, *The Concept of Will (Paurusa) in Yogavasishta* (Ph.D. thesis, Fordham University, 1980). Citations from "Mumukshu Prakarana" are from Chapple's thesis.

[6] The term purushartha is used interchangeably with *paurusa* (free will), *puraskara* (human effort), *yatna* (effort), *prayatna* (great effort), in this work: Chapple, *The Concept of Will*, pp. 129–30.

Those who abandon their diligence and ascribe their circumstances to fate lose all dharma, artha, and kama and are their own enemy. (II. 7. 3)

There is no such thing as fate:

A man is born in this world, grows up, and ages. There is no fate seen here, only progression from childhood to old age. (II. 7. 23)

Liberation or moksha is the outcome of the proper exercise of purushartha:

One is to be released from the abyss of worldly existence by self-power [*swayam balat*]. Having resorted to will and effort, one is released just as a lion escapes from his cage. (II. 5. 15)

There are three powers to draw from: the *Shastras* [learned treatises], the teacher and one's self. Everything is due to one's exertion [purushartha], never fate. (II. 7. 11)

This world arises from the action of man. Thus, Rama, perform with great effort so as you go, you will not fear even the snakes in the trees. (II. 7. 32)

Historians of Indian philosophical thought have commented on the great importance that *Yogavasishta* gives to the notion of purushartha. The emphasis on "the power of human effort," Christopher Chapple writes, "is the hallmark" of this work. T. G. Mainkar, a specialist, has observed that the entire poem is "a vigorous plea" in favor of human effort. According to S. N. Dasgupta, the distinguished historian of Indian philosophy, *Yogavasishta*'s treatment of the relationship between karma and purushartha occupies a "unique" place in the history of Indian philosophy.[7]

Gandhi's approach to the relationship of artha to moksha is similar to *Yogavasishta*'s. However, as we shall see below, his treatment of the relationship of purushartha to fate is somewhat different. The important point to keep in mind, however, is that "the Mumukshu Prakarana" had a lasting impact on him.

1906 marks the next milestone. For it was in that year that he had taken the vow of celibacy. Celibacy, as we shall discuss in chapter 8 below, was his way of integrating or sublimating kama, the third purushartha. Here it is sufficient to note that he did not look upon celibacy (and therefore kama), in isolation from the other three purusharthas. For one thing, it had a dynamic relationship to the pursuit of moksha and dharma. There was nothing new in this as the ancient tradition had also held the same

[7] Cited in Chapple, *The Concept of Will*, p. 26. S. N. Dasgupta, *A History of Indian Philosophy*, vol. II (Delhi: Motilal Banarsidass, 1988), p. 256.

view. What was new, however, was that he placed celibacy in a dynamic relationship with artha as well. The efficacy of agency in the field of artha, he believed, depended on the degree of perfection of celibacy as self-discipline. This new insight into celibacy guided his political life for the rest of his life, especially in the last years, when he had to face such difficult social phenomena as the Hindu–Muslim conflicts, and such political opponents as M. A. Jinnah.

1909 marked an even more important turning point in Gandhi's life. It was in that year that he published *Hind Swaraj*. This work is of critical importance to the present inquiry in three respects. In the first place, it was in this work that he pointed out for the first time that a dynamic relationship ought to exist between the pursuit of swaraj as political free-dom and swaraj as spiritual freedom, for the pursuit of the one assisted the pursuit of the other.

Secondly, it was also in this work that he advocated that a moral link ought to exist between the arts and the political life. The point was made somewhat indirectly, by putting two works on art and art criticism in Appendix I of *Hind Swaraj*. They were Tolstoy's classic, *What is Art?* and Ruskin's "*A Joy for Ever*". The indirect message was that an understand-ing of these works was necessary for an understanding of the philosophy of *Hind Swaraj* taken as a whole. The pleasure derived from the arts made an important contribution to the quality of life lived in the political plane.

Critics have long recognized the importance of Ruskin and Tolstoy for the development of some of Gandhi's economic and political ideas. But for some unexplained reason they have failed to notice their influence on his aesthetic ideas as well. As we shall see later in chapter 9 below, an understanding of his thoughts on the dynamic relationship of the arts to political life is not possible without taking into account Ruskin's and Tolstoy's art theories.

Thirdly, we find *Hind Swaraj* using the concept of purushartha to assess the quality of civilizations. His well-known critique of modern civilization in this work is premised on such a use. What was wrong with modern civilization was that it had made "bodily welfare" its "object of life." The term used for "object of life" here is purushartha.[8] That is to say, modern civilization had a distorted view of what should constitute the object of life. It had excluded spiritual welfare as one of its objects. That was why it was becoming unduly secular and undermining its spiritual foundations. It had introduced a schism between the spiritual ends and the material ends of life. The similes that he used to describe it were

[8] A. J. Parel (ed.), *Gandhi: Hind Swaraj and Other Writings* (Cambridge: Cambridge University Press, 1997), p. 35. Hereafter *Hind Swaraj*.

revealing: it was like the Upas tree that poisoned everything that came under its shadow or like a disease that wasted the body-politic.

For all his criticism of modern civilization, he was not unduly pessimistic about its future. If it was a disease, it was a disease that could be cured. And the cure would consist of making its "object of life" more inclusive. If the pursuit of bodily welfare could be harmonized with the pursuit of spiritual welfare, all would be well with it. This was Gandhi's prognosis as found in *Hind Swaraj*.

We pass the next milestone in 1915, the year when the Sabarmati Ashram was founded. It was meant to be a nursery to raise a community of people committed to adopting the Gandhian paradigm. And the realization of that vision included the harmonious pursuit of the purusharthas. The Ashram's object was definitely political: "to learn how to serve the motherland one's whole life and to serve it."[9] Politics and economics were not "unconnected matters," being linked to dharma and moksha. The study of politics and economics was part of daily Ashram life.[10] Politics was "a part of our being," but "divorced from dharma" it had "absolutely no meaning."[11] That was the full implication of politics being a part of artha.

Celibacy was an important part of Ashram life, thereby underlining its dynamic relationship to the pursuit of politics, ethics, and spirituality.

If the Sabarmati Ashram gave the purusharthas an institutional expression, his analysis of the life of Gopal Krishna Gokhale, as found in his Foreword to *Gokhale's Speeches*, underlined how they could become part of the life of individual citizens. By any standard, Gokhale was an outstanding citizen – college professor, editor of the *Quarterly Journal of the Sarvajanik Sabha*, president of the Indian National Congress, member of the Bombay Legislative Council, the Viceroy's Executive Council, and the founder of the Servants of India Society. No wonder that Gandhi considered him his only "political guru."[12]

The secret of Gokhale's life was that he was able to put the purusharthas into a dynamic relationship within his own life. To begin with, he brought the pursuit of moksha and the political life into a close contact with each other. He had understood the cardinal point that the means chosen for the pursuit of moksha had to vary with the times. To be effective, it had to be "in tune with the times."[13] He realized that, at the present time, politics, economics and social reform were the best means to moksha. The old means – renunciation of the world – had therefore to

---

[9] CW, 13: 91.   [10] Ibid., p. 95.   [11] Ibid., p. 134.
[12] CW, 14: 199. In translating the Foreword I have relied on the Gujarati original.
[13] Ibid., p. 201.

be abandoned. The old way of observing dharma also had to be discarded. Though he never pretended to observe rituals associated with dharma, he was "wise in the truth of the Self," and "his life was full of the true spirit of dharma."[14]

The Foreword also underlined the exemplary aspect of Gokhale's life for every Indian. If he could successfully put the theory of the purusharthas into practice, so could others. "No Indian who aspires to follow the way of true dharma can afford to remain aloof from politics ... one who aspires to a truly religious [*dharmic*] life cannot fail to undertake public service as his life mission."[15]

And if the theory of the purusharthas could be put into practice on a national scale, the quality of Indian politics would improve perceptibly. Politics would no longer be regarded as the struggle for power and domination, it would come to be regarded as means of achieving the public good as well as individual well-being. It would certainly become less violent and more just. Here, allowing his political imagination free rein, he saw a similarity between the ideal envisaged by his theory of the purusharthas and that envisaged by the ancient Hebrew prophet Isaiah – "an ancient seer." The Foreword ended with a paraphrase, in Gujarati, of the famous lines from Isaiah: "And they shall beat their swords into plowshares and their spears into pruning hooks; nation shall not lift up sword against nation, neither shall they know war any more ... The wolf and the lamb shall feed together and the lion shall eat straw like the bullock."[16] Gokhale's ideal of life, the Foreword concluded, "was to labour to bring about this state of affairs."[17]

The autobiography and the *Gita*

Arguably, the best-known statement on the dynamic nature of the relationship of politics to moksha is found in his autobiography (1925–29). The pursuit of moksha is now identified as the pursuit of Truth. "What I want to achieve – what I have been striving and pining to achieve these thirty years – is self realization, to see God face to face, to attain moksha. I live and move and have my being in pursuit of this goal. All that I do by way of speaking and writing, and all my ventures in the political field [artha], are directed to this same end."[18] The telos of the pursuit of moksha is the attainment of Truth, and his life, taken as a whole, is a series of experiments with truth. Most importantly, the Introduction speaks of the exemplary character of these experiments: "what is possible

---

[14] Ibid.   [15] Ibid.   [16] Ibid., p. 202; Isaiah 2: 4 and 65: 25.
[17] Ibid.   [18] CW, 39: 3.

for one is possible for all."[19] The theory of the purusharthas, as he interprets it, has universal application.

The Conclusion to the autobiography confirms the claims made in the Introduction. Those who aspire to moksha "cannot afford to keep out of any field of life. That is why my devotion to Truth has drawn me into the field of politics."[20] To maintain the dynamic relationship of moksha to artha, one needs the support of dharma as well. That was why those who say that dharma had nothing to do with politics did not know what dharma meant.[21] That was not all: the pursuit of moksha understood in this way involved a continuous process of self-purification, which brought into the picture celibacy too.[22] Thus the autobiography begins and ends with a reminder that the purusharthas should act in unison.

However, the most important statement of the subject of the purusharthas is found in his translation of the *Gita* (1931). Its Introduction makes two points very clear: the first is that his interpretation of the purusharthas is going against the traditional interpretation. The second was that it had the full support of the *Gita*.

The common belief is that dharma and artha are mutually antagonistic to each other. 'In worldly activities such as trade and commerce, dharma has no place. Let dharma operate in the field of dharma, and artha in that of artha' – we hear many secular [*laukik*] people say. In my opinion, the author of the *Gita* has dispelled this delusion. He has drawn no line of demarcation between moksha and worldly pursuits.[23]

Elsewhere in the translation he calls purushartha the effort that one makes to attain moksha.[24] And purushartha, understood in this sense is inherent in every human being.[25]

To conclude the foregoing discussion, the quest for the truth about moksha, begun in 1894, formally ended in 1931. In the process he was able to establish that a dynamic relationship existed between all the four purusharthas. The Gandhian paradigm had now acquired its basic features.

A redefinition of the concept

We now turn to Gandhi's attempt to redefine the concept of purushartha. A redefinition was needed, he felt, in order to counteract the popular perception that it applied only to men and that it excluded women. There was of course no philosophic justification for this, and he wanted to do

---

[19] Ibid.   [20] Ibid., p. 401.   [21] Ibid.   [22] Ibid., p. 402.
[23] CW, 41: 98. I have followed the Gujarati text here, as found in M. K. Gandhi, *Anasakti Yoga* (Ahmedabad: Navajivan, 1975), p. 23.
[24] Gandhi, *Anasakti Yoga*, p. 18.   [25] Ibid., p. 11.

something about it. Writing in July 1930 from Yeravda jail, he asked for help from one of his female disciples. "The word purushartha is one-sided in its connotation. Can you think of a neutral word?"[26] It is not known what answer, if any, she was able to give. But we do know that within two weeks he had found an answer. In his letter to Narandas Gandhi, he was able to redefine the concept: "To understand an ideal and then to make a Herculean effort to reach it, no matter how difficult it is, this is purushartha."[27]

The desire to rescue the concept from its gender bias made him explore the matter further. He started with the philosophical anthropology underlying the concept. Humans were body-spirit (purusha or atman) composites. *Gita* V: 13 compares the body to a city – "the city with nine gates" – in which dwells the spirit.[28] Spirit being gender-neutral, things done for its sake could have nothing to do with the gender of the doer. "The word purusha should be interpreted in its etymological sense, and not merely to mean a man. That which dwells in the *pura*, the body, is purusha. If we interpret the word purushartha in this sense, it can be used equally for men and women."[29]

The second thing that Gandhi did with the concept was to make it the *differentia specifica* of human beings. In the West reason was thought to differentiate humans from brutes. Gandhi went one step further to suggest that it was the purusha that separated humans from other living things. Spiritual differences were deeper than rational differences. No brute could ever aspire to moksha. Their activity could never rise to the level of purushartha. "Our only right is to purushartha," he commented. "We can strive and work. All human beings, and animals too, struggle. The only difference is that we believe that behind our struggle there is an intelligent purpose."[30] That purpose transcended the material and the temporal. That purpose was not realized by securing only the bodily welfare. It would be realized only when we realized the welfare of the purusha that dwelt in us. Human activity rose to the level of purushartha only when the interests of the purusha were consciously present in it. "Only effort aimed at the welfare of the atman can be described as purushartha. It has been described as the supreme purushartha. All else is futile expenditure of energy."[31]

---

[26] M. K. Gandhi to Premabehn Kantak, 28 July 1930, CW, 44: 52.

[27] M. K. Gandhi to Narandas Gandhi, 12 August 1930, CW, 44: 80.

[28] R. C. Zaehner (trans.), *The Bhagavad-Gita* (Oxford: Oxford University Press, 1973), 5: 13, p. 208: "[And so,] all works renouncing with the mind, quietly he sits in full control – the embodied [self] within the city with nine gates." The nine "gates" refer to the nine apertures of the human body.

[29] CW, 44: 80.   [30] CW, 32: 350.

[31] Ibid., p. 351. Gandhi here uses the term atman interchangeably with purusha.

Humans then may be redefined as entities that pursue purushartha. Not to serve the interest of the purusha in their strivings is to rob them of their fundamental humanity. Thus the pursuit of wealth or power or pleasure for its own sake, without any reference, however indirect, to the spiritual elements embedded in them, is to pursue them imperfectly. Certainly, wealth should be valued, but not for its own sake, but for the sake of the whole person and the community at large. When it is valued for its own sake, it becomes harmful to human well-being. The same is true of power and pleasure as well. "The truth about ourselves is that we strive for the supreme purushartha and know how to seek the means for it."[32]

In the philosophical anthropology under discussion, an initial struggle between the interests of the body and the aspirations of the soul is taken for a fact, though not for the norm. The fact that purusha is the foundation of personality does not mean that human actions will always meet the standard expected of them. More often than not humans fail to meet the expected standard. The interests of material existence often trump the interests of spiritual life. Yielding to material interests without proper regard to the spiritual interests is reckoned as a human weakness. Hence the notion that purushartha is the inner power by means of which humans overcome themselves. To use his own words: "Our purushartha lies in striving to overcome whatever weaknesses we see in ourselves."[33]

Purushartha, karma, and fate

Arguably, the most important contribution that Gandhi makes to our understanding of the concept of purushartha concerns its relationship to karma and fate. The struggle between free will and fate/destiny (*bhagya*) is perhaps the most difficult inner struggle that humans experience. *Yogavasishta*, as we saw, had alerted Gandhi to this. However, his approach to this struggle was somewhat different from *Yogavasishta*'s. Before we point out where the difference lay, let us first identify Gandhi's position. He identified it in the following four statements:

1. In one sphere, Fate is all powerful, and in another purushartha. Purushartha means striving, and supreme purushartha means escaping from the pairs of opposites.[34]
2. Fate is the fruition of karma. Fate may be good or it may be bad. Human effort [purushartha] consists in overcoming the adverse fate or reducing its impact. There is continuous struggle between fate and human effort [purushartha]. Who can say which of the two really wins?

---

[32] Ibid.   [33] CW, 38: 64.   [34] CW, 32: 360.

Let us, therefore, continue effort [purushartha] and leave the result to God.[35]

3. Between destiny [*bhagya*] and human endeavor [purushartha] there is an incessant struggle. Let us continue to endeavor [purushartha] and leave the result to God.[36]

4. Let us not leave everything to destiny [*bhagya*], nor be vain about our endeavor [purushartha]. Destiny will take its own course. We should only see where we can intervene or where it is our duty to do so, whatever the result.[37]

It is evident that Gandhi saw the question of the struggle between fate and purushartha in the context of the law of karma. According to the latter, action had consequences that could not be escaped.[38] Fate, he pointed out, was the fruit of karma. Accumulated karma acted as fate here and now. Fate may be good or it may be bad. The struggle is with bad fate only.

Gandhi believed that the law of karma operated in a universe subject to divine guidance. God's grace could therefore cancel the results of bad karma. That is to say, God's power was superior to that of karma – a position consistent with his theistic orientation. On this point he differed from *Yogavasishta*, which relied solely on human effort.

A byproduct of his speculations on the relationship of purushartha to karma and fate was that purushartha could overcome caste-related disabilities too. If only the Dalits could activate their purushartha, nothing in the world, neither fate nor karma nor caste, could prevent them from achieving their full potential. Purushartha, then, was the key not only for overcoming fatalism but also all forms of social disabilities. If India remained poor, it was because Indians did not exercise their purushartha in the field of economics. What Indians needed most was a renewal of their faith in the power of purushartha.[39]

Gandhi meets with passive resistance

Gandhi's effort to present the purusharthas as a dynamic system of human ends met with resistance from some Indians. This was not

---

[35] CW, 79: 258. M. K. Gandhi to G. Gurbaxani, 16 March 1945. He had asked Gandhi the following question: "What is fate and how is it related to human effort?" (ibid.). The Gujarati term used for fate is *bhagya*.

[36] CW, 79: 433; from "A Thought for the Day" for 16 March (1945).

[37] Ibid., from "A Thought for the Day" for 17 March (1945).

[38] For an excellent analysis of the doctrine of karma, see Julius Lipner, *Hindus: Their Religious Beliefs and Practices* (London: Routledge, 1994), pp. 230–47.

[39] CW, 15: 200.

surprising, given the millennial hold that the old theory had on people's habits and outlook. His view on artha, that it could not be opposed to kama, dharma, and moksha,[40] was especially difficult to accept. And the resistance sometimes came from totally unexpected quarters. I mention two, one coming from Mahadev Desai, his secretary, and the other from Bal Gangadhar Tilak, the highly respected leader of the extremist wing of the nationalist movement and a major commentator on the *Gita*.

Desai's debate is recorded in his *Secretary's Diary*.[41] He could not see how Gandhi could posit a necessary connection between artha and moksha. He believed that one could successfully pursue moksha regardless of the prevailing social, economic, and political conditions. Moksha concerned only the purusha or atman within. The question was posed as follows: "Would the man who understands that the Indweller [purusha] is apart from the body and who lives a life consistent with his knowledge, ever be swept off his feet by the infatuation of driving back the invading hordes of foreigners?"[42]

Gandhi could not see how earnest seekers after moksha could remain indifferent to the social evils around them. If they were to remain indifferent, there must be something wrong with their notion of spirituality. Even though moksha was the liberation of the purusha, the person who achieved it was a social being whose activities, including spiritual activities, linked him or her with other social beings. The process of attaining moksha had therefore a definite social dimension. It was "impossible" for an actual pursuer of moksha to remain an "unaffected witness" of the social evils around.

Gandhi and Desai agreed to disagree at this point (the debate took place in 1918, in the early days of Desai's life as secretary). However, in later years he came around to see things in Gandhi's way. But this debate is instructive in as much as it gives us an idea of the difficulty that the Gandhian paradigm faces, at least initially, even among Indians.

At the centre of the debate with Tilak was the question whether artha and moksha were compatible with each other. Rephrased, the question was whether "holy men" (*sadhus*) should engage in politics. Tilak implied that they should not, for politics was "a game of worldly people, not of *sadhus*."[43] Its maxim, according to him, was "return wickedness for wickedness." And he believed that there was sanction for this view in

---

[40] CW, 81: 402.
[41] See M. D. Desai, *Day-to-Day with Gandhi: Secretary's Diary*, vol. I (Varanasi: Sarva Seva Sangh, 1968), pp. 181–82.
[42] Ibid., p. 181.   [43] CW, 16: 490–91, n. 2.

Gita IV: 11: "In Whatever way [devoted] men approach Me, in the same way I return their love."[44]

Gandhi took Tilak to task for adopting what looked to him as a thoroughly modern view of politics – politics as an autonomous activity, in which everything was permitted. Such an approach, he pointed out, could only result in the corruption of politics. And he rejected Tilak's interpretation of *Gita* IV: 11, too. "If it be true that God metes out the same measure to us that we mete out to others, it follows that if we would escape condign punishment, we might not return anger but gentleness even against anger. And this is the law not for the otherworldly but for the worldly."[45] Besides, the theory of purushartha required that spiritual values be brought to bear on mundane issues as well: "The epitome of all religions is to promote purushartha, and purushartha is nothing but a desperate attempt to become a *sadhu*, i.e., a gentleman in every sense of that term."[46]

Gandhi's point was that the old distinction between saints and worldly people had lost its meaning. Now it appeared that everyone had a calling to be saints, just as everyone had a calling to be citizens. It is old-fashioned to think that some had a monopoly on moksha while others had a monopoly on politics.

Both Desai and Tilak were defending the old theory while Gandhi was attempting to introduce a new paradigm.

And if resistance to it in India came from the defenders of the old school, it is important to remember that resistance to it in the West comes from the promoters of the new theory that politics is struggle for power and nothing else.

Gandhi's theory of the purusharthas presents a challenge to all those who deny that a dynamic relationship can exist between all the basic human strivings. At the same time, it offers great encouragement to all those who see a basic unity in those very same strivings.

Conclusion

We have now traced the various steps that Gandhi took in his attempt to reconstitute the four purusharthas. Their reconstitution has resulted in the emergence of the Gandhian paradigm. That theory is not something that is imposed on his philosophy but something that underpins it. The rest of this book attempts to substantiate this claim by examining the available data. The outcome of that examination, it is hoped, will contribute towards a paradigm shift in Gandhi studies.

---

[44] Ibid.   [45] Ibid., p. 491.   [46] Ibid.

As the citation at the head of this chapter indicates, the aim of Gandhi's practical philosophy was to create a new legacy in place of the old. He used the theory of the purusharthas to accomplish it. The result is it has become the framework of analysis of his basic ideas. Purushartha, taken in the singular, refers to the inner spiritual power that is present in all human beings. When rightly exercised it can not only overcome all human weaknesses, even fate, but also enable humans to achieve transcendence. Taken in the plural, they refer to the four goals pursued by individuals and cultures. The two meanings taken together constitute Gandhi's theory of the practical.

Part II

Politics and Economics

Politics and Economics (artha) are taken up first because of the new importance that Gandhi attached to them for life in the modern world. Historically, the rise of the renouncer (*sramanic*) movement compromised the importance of artha. Gandhi reversed this trend and restored to artha its due place in the scheme of the four purusharthas.

As a purushartha, artha represents a positive human value and contributes to the material well-being of humans. Only when it is pursued for its own sake, in isolation from the other purusharthas, does it become harmful to humans. What saves self-interest from becoming harmful is precisely its grounding in purushartha.

Gandhi's thoughts on politics and economics were focused on three issues: nationalism, the state, and the economy. The creation and maintenance of a good politico-economic order was humanity's most important secular task. Those who interpret Gandhi as a utopian or as an anarchist may want to pay special attention here.

2   Civic nationalism

"Non-violent nationalism is a necessary condition of corporate or civilized life."[1]

It is axiomatic in political philosophy that the values of artha – wealth and power – can be realized only in a stable political community. Already Kautilya had understood this when he defined the science of artha as that which secured the means of acquiring, preserving, and expanding "a land inhabited by a people."[2] "A land inhabited by a people," or a people living in a specific territory, was his conception of the political community. For Aristotle the political community was the *polis*. For the ancient Romans, it was the republic. For others it was the kingdom or the empire. The nature of the political community has changed over the centuries. Today the nation is the political community par excellence for most peoples around the world.

Gandhi had wholeheartedly embraced the modern idea of nation, albeit a non-violent nation. In this respect, as in some others, he was definitely a modern. Under the impact of modern ideas, the traditional Indian notion of the political community based on hereditary monarchy had lost its credibility and legitimacy. India found itself in a process of evolving from monarchy to nation via colonialism.

His conception of nation was heavily influenced by the civic or liberal notion of nationalism, notably that of Giuseppe Mazzini. *Hind Swaraj* devotes a whole chapter to "Italy and India": Mazzini's manner of unifying Italy is held out to be a model worthy of emulation. His *Duties of Man* is given the honor of being listed in the Appendix to *Hind Swaraj* for study and reflection. Without a national identity, Indians would remain, to use Mazzini's phrase, "the bastards of humanity." The nationalism implicit in *Duties of Man* is built on the idea of the individual as the ultimate unit of the nation. The civic nation exists to protect and enhance the individual.

---

[1] CW, 25: 369.   [2] R. P. Kangle, *The Kautiliya Arthasastra*, 15. 1.2.

Paradoxically, the Raj itself contributed towards the evolution of the concept of Indian nation. One of the conditions necessary for a nation, as noted, is a definite territory. That territory in modern India's case was the creation of the Raj. It was an act of the British Parliament that in 1899 defined the exact territory of modern India.[3]

Gandhi's intellectual integrity in recognizing this fact was exemplary. As he mentioned to Sir Samuel Hoare, the Secretary of State for India, creating a territorial unit out of India was "really the big thing" that the Raj had done for India.[4] As late as June 1947, he reminded Indians of this fact: "It was only when the English came that for the first time the country became one from Dibrugarh to Karachi and Kanya Kumari to Kashmir."[5] Only three days before his assassination he came back to the same idea: "Britain had made of India a political whole and India must continue as such."[6]

Some of the imperial historians also contributed to the formation of Gandhi's thought on nationalism, though in a negative way. Sir John Seeley, for example, had ventured the notion that India was no nation at all but only a geographic expression, like Italy.[7] Gandhi reacted to such assertions rather sharply, which explains why his early writings on Indian nationalism sometimes took on a polemical tone. "The English," he reminds the readers of *Hind Swaraj*, have a habit of writing about the history of other nations. "They write about their researches in most laudatory terms and hypnotize us into believing them. We, in our ignorance, then fall at their feet."[8] "The English have taught us that we were not one nation before. This is without foundation. We were one nation before they came to India."[9]

Indian sources naturally contributed in a positive way towards the formation of Gandhi's notion of the nation. Here, surprisingly enough, he credited the ancient *acharyas* – philosopher-saints – for being India's first "nation-builders." It is remarkable that he did not mention the role of kings and emperors. In fact he was highly critical of the role that the rajahs and maharajas had played in Indian history. Their "tyranny," he asserted, was greater than that of the English.[10]

The *acharyas*, by contrast, played a positive role. For example, they established places of pilgrimage in the four quadrants of the country – Badrinath in the north, Sringeri in the south, Puri in the east and Dwarka

---

[3] Cited in S. Khilnani, *The Idea of India* (London: Hamish Hamilton, 1997), p. 155.
[4] F. Watson, *The Trial of Mr. Gandhi* (London: Macmillan, 1969), p. 214.
[5] CW, 88: 151. Similar sentiments expressed in CW, 88: 350.   [6] CW, 90: 504.
[7] J. R. Seeley, *The Expansion of England* (London: Macmillan, 1883), p. 257. That Gandhi had read Seeley is evident from CW, 1: 285, and CW, 3: 462.
[8] Parel, *Hind Swaraj*, p. 56.   [9] Ibid., p. 48.   [10] Ibid., p. 76.

in the west. His claims on their behalf were sometimes quite imaginary. Their intentions in this regard, he claimed, were not so much religious as social. Religious worship did not require long-distance travel. However, these "leading men" or these "far-seeing ancestors of ours," as he called them, thought otherwise. "They knew that worship of God could have been performed just as well at home." Yet they traveled throughout India, "either on foot or in bullock carts," and learned one another's languages. They did all this because "they saw India as one undivided land, so made by nature. They, therefore, argued that it must be one nation. Arguing thus they established holy places in various parts of India and fired the people with the idea of nationality in a manner unknown in others parts of the world."[11] The use of the word "nationality" here may be a little far-fetched, but the idea is that the *acharyas* did play a role in creating an awareness among Indians that transcended their particular region.

Gandhi found a second tool in the Indian sources that helped him greatly to articulate his nationalist thought. I refer to the term *praja*, which he consistently uses in *Hind Swaraj* (for example), for the term nation. *Prima facie*, Gandhi's claim that India was a nation before the British came on the scene sounds anachronistic, to say the least. For everyone knew that nationalism had its origin in the eighteenth century in Europe, whence it radiated to other parts of the world including India. How then could he assert that India was a nation before that date? The charge of anachronism is legitimate until we pay attention to the Gujarati word that he used for "nation" – *praja*.

In Gujarati, as in other Indian languages, *praja* is a civic term, meaning the subjects of a rajah. India had always had rajahs and to that extent Indians had always been a *praja*. The idea of *praja* was well suited for Gandhi's purpose: it transcended such pre-political identities as caste, religion, language, region and the like. Thus a Hindu king could have as his subjects (*praja*) Hindus as well as Muslims, Sikhs, Christians, Buddhists, Jains, Parsis, and Jews. They were all equally his subjects. What Gandhi has done to the term, however, is to invest it with a new, modern meaning – that of nation. Additionally, it also suited his idea of civic nationalism – being neutral in regard to religion, race, language and other particularities.

From a historical perspective Gandhi's claim that Indians in the past had something of a sense of common identity was not far-fetched at all – whatever Seeley and others might have thought. For we find Alberuni, writing in the eleventh century, speaking of the whole of India,

---

[11] Ibid., pp. 48–49.

Bharata-Varsha, as an *oicumene* – a self-conscious, civilizational unit. It was composed, he informs us, of nine different regional parts, called Nava-Khanda-prathama.[12] This *oicumene* had a common worldview, a common way of organizing social life, a common political thought. The civilizational community mentioned here could form only part of the basis of the future national community. The "four sites argument," being based on a pre-Muslim notion of India, needed the necessary adjustment to a post-Muslim India, an issue that Gandhi takes up later in his argument. Alberuni also spoke of the places of pilgrimage such as Kailasa, Benares, Multan, and Kashmir, as well as the names of famous temples such as Somnath.[13]

Has Islam unmade the nation?

The *praja* that Gandhi spoke of applied, no doubt, to the pre-Muslim period of Indian history. The question now arises as to whether one could still speak of an Indian *praja after* the coming of the Muslims? In raising this question he acknowledged that the Muslim question was the fundamental question of modern Indian nationalism. "You have described to me the India of the pre-Mohamedan period," the Reader in *Hind Swaraj* observes, "but now we have Mohamedans, Parsees, and Christians. How can they be one nation?"[14] Hindus and Muslims are "old enemies." Local proverbs prove it. Their religious customs are radically different. "We thus meet with differences at every step. How can India be one nation?"[15] The historical realism exhibited here can hardly be improved. He capped it by raising the fateful question: "Has the introduction of Mohamedanism not unmade the nation?"[16] The simplicity and the directness of this question are stunning. Its prophetic quality can hardly be missed. And he raised it in 1909, four decades before the definitive answer was given. The contrast between what colonialism had accomplished and what separatist Islam would do could not have been drawn more sharply: if colonialism integrated India territorially, separatist Islam now threatened to disintegrate it.

---

[12] See E. C. Sachau (ed.), *Alberuni's India: An Account of the Religion, Philosophy, Literature, Geography, Chronology, Astronomy, Customs, Laws and Astrology of India about A.D. 1030*, two vols. in one (Delhi: S. Chand and Co., 1964), vol. I, pp. 294–305. The original Arabic for the Greek term *oicumene* is *ma'mura*, meaning "the inhabited world." I owe this point to Professor R. Euben of Wellesley College, MA.

[13] Ibid., vol. II, pp. 142–48. The pillage of Somnath temple by Mahmud of Ghazni is mentioned at p. 103.

[14] *Hind Swaraj*, p. 49.   [15] Ibid., pp. 49–50.

[16] Ibid., p. 51. The Gujarati original for "unmade the nation" is *"praja-bhang"* – "break up" the nation, something more expressive than just "unmake."

Gandhi dedicated the rest of his life to answering his own question in the negative. There was no good reason, he argued, why Islam should break up India. Indeed there were many good reasons why it should not. If India was one nation before the introduction of Islam, it should remain the same after its introduction. This was Gandhi's civic nationalist mantra. And it rested on two main ideas. The first was that Indian civilization was an open civilization and that it had the capacity to assimilate foreign elements. The second was that religion was not the basis of civic nationalism.

As for the first idea, Indian culture was, and still is, open and assimilative. It started as a Hindu culture, it then assimilated elements of Buddhist and Jain cultures; later it assimilated elements of Islamic, Christian, Sikh, and Parsi cultures, and modern Western culture itself. The "idea of India," from the very beginning, has been the idea of the one and the many. India was never one without being many. Gandhi believed in this with all his heart and mind. "India cannot cease to be one nation because people belonging to different religions live in it. The introduction of foreigners does not necessarily destroy the nation as they merge in it. A country is one nation only when such a condition obtains in it. India has ever been such a country."[17]

The second idea, that of religion, takes us to the heart of Gandhi's religious thought, which we shall see in detail in chapter 6. Here it is sufficient to note that he emphatically denies that religion is the basis of Indian nationalism. Religion in one respect – as the quest for liberation – was of course a personal matter. In that sense he was quite correct in saying that "there are as many religions as there are individuals."[18] Those who were conscious of this did not interfere with one another's religion. If they did, they were not fit to be members of a civic nation.[19]

Institutional religion was a different matter. Whereas religion as a means of the pursuit of liberation was an individual affair, institutional religion, with its codes and practices, beliefs and dogmas, bound its members together, giving them a sense of identity and solidarity. However, he could not accept institutional religion as the basis of civic nationalism. "In no part of the world are one nationality and one religion synonymous terms: nor has it been so in India." For institutional religions are "different roads converging on the same point."[20] Besides, there is a universal religion that underlies all organized religions;[21] that is to say all organized religions teach comparable doctrines on such basic virtues as love, compassion, and justice. Besides, there are in religions core issues and peripheral issues. If the followers of various religions focus on the

---

[17] Ibid., p. 52.   [18] Ibid., p. 53.   [19] Ibid.   [20] Ibid.   [21] Ibid., p. 42.

core issues, there should be no basis for any serious conflict between institutional religion and civic nationalism.

Gandhi was aware that the religious extremists often focused their attention on the peripheral issues. Already in *Hind Swaraj* he had identified "mullahs" and "*shastris*" (Hindu religious experts) as the fomenters of disunity and hatred.[22] They were unwilling to concede that modern India was a multi-religious nation. "If the Hindus believe that India should be peopled only by Hindus, they are living in a dreamland. The Mohamedans also live in a dreamland if they believe that there should only be Mohamedans there."[23]

While he rejected institutional religion as the social basis of civic nationalism, he readily accepted the view that religious ethics that taught individual freedom and social equality could only strengthen the spirit of civic nationalism. This was the reason why he published in 1926 in *Young India* an article entitled "Nationalism and Christianity" by Malcolm Muggeridge, then spending a term in India at the Union Christian College, Alwaye, Kerala. The latter was advancing the thesis that it was the duty of every Indian Christian to be a nationalist and be against British rule. It would be possible "for us to be Christians in India" only when India was free. For only free individuals could understand Christ, let alone follow him. In his view, the following would be Jesus' message for Indian Christians: "Let each man in his own mind be free; when you are free in your own minds, you will get *swaraj* [national independence]." Any one listening to Jesus thus speaking "would tear savagely at our bonds." Indian Christians, therefore, should fight colonialism "with body and mind and soul," until it withered away, "burnt by the strong light of truth."[24]

The role of the Indian National Congress

One of the major contributions that Gandhi made to the evolution of Indian nationalism was to transform the Indian National Congress (1885) into a vehicle of civic nationalism. He used it to give institutional expression to the two ideas we discussed above, namely the open character of Indian civilization and the religious neutrality of civic nationalism. The Congress was already noted for its freedom from religious partiality. For example, between 1885 and 1917, it had as its presidents,

---

[22] Ibid., p. 56.

[23] Ibid., p. 52, n. 88. The English text omits the last sentence from the original Gujarati text.

[24] M. Muggeridge, "Nationalism and Christianity," *Young India*, 8 (22 July 1926), pp. 258–59.

besides Hindus, as many as five Britons, four Muslims, three Parsis, and one Indian Christian. Nowhere in the history of nationalism could one find a matching record.

Gandhi built on that tradition when he took up its leadership in 1920. However, several important changes were also introduced. The first was the introduction of the 1920 constitution. According to its first article the means used to achieve national independence would only be peaceful, not violent. Only a decade before the Congress had been split between the moderates and the extremists. The moderates believed in gradual constitutional changes. The extremists believed in violent changes brought about by open rebellion and even terrorist rebellion. Vinay Damodar Savarkar was a leader of a secret terrorist society in Maharashtra, and Aurobindo Ghosh was sympathetic to another such society in Bengal. Gandhi, managing to stay clear of these two factions, succeeded in moving the Congress to adopt a non-violent form of nationalism.

Article four of the new constitution met the problem of linguistic nationalism head on. It made the language territory the regional base of the Congress. Twelve such linguistic units were recognized.[25] This reflected Gandhi's strongly held view that the linguistic community was a primary human community and that civic nationalism must take this fact into full account. At the same time he was also of the firm belief that a linguistic community, however basic it was for human existence, was not per se a political community. Therefore, as far as India was concerned, the linguistic community and the national community could not be co-terminus. To facilitate communication between the linguistic provincial units, English was adopted as the link language, until such time as Hindustani would be ready to replace it.

Article 29 of the new constitution met religious nationalism also head on. No policy affecting the interests of Hindus and Muslims would be introduced into the Congress executive unless it had the prior agreement of its Hindu and Muslim members. The same principle implicitly applied to policy affecting other religions too.

Even more important than the revision of the constitution of the Indian National Congress was the formal linking of the philosophy of human rights to Indian civic nationalism. This he was able to achieve in a signal way by getting the resolution on fundamental rights and social policy accepted by the Congress at its 1931 annual meeting in Karachi.[26] His precise role, especially in relation to that played by Jawaharlal Nehru, in getting the Congress to accept this resolution will be taken up in the next

[25] CW, 19: 191.   [26] For the text of this resolution see CW, 45: 370–72.

chapter. Here our concern is to highlight the ideological stamp that it put on Indian civic nationalism. For the first time in Indian political history, the individual, regardless of religious or linguistic or gender or racial or caste distinctions was acknowledged as the basic unit of the nation. To be an Indian meant to be a bearer of certain inalienable rights. As G. Austin has rightly pointed out, this resolution was "the spiritual, and in some cases the direct, antecedent" of the Directive Principle of the 1950 Indian constitution.[27]

Gandhi's civic nationalism was based on the belief that it was possible to remain faithful to one's own religion and at the same time be respectful of the religion of others. This idea found a strong expression in the *Constructive Programme: its Meaning and Place* (1941), his second most important political tract behind *Hind Swaraj*. In it he urged members of the Congress, whatever their religion might be, "to represent in [their] own person" all that was best in other religions. They had to feel their identity with every one of the millions of the inhabitants of India. In order to realize this, they would have to cultivate "personal friendship" with persons representing faiths other than their own. They should have the same regard for the other faiths as they have for their own.[28]

Gandhi was of the view that India had the historical, moral and intellectual resources to develop into a civic nation. Its religious and linguistic diversity was in his judgment an asset rather than a liability. Such pluralism was healthy so long as it was fed by an All-India consciousness, just as the latter would be healthy when it was nourished by the larger purpose of the universe.[29] As far as the Indian nation was concerned, Hindus, Muslims, Christians, Sikhs, Buddhists, Parsis, Jains, and Jews were equally Indians. Such awareness should enable each group to follow its religion scrupulously without interfering with the religion of the others. As he wrote to Dr. B. S. Moonje, for "the service of India, Mussalmans, Jews, Christians should be Indians, even as Hindus should be Indians."[30]

Gandhi's defense of civic nationalism can adequately meet the charge made by some that nationalism as such is alien to India or that it is at best derivative and imitative.[31] The fact is that he domesticated nationalism,

---

[27] G. Austin, *The Indian Constitution: Cornerstone of a Nation* (Delhi: Oxford University Press, 1966), p. 56.

[28] CW, 75: 147.   [29] CW, 28: 120.

[30] CW, 38: 232. Civic nationalism enabled him to lose his caste consciousness (CW, 72: 310). His civic nationalist consciousness prompted him at the Second Round Table Conference to remind Ramsay Macdonald, the Prime Minister, that as the representative of the Congress Party he was an Indian not a Hindu (CW, 48: 374).

[31] See P. Chatterjee, *Nationalist Thought and the Colonial World: A Derivative Discourse?* (London: Zed Books, 1986).

not in terms of dharma, as Ranajit Guha argues, but in terms of artha, as we argue here.[32] Ashis Nandy has expounded how Tagore's nationalism evolved from being "Brahminic" at first, to being inclusive later, as when he wrote the national anthem, to the final stage of rejecting it as altogether illegitimate.[33] Bhikhu Parekh and, following him, David Arnold and David Hardiman, think that Gandhi believed that India was not a nation but a civilization.[34]

Gandhi was realistic enough to recognize that civic nationalism in India needed constant nurturing. He would have agreed with Ernest Renan that "the existence of a nation is a plebiscite of every day" – something that needed constant affirmation.[35]

In this regard, the metaphor of "the clay pot" that he used for Indian civic nationalism is worthy of our attention. "A clay pot would break through impact; if not with one stone, then with another. The way to save the pot is not to keep it away from the danger point, but to bake it so that no stone would break it. We have to make our hearts of perfectly baked clay."[36] That is to say, civic nationalism needed constant nurturing. A deepening of the emotional ties between different sub-national groups would be needed to make it flourish. These groups spread over India – from Kashmir to Kerala, Nagaland to Gujarat – would have to take deliberate steps to strengthen their emotional bonds. Anything that one sub-group did to diminish the self-esteem of another would weaken the whole political community. In this regard, the Hindi-speaking groups of the north have a special responsibility resting on their shoulders. They have to be careful not to appear, and indeed not to be, the new ruling bloc of modern India. Language and religion are sources of deep group loyalty. Civic nationalism, if it were to flourish, would have to pay close attention to this fact. The pot can break easily from stones thrown by one sub-group at another.

Though aware of the potential threats that civic nationalism faced in India, Gandhi remained steadfast in his belief that this form of national-ism alone could provide the kind of political community that Indians needed if they were to develop their purushartha. He used another

---

[32] R. Guha, *Dominance Without Hegemony: History and Power in Colonial India* (Cambridge, MA: Harvard University Press, 1997), p. 36.

[33] A. Nandy, *The Illegitimacy of Nationalism: Rabindranath Tagore and the Politics of the Self* (Delhi: Oxford University Press, 1996).

[34] B. Parekh, *Gandhi* (Oxford University Press, 1997), p. 20; D. Arnold, *Gandhi* (London: Longman, 2001), pp. 104, 217–18; D. Hardiman, *Gandhi in His Times and Ours* (Pietermaritzburg: University of Natal Press, 2003), p. 16.

[35] E. Renan, "Qu'est-ce qu'un nation?," cited in H. Kohn, *Nationalism: Its Meaning and History* (New York: Van Nostrand, 1955), p. 139.

[36] *Hind Swaraj*, p. 57.

metaphor, one that subsequently became famous, to express this hope – that of the oceanic circle.[37]

Independent India, fully developed into a civic nation, would be an oceanic circle. The term "oceanic" signified inclusiveness of all the subgroups – religious, linguistic, regional, tribal, etc. – that made up India. The term "circle" signified the closed character of the civic nation. Any nation, civic or otherwise, had to be closed to some degree from other nations. Otherwise it could not qualify as a nation. However, since civic nationalism by definition was non-violent, its closed character did not pose any threat to other nations.

What makes this metaphor admirably suited to describe Gandhi's civic nationalism is the position that it ascribes to the individual citizen. It recognizes the individual citizen as the ultimate unit of the nation. The individual is the center from which the circle is drawn. But Gandhi's individuals are not the "possessive" individuals that C. B. Macpherson speaks of, the radical individuals of Hobbes and Locke.[38] On the contrary, they are "never aggressive in their arrogance but ever humble sharing the majesty of the oceanic circle of which they are integral units."[39] They are held together by a "free and voluntary play of mutual forces." No one would want "anything that others cannot have with equal labor," thereby guaranteeing its egalitarian character, and rejecting all notions of hierarchy. It would not be a pyramid, the base supporting the apex. On the contrary the authority needed for governance would be derived from the people as a whole. The citizen may belong to as many sub-groups as he or she may wish; he or she may draw as many concentric circles as he or she may desire – the oceanic circle has room for all. And this applies to Muslims as well; they, like any other group, may draw as many concentric circles as they wish, provided they do not go outside the circumference of the oceanic circle. It is on such an optimistic note that Gandhi's analysis of Indian nationalism ends.

Ethnic nationalism

It was one thing for Gandhi to interpret Indian nationalism in terms of civic nationalism, but quite another to expect others to accept his interpretation. As Antony Copley reminds us, there were in pre-Independence

---

[37] CW, 85: 32–33. In 1946 Gandhi was asked by a journalist to give an idea of his vision of independent India. The oceanic circle was the metaphor that he used in his response.

[38] See C. B. Macpherson, *The Political Theory of Possessive Individualism: Hobbes to Locke* (Oxford: Clarendon Press, 1962).

[39] CW, 85: 33.

India "varieties of nationalism."[40] Hindu extremists and Muslims separatists had their own variety. They most vigorously challenged Gandhi at
every turn. The one led to his assassination and the other to the vivisec-
tion of the body politic. Modern India emerges out of the contest between
these three forms of nationalism – the civic, the ethnic, and the religious.

Here we digress briefly in order to clarify the meanings of these forms of
nationalism.[41]

To start with nationalism itself: it is an ideology that claims that the
nation is the basis of the political community. A nation is conceived of as a
people who inhabit a certain territory and who feel conscious of their
identity and of their differences from other peoples similarly constituted.
Whether or not a nation should have its own state is an open question
with no definite answer. For there are multinational states, such as
Canada, that choose to form a single federal state, while there are also
nations that choose to have their own sovereign state. What gives a nation
its sense of identity are a shared sense of history and culture, and a shared
sense of justice, rights, and duties. A common religion is not a necessary
condition of national identity, as there are multi-religious nations such as
the United States. Catholics in South America do not form a single
nation; they form different nations, even though they profess the same
religion. Similarly, a common language is not a necessary condition of
nationality as people speaking different languages form a single nation, as
in the case of Belgium or Switzerland. The same is true of race or
ethnicity.

A civic nation is a people who, in addition to sharing a common history,
culture, sense of justice, rights, and duties, attach the greatest importance
to the dignity and sanctity of its individual members. The individuals in a
civic nation are valued independently of their religious or linguistic or
racial or ethnic particularities. They are valued simply because they are
free agents capable of self-determination and self-development. The civic
nation exists to protect and promote the liberties and rights and dignity of
its members. This is the only type of nation that can promote harmony
between every member and every group within it.

An ethnic nation, by contrast, is a people who hold that having the
same ethnic or racial background and a culture emanating from it are
the necessary and sufficient conditions of their being a nation. Those
who are of a different racial or ethnic background and culture are either

---

[40] A. Copley (ed.), *Hinduism in Public and Private: Reform, Hindutva, Gender, and Sampraday* (Delhi: Oxford University Press, 2003), pp. 6–15.

[41] For a short list of essential books on nationalism, see the Bibliography to this book.

"cleansed" or persecuted or considered second class. Harmony between the national group and the rest is not possible in an ethnic nation.

A religious nation is a people who hold that having the same religious background and a culture that stems from it are the necessary and sufficient conditions of their being a nation. Those who belong to a different religion or those who are considered heretics are either persecuted or treated as second class. Harmony between the national group and the rest is not possible in a religious nation.

India at the turn of the twentieth century was faced with the hard task of choosing between these three forms of nationalism.

By the third quarter of the nineteenth century, a significant number of Hindus felt attracted to ethnic nationalism. This was due in large measure to their adverse reaction to Islam, notably in the Punjab and Bengal, the two areas that paid dearly for it in 1947. The Arya Samaj (Society of Aryans) founded in 1875 by Swami Dayanand Saraswati, a Gujarati like Gandhi, gave Hindu ethnic nationalism its first organizational structure. It popularized the slogan of one religion (Hinduism), one language (Hindi) and one nation (Hindustan). The Hindu Mahasabha, founded in 1919, followed this lead, and established itself as a political party in opposition to both the Indian National Congress and the Muslim League. Vinaya Damodar Savarkar (1883–1966), a Maharashtrian Brahmin, gave Hindu ethnic nationalism its basic ideology, the ideology of *Hindutva* (Hinduness). His *Hindutva, Who Is a Hindu?* (1923) remains its fundamental text. He was assisted by another Maharashtrian Brahmin, Keshav Baliram Hedgewar (1889–1940). In 1925 he founded the Rashtriya Swyamsevak Sangh (the RSS), the militant organizational wing of *Hindutva* nationalism. Yet another Maharashtrian Brahmin, Mahadev Sadashiv Golwalkar (1902–73) in his *We or Our Nationhood Defined* (1939) gave Hindu ethnic nationalism the second most important articulation.

Hindutva, Who Is a Hindu? is in part an analysis of India's past from the point of view of Hindu ethnic nationalism, and in part a manifesto for future action. India of the past was the creation of a racially superior people, the Aryans. They came to be known to the outside world as Hindus, the people beyond the Indus River. Their identity was created by their race (*jati*) and their culture (*sanskriti*). "All Hindus claim to have in their veins the blood of the mighty race incorporated with and descended from the Vedic fathers."[42] They created a culture – an ensemble of mythologies, legends, epic stories, philosophy, art and architecture,

---

[42] V. D. Savarkar, *Hindutva, Who Is a Hindu?* (6th edn, New Delhi: Bharti Sahitya Sadan, 1989), pp. 84–85.

laws and rites, feasts and festivals.[43] They have a special relationship to India: India is to them both a fatherland and a holy land. Only those who can claim India in this way can possess *Hindutva*. This automatically excludes Indian Muslims, Christians, Parsis, and Jews, for their holy land lies elsewhere. But it includes Buddhists, Jains, and Sikhs. There is a subtle effort here to erase the distinct identities of these last groups, and to absorb them into the Hindu fold, something at least the Buddhists and the Sikhs have vigorously denounced.

Savarkar was particularly hard on historical Buddhism and Islam. His complaint against Buddhism was that it made India militarily weak, and a helpless prey of foreign invaders. Its "mealy mouthed formulas of *ahimsa* [non-violence]," its "mumbo-jumbo" of universal brotherhood, and its exchange of "the sword for the rosary" robbed India of its national virility.[44]

As for Islam, the day Mohammad of Ghazni crossed the Indus, a "conflict of life and death began."[45] The hatred towards this particular foe ought to unite all those who possess *Hindutva*.

Hindu culture was presented as a self-sufficient culture, not needing any input from other cultures – an unhistorical, narcissistic, and false account of India's past. Savarkar's manifesto for the future was equally flawed. India must become a Hindudom, and debar Indian Muslims and Indian Christians from Indian nationhood. Hinduize all politics and militarize Hindudom was his slogan. He saw in Gandhi's civic national-ism nothing but a betrayal of the true nationalism of the Hindus.

Golwalkar's *We or Our Nationhood Defined* brought out quite explicitly the fascist potential of Hindu ethnic nationalism. Hindus, according to Golwalkar, were a race, and only they, "naught else," should constitute the nation.[46] He was greatly influenced by the Nazi idea of nationalism: "To keep up the purity of the race and its culture, Germany shocked the world by her purging the country of the Semitic race – the Jews. Race pride at its highest has been manifested there. Germany has also shown how well nigh impossible it is for races and cultures, having differences going to the root, to be assimilated into one united whole, a good lesson for us in Hindustan to learn and profit by."[47]

He had nothing but contempt for civic nationalism. The idea that "the nation was composed of all those who happened to reside in India" was nothing but political poison.[48] Buddhists were traitors "to mother

---

[43] Ibid., pp. 91–102.   [44] Ibid., pp. 18–26.   [45] Ibid., p. 42.
[46] M. S. Golwalkar, *We or Our Nationhood Defined* (4th edn, Nagpur: Bharat Prakashan, 1947), p. 2.
[47] Ibid., p. 43.   [48] Ibid., p. 19.

society and mother religion."[49] It was because Kandahar (in present-day Afghanistan) was a Buddhist territory that it fell so easily to the Muslims. As for Muslims and Christians, they have a choice of either adopting Hindu culture and becoming Hindus or else of remaining "wholly subordinated to the Hindu nation," claiming no privileges, "not even citizen's rights."[50] The attempt to create a civic nation out of India would be like the attempt to create a "novel animal," by joining the head of a monkey and the legs of a bullock to the body of an elephant.[51]

Savarkar, a bitter opponent of Gandhi's civic nationalism, was the president of Hindu Mahasabha during the critical years from 1937 to 1943. Its election manifesto, cited below, gave a clear idea of what its ethnic nationalism really meant:

Hindustan is the land of the Hindus from time immemorial. The Hindu Mahasabha believes that Hindus have a right to live in peace as Hindus, to legislate, to rule, to govern themselves in accordance with Hindu genius and ideals and establish by all lawful and legal means a Hindu state based on Hindu culture and tradition, so that Hindu ideology and way of life should have a homeland of its own.[52]

The opposition of Hindu ethnic nationalism to Gandhi and his civic nationalism was uncompromising. It was no accident that Nathuram Godse, a follower of this ideology and a devout admirer of Savarkar, turned out to be Gandhi's assassin. He justified his murder as a condign punishment for what in his judgment Gandhi had done to the Hindus: "All his experiments," he asserted, "were at the expenses (sic) of the Hindus."[53] If Hindu ethnic nationalism sounds the tocsin of India's civic nationalism, it should not come as a surprise; and there is every reason that it should be taken seriously. By murdering Gandhi it signaled that it wanted to get rid of more than just the man: it wanted to get rid of his civic nationalism as well.

We mention only in passing Sri Aurobindo's concept of nationalism and the Indian political community. The reason is that, though very different from Gandhi's, it did not directly confront his (at least in his lifetime). But it did claim that religion as spirituality, as the pursuit of *sanatana dharma* (eternal religion or eternal law) was of the essence of

[49] M. S. Golwalkar, *Bunch of Thoughts* (2nd edn, Bangalore: Jagarna Prakashan, 1980), p. 94.
[50] Golwalkar, *We or Our Nationhood Defined*, pp. 55–56.
[51] Golwalkar, *Bunch of Thoughts*, pp. 197–98.
[52] Cited in K. K. Klostermaier, *A Survey of Hinduism* (2nd edn, Albany: State University of New York Press, 1994), p. 463.
[53] Godse's statement, cited in A. Nandy, *At the Edge of Psychology: Essays in Politics and Culture* (Delhi: Oxford University Press, 1990), p. 71.

Indian nationalism. As he wrote in 1907 in his journal *Bande Mataram,* "This great and ancient nation was once the fountain of human light, the apex of human civilization, the exemplar of human courage, the perfection of good government and settled society."[54] Five years later he made the point even more sharply: India was "the center of religious life of the world and its destined savior through the *sanatana dharma.*"[55] It was his life mission to help the Indian nation to realize this goal.

What is striking from the perspective of this book is that Sri Aurobindo could see no way of combining the pursuit of the spiritual and that of the political. For him the essence of the Indian mind was spirituality – not the whole of it, but "the master-key" to it.[56] As he explained to Joseph Baptista, an Indian nationalist leader, while he did not look down on politics, he nevertheless did not know how to harmonize it with the spiritual life. Consequently, he had to place his "entire stress" on the latter.[57] That was why, in 1920, he turned down the invitation to be the president of the Indian National Congress: he could not leave his spiritual life for politics, as he had taken up the pursuit of the spiritual as his mission for the rest of his life.[58]

That the ideologues of *Hindutva* nationalism have appropriated Sri Aurobindo's nationalism is not the worst of it. What is truly tragic is the fact he contributed to the perpetuation of the myth that India, as a nation, was a spiritual substance. Artha, for all his appreciation of it, remained alienated from dharma and moksha. The reality of the presence of Muslims in India did not influence his nationalist thought as it did Gandhi's.

Muslim separatist nationalism

The Indian Muslim reaction to Gandhi's civic nationalism was by no means uniform. There were several reactions, two of which became historically very important. The first was of course the reaction of the religion-based nationalism of the Muslim League led by Muhammad Ali

---

[54] Cited in P. Heehs, "The Centre of the Religious Life in the World: Spiritual Universalism and Cultural Nationalism in the Work of Sri Aurobindo," in Copley (ed.), *Hinduism in Public and Private,* p. 73.

[55] Ibid., p. 66.

[56] P. Heehs, "Shades of Orientalism: Paradoxes and Problems in Indian Historiography," *History and Theory,* 42 (2003), p. 187.

[57] Sri Aurobindo, *On Himself: Complied from Notes and Letters* (Pondicherry: Sri Aurobindo Ashram, 1989), p. 430.

[58] Sri Aurobindo to Dr. Munje, 30 August 1920, ibid., p. 433.

Jinnah, and the second was the reaction of Abul Kalam Azad, who adapted civic nationalism to the needs of South Asian Muslims.

Jinnah's adherence to a religion-based nationalism appears paradoxical, since he was, up to at least 1920, a civic nationalist himself. Gandhi's emergence as the leader of the Indian National Congress had the effect of alienating him from that party, and eventually from civic nationalism itself. Yet personal antipathy alone does not explain why the "Muslim Gohkale" metamorphosed into a modern-day Saladin – to use Akbar Ahmed's hyperbole.[59] Historians have tried to explain the paradox that Jinnah presents. Ayesha Jalal has hypothesized that his demand for Pakistan was part of a strategy that he used in the poker game of nationalist politics. The Pakistan Resolution of 1940 was "a bargaining counter" to ensure the interests of Muslims everywhere in India, not just the Muslim-majority provinces. In her view, his rhetoric did not reflect what he really wanted, which was a loose federation with a weak centre.[60]

Certainly, strategy did play a role in Jinnah's politics, as it did in the politics of every other astute politician. It can explain some things but not everything. In Jinnah's case there was the additional fact of his sound grasp of Islamic philosophical principles lying behind the strategy. As a cultural Muslim – as distinct from a theological one – his political thought was consistent with the Islamic principles of community, culture, governance and separatism. Francis Robinson, following Quentin Skinner, has made the key point that the Muslim elite of India operated from within a specific "ideological framework" of understanding and communication.[61] According to that framework, separatism was "a special characteristic of Muslims," there being a "fundamental connection between Islam and political separatism."[62] The Islamic idea of community (the *umma*), and law and governance (the *Sharia*) encouraged Muslims everywhere, but especially in India, to consider themselves as separate from, and superior to, non-Muslims. Muhammad Ali's notorious remark that even a Muslim of low character was superior to any non-Muslim, Mahatma Gandhi included, was certainly in bad taste.[63] But it also

---

[59] Akbar S. Ahmed, *Jinnah, Pakistan and Islamic Identity: The Search for Saladin* (London: Routledge, 1997).

[60] Ayesha Jalal, *The Sole Spokesman: Jinnah, the Muslim League and the Demand for Pakistan* (Cambridge: Cambridge University Press, 1985), p. 57; and *Self and Sovereignty: Individual and Community in South Asian Islam since 1850* (London: Routledge, 2000), pp. xiii–xiv, 397–400.

[61] See his essay on "Islam and Separatism," in his *Islam and Muslim History in South Asia* (New Delhi: Oxford University Press, 2000), pp. 177–209, at p. 180.

[62] Ibid., pp. 177 and 204.   [63] Ibid., pp. 195–96.

pointed to the lengths to which the Muslims separatist ideology was capable of going.

Now, civic nationalism also had a theory of political community. How it related to the Muslim theory became critical to Jinnah. Beyond strategy and tactic, he thought in terms of certain Muslim ideas, two of which he used in his encounter with Gandhi.

The first was that Hindus and Muslims belonged to separate civilizations, a point he had already made in his 1940 Lahore speech. There he enunciated his version of the clash of civilizations thesis. Hindus and Muslims belonged to two clashing civilizations because they belonged to clashing communities. To cite from his Lahore speech:

> The Hindus and Muslims belong to two different religious philosophies, social customs, literatures. They neither intermarry nor interdine together and, indeed, they belong to two different civilizations which are based mainly on conflicting ideas and conceptions. Their outlook on life and of life are different ... To yoke together two such nations under a single state ... must lead to growing discontent and final destruction of any fabric that may be so built up for the government of such a state.[64]

His letter of 17 September 1944 to Gandhi reflected the above point quite accurately:

> We maintain and hold that Muslims and Hindus are two major nations by any definition or test of a nation ... we are a nation with our own distinctive culture and civilization, language and literature, art and architecture, names and nomenclature, sense of value and proportion, legal laws and moral codes, customs and calendar, history and traditions, aptitudes and ambitions; in short, we have our own distinctive outlook on life and of life ... I am convinced that true welfare not only of the Muslim but the rest of India lies in the division of India as proposed by the Lahore Resolution.[65]

What we see here is theory, not strategy – theory whose telos is partition. For nearly a thousand years, he reminded Gandhi, Muslims had managed to maintain their separate cultural identity. They were now going to assert their separate political identity as well.

The second idea that he used against Gandhi was the Muslim idea of self-determination. Put very simply, it is that, wherever Muslims are in a majority, they have the canonical right to establish a government of their own, regardless of the wishes of the non-Muslims inhabiting the same territory. His letter of 21 September 1944 to Gandhi reflected this point:

---

[64] Cited in C. H. Philips, (ed.), *The Evolution of India and Pakistan 1858–1947* (London: Oxford University Press, 1962), p. 354.

[65] CW, 78: 407–8.

can you not appreciate our point of view that we claim the right to self-determination as a nation and not as a territorial unit, and that we are entitled to exercise our inherent right as a Muslim nation, which is our birthright? ... The right of self-determination which we claim postulates that we are a nation, and as such it would be the self-determination of the Mussalmans, *and they alone are entitled to exercise that right.*[66]

Other instances of Jinnah's approach to separatism could also be mentioned. The most significant of these was his willingness to resort to jihad, if necessary. According to Humayun Mirza, only three months before Pakistan was granted independence, he had explored the possibility of instigating a jihad. Iskandar Mirza (then an official in the colonial government, later the first president of Pakistan) was given Rs 20,000 to explore the possibility of a jihad, with the promise of Rs 10 million to follow. The idea was dropped, as Pakistan came into being three months after these negotiations took place.[67]

There is little doubt that Jinnah's separatism contributed its share to the partition of India. Once partition was achieved, however, his religion-based nationalism took a U-turn: he now wanted the new state to act as if it were the organ of a civic nation. He wanted it to be neutral towards religion, and its citizens to be defined in terms of rights rather than religion. This was the ideology underlying his speech of 11 August 1947 in the Pakistan Constituent Assembly, referred to by Akbar Ahmed, with exaggeration, as his Gettysburg Address.[68] He exhorted the constitution-makers of Pakistan to create a civic nationalist state within a separatist Muslim nation:

You are free; you are free to go to your temples, you are free to go to your mosques or to any other place of worship in this State of Pakistan. You may belong to any religion or caste or creed – that has nothing to do with the business of the State ... We are starting in the days when there is no discrimination, no distinction between one community and another ... I think we should keep in front of us as our ideal and you will find that in the course of time Hindus would cease to be Hindus and Muslims would cease to be Muslims, not in the religious sense, because that is the personal faith of each individual, but in the political sense as citizens of the State.[69]

---

[66] Jinnah to Gandhi, 21 September 1944, CW, 78: 410–11. Italics added.

[67] See H. Mirza, *From Plassey to Pakistan* (rev. edn, Lanham, MD: University Press of America, 2002), p. 151. As Pakistan was granted independence in August 1947, the proposed jihad was called off (ibid.).

[68] Ahmed, *Jinnah, Pakistan and Islamic Identity*, pp. 173–75.

[69] Cited in Stanley Wolpert, *Jinnah of Pakistan* (New York: Oxford University Press, 1984), pp. 339–40.

Two notions of nationalism, then, co-existed in Jinnah's mind in a state of unresolved tension, one pulling in the direction of Muslim separatism and the other in the direction of Hindu–Muslim amity. The speeches of March 1940 and August 1947 reflect this tension. Unfortunately, the unresolved tension in the founder's mind was perpetuated in the nation-state that he founded. The latter remained unable to decide which nationalism it really wanted – a religion-based one or one that was neutral towards religion. The unresolved problem of Kashmir is, above all, a relic of the ideology of Muslim separatism. The principle of self-determination that is invoked by the *separatist* Muslims there is, at bottom, the Muslim version of it: because the Muslims are a majority there, they have the canonical right to a Muslim state, regardless of the wishes of non-Muslims.

Amity between Muslims and non-Muslims in South Asia is not possible on the basis of a religion-based theory of nationalism; it is possible only if a Gandhian-type civic nationalism is grafted to a non-separatist interpretation of Islam. The person who understood this important point was not Jinnah, but Abul Kalam Azad.

Azad and civic nationalism

Azad will go down in Indian history as the person who dared to break the separatist mould of South Asian Islam. With him Indian Muslim thought took a historic forward step. He argued on Islamic grounds that being a Muslim and being an Indian were compatible attributes. Though he had started his career as a Muslim revivalist, by 1920, he had come under the influence of Gandhi and his civic nationalism. In 1923, at the age of thirty-five, he became the president of the Indian National Congress – the youngest to assume that post in its history. And he became president again in 1939, for an unprecedented seven-year term.

His greatest contribution to civic nationalism was the adaptation of Muslim theology and jurisprudence to the needs of South Asian Muslims. He found support for this in the *Quran*: so long as Indians were not hostile to Islam, Muslims had an obligation to be non-separatists. The *Hadith*, the traditions of the Prophet, also, according to him, supported the move towards composite nationalism. The Prophet had entered into a covenant with the Jews and pagans of Medina. This, he argued, had normative value for contemporary Indian Muslims as well. That covenant produced "one nation," an *umma wahida*, regardless of the religion of those who entered into it.[70]

---

[70] Ian Henderson Douglas, *Abul Kalam Azad: An Intellectual and Religious Biography*, edited by Gail Minault and Christian W. Troll (Delhi: Oxford University Press, 1988), p. 176.

According to Azad, the basic message of the *Quran* was "the oneness of religion" (*wahadat–e-din*). *Din*, interpreted as devotion to God and righteous living, was found in all religions. In so far as this was true, it provided the basis for the peaceful co-existence of all religions. The *Sharia*, by contrast, was subject to change, depending on the needs of time and place. It was therefore possible to adapt it to the needs of civic nationalist Indian Muslims. Islam, in his view, was more an "attitude of submission, surrender and obedience" to God than a religio-cultural system defined by the boundaries of law.[71] To submit to God did not mean denial of one's nationality, but its sanctification.[72]

Given all this, there was no justification for continuing with the separatist mode of Muslim thought. A new ideological frame of reference was now available. The suggestion that religious affinity could unite all Muslim countries into one world-state was, he claimed, "one of the greatest frauds" foisted on Muslims.[73]

Azad's theology harmonized with Gandhi's civic nationalism. Besides, it gave Indian Muslims a solid reason for becoming an integral part of the civic nation of India. In so far as this is the case, there is every reason to consider him as one of the great founders of modern India.

Conclusion

What type of political community in the modern world can best generate and promote internal political harmony is the fundamental question that Gandhi raises in this chapter. The answer is simple and unequivocal: only a political community animated by the principles of civic nationalism can do it. It alone can knit together the Dalits and non-Dalits, and people belonging to different religious, ethnic and language communities. Ethnic nationalism and religious nationalism set religion against religion, ethnic group against ethnic group, linguistic group against linguistic group. They cannot do otherwise, for it is in their nature to tear communities apart. This is Gandhi's main contention.

It is true that historically, in 1947, civic nationalism in India failed to unite all Indians into a political community. It lacked the emotional resources to stand up to religious separatism and ethnic nationalism. But the failure was not total. For civic nationalism appealed to a significant number of Indian Muslims who refused to identify religion and nation. They now count over 100 million. With the help of Gandhi's

---

[71] Ibid., p. 291.   [72] Ibid., p. 277.
[73] Maulana Abul Kalam Azad, *India Wins Freedom: An Autobiographical Narrative* (New Delhi: Orient Longman, 1959), p. 227.

civic nationalism, reinforced by Azad's philosophy, they could set aside the framework of separatism and become part of the civic nation that India is. Should this happen, their example would have a normative value for Muslims in the rest of the word.

Gandhi's civic nationalism is also the key to harmonious relations between nation-states. As he wrote in his introduction to Muggeridge's essay, mentioned above, internationalism presupposed nationalism. He was not thinking of "the narrow, selfish, greedy" kind that passed under the name of nationalism, but the nationalism that, whilst it insisted upon its own freedom and growth, disdained to attain them at the expense of other nations.[74]

---

[74] M. K. Gandhi, Introduction to M. Muggeridge, "Nationalism and Christianity," *Young India* (22 July 1926), p. 258; CW, 31: 181.

3   The state

"But today my corporate activity is undoubtedly devoted to the attainment of parliamentary swaraj in accordance with the wishes of the people of India."[1]

The state according to Gandhi is an institution necessary for the realization of the values of artha. A political community without the state disintegrates into chaos. There is nothing more despairing for an individual than to be stateless. Colonialism had taught him a hard lesson in state appreciation. The establishment of a sovereign state for the whole of India was the ultimate goal of the nationalist movement that he led from 1920 to 1947.

There is a frequently quoted statement of Gandhi according to which the state "represents violence in a concentrated and organized form. The individual has a soul, but the state is a soulless machine; it can never be weaned from violence to which it owes its very existence."[2] Based on this statement many have jumped to the conclusion that he was against the state as such, and not just the absolutist, Hobbesean/Machiavellian state. The fact is that he did defend the state, the constitutional state, a "parliamentary swaraj," to use his terminology. This Gandhian state will be centralized enough to provide for internal order and external security, and coercive enough to meet all its constitutional obligations. In *Hind Swaraj* we see him rejecting only the absolute and aggressive model of the state,[3] and the modern notion of "national interest" (*prajana swarth*) as the supreme rule of state conduct.[4] However, he defends the parliamentary swaraj that recognizes the ethical supremacy of the moral law (dharma) over state law. The notion that the state is above the moral law is, in his view, "a new-fangled notion."[5] Briefly, Gandhi wants a state that meets the requirements of artha and civic nationalism. Only in such a state can citizens and social groups live and flourish in peace and security.

---

[1] Preface to the 1921 edition of *Hind Swaraj*, CW, 19: 278.
[2] N. K. Bose, *Selections From Gandhi* (Ahmedabad: Navajivan, 1957), p. 41.
[3] *Hind Swaraj*, pp. 27–28.   [4] Ibid., p. 87.   [5] Ibid., p. 91.

The two major functions that Gandhi attached to the state were the protection of the rights of its citizens and the guarding of their security from external aggression.

The state as the protector of human rights

Gandhi went far beyond Kautilya in identifying the basic functions of the state. For Kautilya the state's main function was external expansion through war and internal stability through punishment (*danda-niti*). For Gandhi the emphasis shifted from war to peace, and from punishment to rights. The state in its internal aims existed in order to protect the rights of the individuals.

There are two documents that are of fundamental importance here. The first refers to the "Declaration of Independence" that he wrote in 1930 to tell the world that India would be satisfied with nothing less than complete independence (*purna* swaraj). Echoes of the American Declaration of Independence could be heard here without difficulty. Its preamble read as follows:

We believe it is the inalienable right of the Indian people, as of any other people, to have freedom and to enjoy the fruit of their toil and have the necessities of life, so that they may have full opportunity for growth. We believe also that if any government deprives a people of these rights and oppresses them, the people have a further right to alter it or to abolish it. The British Government in India has not only deprived the Indian people of their freedom but has based itself on the exploitation of the masses and has ruined India economically, politically, culturally and spiritually. We believe, therefore, that India must sever the British connection and attain *purna* swaraj or complete independence.[6]

Attached to this preamble was a list of complaints against the colonial state – "the fourfold disaster," as he called them. Only a sovereign Indian state could undo the damage done by colonialism.

The second document is the famous 1931 "Resolution on Fundamental Rights and Economic Changes," already referred to in the last chapter.[7] There is some confusion in the existing literature regarding its authorship and ideological orientation. Stanley Wolpert thinks that it was drafted and

---

[6] For the text of the Declaration see CW, 42: 384–85. A first draft for comments was sent to Jawaharlal Nehru on, 10 January 1930; see ibid., p. 382–83. Gandhi was very proud of his authorship of this text. "I was its author," he wrote in *Harijan* on 16 January 1940. "I wanted the people not merely to repeat the mantra of independence but to educate the people as to its why and wherefore [sic]," CW, 71: 116. Stanley Wolpert attributes its authorship to Nehru; see Wolpert, *Nehru: A Tryst With Destiny* (New York: Oxford University Press, 1996), p. 106.

[7] See p. 37 above.

introduced to the Congress by Nehru and that Gandhi supported it just to mollify him.[8] Leonard Gordon refers to the Leftist view that it reflected the influence of M. N. Roy, a Communist intellectual, on Nehru on this matter.[9] According to Judith Brown, Gandhi and Nehru had jointly drafted it.[10] As for Nehru, he categorically claimed that Roy "had absolutely nothing to do with it."[11] S. Gopal, Nehru's authorized biographer, was of the opinion that the resolution had nothing socialistic about it, and that only the secret police could have imagined that Roy had a hand in its drafting. As a matter of fact Roy had roundly denounced it "as confused, compromising with foreign imperialism and native feudalism and 'an instrument of deception.'"[12]

The notion that Gandhi was a reluctant partner in promoting human rights hardly deserves serious consideration. As everyone knows, the idea of rights was at the heart of satyagraha, which *Hind Swaraj* had defined as a new method of defending rights.[13] His campaigns in both South Africa and India were directed towards the securing of the rights of the parties concerned. As for the 1931 Resolution, apart from his role in its genesis as Nehru described it, it was he who introduced its final draft to the Congress, with a moving speech made in Hindi – so that he could reach more than just the English-speaking elite:

This resolution is meant for those who are no legislators, who are not interested in intricate questions of constitution, who will not take an active part in the administration of the country. It is meant to indicate to the poor, inarticulate Indian the broad features of swaraj or *Ramarajya*. . . . by passing this resolution we make it clear to the world and to our own people what we propose to do as soon as we come to power.[14]

---

[8] Wolpert, *Nehru: A Tryst With Destiny*, pp. 128–29, and *Gandhi's Passion: The Life and Legacy of Mahatma Gandhi* (New York: Oxford University Press, 2001), p. 159.

[9] Leonard Gordon, *Brothers against the Raj: A Biography of Indian Nationalists Sarat and Subhas Chandra Bose* (New York: Columbia University Press, 1990), p. 244.

[10] J. M. Brown, *Gandhi: Prisoner of Hope* (New Haven: Yale University Press, 1989), p. 251.

[11] J. Nehru, *An Autobiography* (new edn, London: The Bodley Head, 1958), p. 268. The following is his account of the authorship of the resolution: "During my early morning talks in Delhi with Gandhiji in February and March of 1931, I had referred to this matter [the matter covered by the resolution], and he had welcomed the idea of having a resolution on economic matters. He asked me to bring the matter up at Karachi, and to draft a resolution and show it to him there. I did so at Karachi, and he made various changes and suggestions. He wanted both of us to agree on the wording, before we asked the Working Committee to consider it. I had to make several drafts and this delayed matters for a few days, and we were otherwise preoccupied with other matters. Ultimately, Gandhiji and I agreed on a draft . . ." Ibid., pp. 267–68.

[12] S. Gopal, *Jawaharlal Nehru: A Biography*, vol. I, *1889–1947* (Delhi: Oxford University Press, 1975), p. 152.

[13] *Hind Swaraj*, p. 90.   [14] CW, 45: 372.

This resolution's historic contribution to the evolution of the state in India is widely recognized. Granville Austin called it the "spiritual" antecedent of the Directive Principles of the new Indian constitution.[15] Susan Bayly saw it as "one of the major documents" of the entire nationalist movement.[16]

It can be divided into parts.[17] The first enumerated the negative liberties of the citizen, such as freedom of speech and conscience, neutrality of the state in religious matters, etc. The second part presented the state as a promoter of positive liberty. It covered areas of social policy relating to the adult franchise, protection of women in the work place, free primary education, right to form labor unions, to a living wage, and progressive income tax, etc. There was a warning to the upholders of the old regime – the rajahs, maharajas, and landlords: they had to share their wealth and reduce social disparities lest legislation should overtake them.[18] The state that Gandhi envisaged here was hardly the "soulless machine" that he once called the modern state.

A constitutionally limited state

The state that Gandhi defended was the limited liberal state – limited by the very fundamental rights that it was required to protect. The presumption here was that even a liberal state was liable to abuse its power from time to time. The citizens, therefore, had to hold in reserve the right to resist such abuses. Gandhi invented one of the most famous techniques of responding to such abuses, viz., satyagraha. Satyagraha was the Gandhian, non-violent, way of defending rights. It was comprised of three basic elements: non-violent civil disobedience, voluntary acceptance of condign punishment due to the act or acts of civil disobedience, and the improvement of the quality of justice that would result from the practice of satyagraha.

It is very important to keep in mind that satyagraha presupposed the legitimacy of the coercive state. It required that the citizens be habitually law-abiding. Only they had the right to civil disobedience in the Gandhian sense of disobedience, who knew "how to offer voluntary and deliberate obedience to the laws of the state" in which they lived.[19] The habit of obedience to the state is an important condition for exercising

---

[15] Austin, *The Indian Constitution*, pp. 56–57.
[16] S. Bayly, *Caste, Society, and Politics in India from the Eighteenth Century to the Modern Age*, The New Cambridge History of India, IV. 3 (Cambridge: Cambridge University Press, 1999), p. 244.
[17] For the text see CW, 45: 370–2.   [18] Ibid., p. 373.   [19] CW, 15: 436.

the right to civil disobedience. Without this habit a people could lose their independence and be conquered by more disciplined states.[20] The *satyagrahi*, therefore, had to remain a "friend" not "enemy" of the state.[21] Only those who habitually obeyed the law were entitled to disobey it.[22] Before civil disobedience could be practiced on a vast scale, people had to learn the art of civil or voluntary obedience.[23] No society could survive without penal institutions. "We are not out to abolish jails as an institution," he once wrote. "Even under swaraj we would have our jails."[24]

By providing for resistance to itself, the Gandhian constitutional state strengthens, not weakens, its moral basis. It is worth observing here that John Rawls' idea of non-violent civil disobedience "within the limits of fidelity to law," is compatible with the Gandhian idea of civil disobedience.[25] According to Rawls, a "general disposition" to engage in justified civil disobedience contributes to the stability, and not the instability, of a well-ordered society, or one that was nearly just. Justified civil disobedience under these conditions can act as "a final device to maintain the stability of a just constitution."[26] Both Rawlsian civil disobedience and Gandhian satyagraha help to improve the moral temper of the state.

Given the compatibility of satyagraha with the constitutional state, the charge that satyagraha promotes anarchism misses the mark by a wide margin. Sir C. Sankaran Nair (1857–1934), President of the Indian National Congress for 1897 and member of the Viceroy's Executive Council for 1915, had accused Gandhi of being an anarchist. He even wrote *Gandhi and Anarchy* (1922), to make his case. Curiously enough, his claim rested on a misunderstanding of Gandhi's position on the relationship of artha to moksha. Sir Sankaran reasoned that because Gandhi's ultimate goal was "spiritual self-fulfillment," or moksha, he had to be, for that reason, against "any government" and had to choose "anarchy and soul force" as substitutes for law and imposed order.[27] Even Joan Bondurant found herself asserting that satyagraha could "reconcile" the state with the idea of anarchism or at least pave the way for the "realization of the fundamental objectives of anarchism."[28] All these criticisms go against Gandhi's repeated claim that satyagraha was "the

[20] CW, 89: 196.   [21] CW, 22: 19.   [22] CW, 15: 436–37.
[23] R. Iyer, *The Moral and Political Writings of Mahatma Gandhi* (3 vols., Oxford: Oxford University Press, 1986–87) vol. III, p. 597.
[24] CW, 22: 19.
[25] J. Rawls, *A Theory of Justice* (Cambridge, MA: Harvard University Press, 1973), p. 366.
[26] Ibid., pp. 383–84.
[27] C. Sankaran Nair, *Gandhi and Anarchy* (Delhi: Mittal Publications, 1995), pp. 16, 27, 64.
[28] J. Bondurant, *Conquest of Violence: The Gandhian Philosophy of Conflict* (rev. edn, Berkeley: University of California Press, 1967), pp. 172–73.

purest form of constitutional agitation."[29] The mistake here was to isolate satyagraha from its necessary correlate, the state. In doing so, the therapeutic or corrective function of satyagraha got lost.

The end result of satyagraha, as Gandhi saw it, would be the emergence of an improved constitutional order, not its replacement by statelessness or anarchy. As K. M. Munshi, one of the framers of the 1950 Indian Constitution had pointed out, Gandhi asserted time and again that satyagraha was constitutional. The goal of resistance to the state was the improved constitutional order, and not the replacement of the state by statelessness. The voluntary acceptance of the penalty for civil disobedience proved both the legitimacy and validity of the state, and the constitutionality of civil disobedience.[30] And as "the Satyagraha Pledge" of 1919 stated, disobedience to unjust laws, the non-violent securing of the rights and the preservation of the state all went together.[31]

The constitution and satyagraha played complementary roles in Gandhi's philosophy. He spoke of the difference between what he called the "constitutional swaraj" and "organic swaraj." The first created a liberal, coercive state; the second developed the satyagraha technique of resisting it, should it deviate from its liberal path. The first required the involvement of the elite – "the learned and politically astute leaders" – and the second required the involvement of "the ordinary, illiterate masses."[32] To run smoothly, the Gandhian state needed the active involvement of both the elite and the masses. Action on the part of the state and the corrective, non-violent, resistance on the part of the citizens restrained the state's tendency to expand its power and to dominate the whole of social life.

The state as the defender of national security

To provide for the security of the nation against external aggression, Gandhi firmly believed, was one of the major responsibilities of the state. The questions of war and peace, no less than those of independence, presupposed the existence of the state. He had both historical and theoretical reasons for believing this. From the historical perspective, it was India's inability to have a state for the whole of India, capable of defending itself, that was part of the reason for colonialism. Swaraj, therefore, meant, among other things, the establishment of an Indian

---

[29] CW, 22: 19.
[30] See K. M. Munshi, *Indian Constitutional Documents* (Bombay: Bharatiya Vidya Bhavan, 1967), vol. I, pp. 195–96.
[31] CW, 15: 101.   [32] CW, 37: 249.

state that would rectify this terrible mistake of the past. That Gandhi had strong and consistent views on national defense may come as a surprise to those who view him, quite incorrectly, as a radical pacifist.

On theoretical grounds, he held the view that the international system constituted a community of states and not anarchy. The states therefore had the obligation to behave like responsible, cooperative, world citizens. This view was articulated in a formal document, his 1924 presidential address to the Indian National Congress. "The better mind of the world desires today not absolutely independent states warring one against another but a federation of friendly interdependent states. The consummation of that event may be far off. I want to make no grand claim for our country. But I see nothing grand or impossible about our expressing our readiness for universal interdependence rather than independence ... I desire the ability to be totally independent without asserting the independence."[33] Being responsible members of the international community meant that states ought not to pursue national interest as the sole rule of international relations. Indeed, they should follow their national interest only within the bounds of universally accepted norms.

A second principle that guided his thought was that states had the right to self-defense, if necessary, by military means. The use of force in international relations, as we shall see later in chapter 7, was consistent with his general ethical theory of non-violence. He was strongly critical of the compulsory disarming of Indians by the colonial power. It made them "unmanly," and lacking in the spirit of resistance and the capacity for self-defense.[34] It would therefore be the first duty of an independent Indian state to give military training to its citizens. Although he himself would not join the army, he considered it his "duty to vote for the military training of those who wished to take it."[35] An independent Indian state would have to follow "some kind of mild war policy."[36]

He formally expressed these views with force and eloquence in 1931 at the Second Round Table Conference. "I think that a nation that has no control over her own defense forces, and over her external policy is hardly a responsible nation. Defense, its Army, is to a nation the very essence of its existence, and if a nation's defense is controlled by an outside agency, no matter how friendly it is, then that nation is certainly not responsibly governed." He came to this conclusion, he emphasized, "with the greatest deliberation."[37] It was his "fundamental position," his "dream," to restore that power to the Indian state. "It is the dream I should like to cherish up to the end of my time ... That is really my ambition and,

---

[33] CW, 25: 482.   [34] CW, 42: 385.   [35] CW, 37: 271.   [36] CW, 87: 202.
[37] CW, 48: 304.

therefore, I say I would wait till eternity if I cannot get control of Defense. I refuse to deceive myself that I am going to embark upon responsible government although I cannot control my Defense."[38] There can be no swaraj without adequate defensive military power. India once had such power. The Rajputs, he pointed out, were responsible for "a thousand Thermopylaes, and not one little Thermopylae as in Greece."[39]

His third principle concerned the duty of citizens to contribute to the defense of the state. It was on the basis of this principle that he justified his participation, in a noncombatant role of course, in the Boer War and the Zulu Rebellion. He invoked the same principle during the First World War, when he actively recruited for the Indian army. In this context, he severely criticized the world-renouncing spiritual elite of India – the pundits, the *shastris*, and *Sankaracharyas* (the successors of the first Sankara) – for neglecting artha in the life of the nation. Unless their "pseudo-philosophy" was rooted out of the Indian soil, there would be no peace in the country.[40]

His support for the First World War should be seen in the context of India's colonial condition. One of the requirements necessary to come out of that condition was India's capacity for self-defense. Only if India possessed that capacity could India deal with Great Britain on equal terms. To get that capacity one had to have military training and to have military training one had to have an army. Therefore, it was the duty of every Indian who desired independence to enlist in the army.

Gandhi was severely criticized by C. F. Andrews and others for this kind of reasoning. But he stood his ground. For he believed that war was a permanent feature of the international system. In the embodied condition, it could not be otherwise. His response was firm: "under exceptional circumstances war may have to be resorted to as a necessary evil, even as the body is. If the motive is right, it may be turned into the profit of mankind, and ... an *Ahimsaist* [a practitioner of non-violence] may not stand aside and look with indifference, but must make the choice and actively cooperate or actively resist."[41] This is the new Arjuna speaking.

However, the horrors of the Second World War produced a profound impact on Gandhi's thinking on war and the state's right to self-defense by military means. Still he did not see pacifism as a solution to the questions of war and peace. What he did see was the need to rethink the right to self-defense by military means. But rethinking here did not mean

---

[38] Ibid., pp. 306–7.   [39] Ibid., p. 307; the reference is to Colonel Tod's *Memoirs*.
[40] M. K. Gandhi, "Recruiting Appeal: Bulletin No. 2," in Desai, *Day-to-Day with Gandhi*, p. 357.
[41] Gandhi to C. F. Andrews, 6 July 1918 (ibid., p. 177).

abandoning the principle, only modifying its methods of application. He began to think in terms of developing civilian means of exercising that right side by side with the military means. All decent states from now on would have the duty to pursue commonly agreed-upon methods of disarmament, even while they maintained the right to defend themselves by military means.[42]

During the last years of the Second World War Gandhi was willing for India to join the Allies as a free, equal, sovereign state. However, that was not to be. There was no question of Great Britain granting independence to India in the middle of the war. Hence his act of defiance, and the launch of the "Quit India" campaign. It failed, and all that Gandhi got for his troubles was yet another term in jail.

It was not so much the physical departure of the British during the war that he wanted as a change in the political status of India as a colony. He understood the requirements of military necessity that Great Britain faced in India during the war. He would, therefore, have been satisfied with the establishment of a "provisional" government by a new Indian state. The latter would then freely enter into treaty relations with the Allies, and allow Allied troops to operate from the Indian soil.[43] The idea behind the "Quit India" agitation was the urgent need to restore full sovereignty to the Indian state.

Already in 1947 the new Indian state found itself faced with a military crisis in Kashmir. Though he would have preferred the civilian mode of self-defense here, the decision of the new state to use military means of self-defense had his tacit support. For he realized that "ordinarily government was impossible without the use of force." That was why, as he often said, those who wanted "to be good and do good in all circumstances must not hold power."[44] If friendly negotiations failed and justice could not be had, then resort of armed resistance would become inevitable. Gandhi's practical realism made him realize that a responsible state could not in principle abandon the right to self-defense by military means. His realism dictated that an independent India had to have the necessary military capacity to defend itself even when it tried to develop civilian means of national defense.

The secularity of the state

Gandhi was a strong supporter of the secular state. As we saw in the previous chapter, civic nationalism required that institutional religion be

---

[42] CW, 84: 89.   [43] CW, 76: 313, 282–84, 454.   [44] CW, 90: 510–11.

not the basis of the political community. The state that was to preside over a civic nation had to be neutral towards all religions. The second article of the "Resolution on Fundamental Rights and Social Changes" had stipulated the neutrality of the state towards all religions.[45] There was no ambiguity whatsoever about his stand on the matter. "Religion is a personal matter. It ought not to affect the political field."[46]

The state's competence, apart from protecting rights, was limited to securing the material conditions of life – national security, the collection and management of revenue, public health and sanitation, police, criminal and civil justice, etc. In matters affecting religious belief, manner of worship, etc. "a secular state [had] no concern."[47] "If I were a dictator," he once told an interviewer, "religion and state would be separate. I swear by my religion. I will die for it, but it is my personal affair. The state has nothing to do with it. The state would look after your secular welfare, health, communication, foreign relations, currency and so on, but not your, or my, religion. That is everybody's personal concern."[48]

Gandhi's concept of secularism, it is worth repeating, has its basis in the theory of the purusharthas. Artha is distinct from, but not opposed to, dharma or moksha. The three, being purusharthas, belong to a system of valid ends, and for this reason are required to work out a *modus vivendi*. His secularism is, therefore, philosophically different from the laic, antireligious secularism that arose in Europe after the Enlightenment.[49]

The state and civil society

Gandhi's theory of the state has an important bearing on the state's relationship to civil society. His *Constructive Programme* is devoted to this question.[50] "Constructive work" is his phrase for voluntary work done by Non-Governmental Organizations (NGOs). Freedom is maximized and violence minimized when the state and NGOs work in harmony.

The state represents a necessarily coercive order, while the NGOs represent the non-violent voluntary order. They complement each other. Organized voluntary work brings swaraj to its perfection.[51] The state does its work through the bureaucracy and NGOs through highly motivated, voluntary agencies.

---

[45] CW, 45: 370–71.   [46] CW, 74: 27.
[47] CW, 75: 237; Again, "religion was a personal matter," CW, 89: 79, 112.
[48] CW, 85: 328.
[49] For a sophisticated discussion of secularism in modern India, see R. Bhargava (ed.), *Secularism and Its Critics* (Delhi: Oxford University Press, 1998).
[50] CW, 75: 146–66.   [51] Ibid., p. 146.

Constructive work complements satyagraha too. The one seeks to remove a particular social evil, while the other seeks to remove the evils of a particular piece of legislation. Given the state's propensity to abuse its power, civil disobedience will always be needed. But a society cannot live by civil disobedience alone. In order to flourish it needs constructive work as well.

Constructive Programme identified eighteen areas that were particularly suitable for the action of NGOs. They included areas of conflict produced by religious, linguistic, racial, caste, and gender differences; areas of public health and hygiene, village crafts, agriculture, adult education, etc. The list reflected the priorities of the 1930s and 1940s. It was not meant to be exhaustive or final. What areas would be appropriate for NGO action would depend on time and place. The point was that the more NGOs got into action, the less violent society would become.

Gandhi's insight was that if the state was to become less violent it had to act in tandem with organs of civil society. At the same time, he did not want the state to wither away and leave the field solely to the organs of civil society. Some, such as Gene Sharp, have argued that Gandhi would have preferred civil society as an alternative to the state.[52] Nothing could be farther from the truth. Gandhi wanted the two to work together on the basis of the principle of subsidiarity. According to that principle, the state may not intervene where voluntary agencies can do the job. For example, the cause of secularism would be strengthened if the people, on their own, established organizations that promoted amity between different religious groups. The same was true of matters affecting racial and ethnic relations. Gandhi writes: "I admit that there are certain things which cannot be done without political power, but there are numerous other things which do not at all depend upon political power. That is why a thinker like Thoreau said that 'that government is the best which governs the least.' This means that when people come into possession of political power, the interference with the freedom of the people is reduced to a minimum. In other words, a nation that runs its affairs smoothly and effectively without much state interference is truly democratic. Where such condition is absent, the form of government is democratic in name [only]."[53]

Gandhi saw yet other benefits accruing from NGOs – decentralization and diffusion of power. The power that would otherwise be concentrated in the hands of the state would now be shared with NGOs. In this way

[52] G. Sharp, *Gandhi As A Political Strategist* (Boston: Porter Sargent Publishers, 1979), p. 80.
[53] CW, 62: 92.

the sphere of non-violence would expand, and that of coercive power contract. The more vibrant the civil society, the less violent the state would be.

For such a state of cooperation to flourish between the state and civil society, the average citizenry would have to reach an optimal level of material and moral development. But a beginning had to be made for which civil society would depend on individual leaders of exceptional moral insights. Gandhi was one such individual, and his influence on the development of NGO activities in India had been, and still is, immense.[54]

We are now in a position to survey the full scope of Gandhi's state-theory. A good society needs both the state (acting through coercive power) and a vibrant civil society (acting through non-violent power). The two can exercise mutually beneficial influence on each other. Maintaining the balance between the two is part of good statecraft. When the state is in right balance with civil society, there would be what Gandhi called *su-rajya*, the good state.[55] In *su-rajya* there would be minimum necessary coercion and the maximum possible civic freedom, i.e., harmony between artha, dharma, and moksha.

The state, the ideal state or *Ramarajya*

There was a strong streak of idealism running underneath Gandhi's attempts to create the actual, historic state in modern India. He often expressed that idealism by the term *Ramarajya*, literally, "the reign of Rama," the prince of Ayodhya, the hero of the epic *Ramayana*, and the seventh avatar of Vishnu. Figuratively, the term meant the "reign of ideal justice," "perfect democracy," or "the reign of self-imposed law of moral restraint."[56]

Gandhi was often misunderstood here. He was criticized for using a term with such an obvious Hindu connotation. The separatist Muslims accused him of being a Hindu nationalist in civic nationalist disguise. The Hindu nationalists, in their turn, welcomed the term, claiming that their ideology was no more sinister than his.

Gandhi was deeply troubled by all this. He denied that he had attached any sectarian meaning to the term. He certainly did not mean by *Ramarajya* a Hindu Raj. What he meant was "Divine Raj," the kingdom of God in human hearts, the sort of thing that Tolstoy meant in his work *The Kingdom of God Is Within You*. He was not even referring to the Rama

[54] For an excellent account of Gandhi's influence on Indian NGOs, see R. Sooryamoorthy and K. D. Gangrade, *NGOs in India* (Westport, CT: Greenwood Press, 2001).
[55] CW, 90: 24.   [56] CW, 80: 300.

of history, but to an imagined, spiritual Rama, the symbol of perfection. "Whether the Rama of my imagination lived or not on this earth," he wrote, "the ancient idea of *Ramarajya*" meant for him "perfect democracy" in which there would be perfect equality between all members of the nation.[57] He could not find a better alternative that would convey to the millions of Hindus what Christians meant by "the kingdom of God" and the Muslims meant by the phrase "Khudai Raj" (God's reign). What the three traditions – the Hindu, Christian, and Muslim – were trying to portray was the ideal of perfect justice.[58] Under these circumstances, not to use the term for fear of political incorrectness would have been "self-suppression and hypocrisy."[59]

Theologically, then, the term stood for the reign of perfect justice within the human heart. Such a reign could never be fully realized in the institutions of society. Therefore his ideal of *Ramarajya*, best understood within the bounds of his theory of the purusharthas, has nothing to do with theocracy of any kind. At the same time, according to that same theory, sanctity was within the reach of ordinary citizens operating in the field of artha, regardless of their religious affiliation. Genuine sanctity, according to Gandhi, was compatible with genuine democracy. Neither theocracy nor secularism can see how this is possible. That is why both the secularists and theocrats are uncomfortable with and suspicious of the Gandhian concept of *Ramarajya*. However, the theory of the purusharthas, properly applied, can help remove the basis for both the discomfort and the suspicion.

Gandhi, anarchy, and statelessness

One of the contributions that the theory of the purusharthas makes is to give legitimacy to the institution of the state. The state is a requirement of artha. Yet we see among Gandhi scholars a certain reluctance to grant legitimacy to his theory of the state. They sometimes attribute utopianism and anarchism to his practical philosophy. This, in our view, is due to a misunderstanding of his theory of the purusharthas.

Raghavan Iyer, for example, saw a conflict between the demands of truth and non-violence on the one hand and those of the state on the other. Being allegedly a soulless machine, the state was liable to overstep its boundary and smother the individual. The individual would feel fully secure in a condition of enlightened anarchy. Iyer is inclined to the opinion that "an anarchist view of the State" was the ultimate ideal that Gandhi preferred, but on practical grounds he settled for a minimally

[57] CW, 41: 374.   [58] CW, 85: 135.   [59] Ibid.

coercive state. In other words, on the question of the state, Gandhi's practice did not tally with his theory.[60] The movement of Gandhian political thought was towards a stateless society.[61]

Iyer is repeating the old mistake of positing an unnecessary opposition between the pursuits of dharma and artha – a mistake that Gandhi wants everyone to avoid. The state, being a part of artha, is a positive institution necessary for human flourishing. Besides, even the Shastras were opposed to anarchism.[62] Writing in 1940, Gandhi feared "the dread prospect of anarchy" threatening India.[63] The best way to meet that threat was the establishment of a constitutional state according to the wishes of the people of India.

Bhikhu Parekh holds that Gandhi was unhappy with not just the modern state, but the state as such. And the reason, ultimately, was the alleged opposition between the purusharthas. The state "by its nature," says Parekh, is incompatible with man's moral and spiritual pursuits. The soul and the modern state, which is a soulless machine, cannot co-exist. Humans, therefore, have to find "an alternative way of structuring their organized life." The modern state is particularly unsuited for India. For India has a spiritual civilization, whereas the state is "uniquely a product of materialist civilization."[64] Again, "For Gandhi, the vital task today was to explore alternatives not just to the contemporary forms of government but to the very institution of the state." "Like many a moral idealist Gandhi found it difficult to appreciate the role of coercion in social life and to come to terms with the state."[65]

According to Partha Chatterjee the state could never be "the appropriate machinery" for carrying out Gandhi's programme. He would rather have the state abdicate its "presumed responsibility" and clear the way "for popular non-state agencies to take up the work of revitalizing the village economies." Thus, after collaborating with the Indian bourgeoisie for several decades, he "in the last years of his life resumed to struggle [sic] for Utopia." In the end, according to Chatterjee, he

---

[60] R. Iyer, *The Moral and Political Thought of Mahatma Gandhi* (Santa Barbara, CA: Concorde Grove Press, 1983), p. 254.

[61] Iyer, *The Moral and Political Writings of Mahatma Gandhi*, vol. III, pp. 595–609. The texts collected here are taken out of their specific contexts, not to mention Gandhi's general theory of the state.

[62] CW, 13: 240.   [63] CW, 72: 202.

[64] B. Parekh, *Gandhi's Political Philosophy* (Notre Dame, IN: Notre Dame University Press, 1989), p. 112.

[65] Parekh, *Gandhi*, pp. 81, 90.

allegedly posited an opposition between "political swaraj" and "true swaraj,"[66] in our terminology, between artha and moksha. Gandhi, as we have seen, posits no such opposition between the political and the spiritual.[67]

Granville Austin's analysis of Gandhi's position on the constitution and the state is also based, ultimately, on his perception that moral action (dharma) is self-sufficient even in the field of politics, and that it could produce political results independently of artha. Austin wrote: "Gandhi believed that the achievement of social justice as the common lot must proceed from a character reformation of each individual, from the heart and mind of each Indian outward into society as a whole. The impetus for reform must not come downward from government, and a reformed society would need no government to regulate or control it."[68] But such a view goes against Gandhi's theory of the purusharthas. Artha, as a purushartha, is constitutive of the good of society, and no matter how morally virtuous members of society are, society will need all that artha entails, including the state. Besides, it is not true that according to Gandhi an individual who does not actively participate in the political affairs can be counted as virtuous. He or she may be considered virtuous in the old, renouncer's sense of virtue, but not in the new, Gandhian civic sense. For Gandhi, to be virtuous one had to engage in public life. Gokhale the statesman was his model of a virtuous person. He was virtuous because he was a statesman, and he was a statesman because he was virtuous.

Gandhi did not participate in the deliberations of the Constituent Assembly, convened on 9 December 1946. He felt his presence was more urgently needed in riot-torn Bengal than in Delhi. He was confident, however, that his colleagues – Jawaharlal Nehru, B. R. Ambedkar, Vallabhbhai Patel, Rajendra Prasad, Rajaji, Maulana Azad, and J. B. Kripalani – were fully competent to guide the proceedings of the Assembly.[69] He was not in the least interested in promoting what some critics had called "a Gandhian constitution," in opposition to the proposed constitution. On the contrary, he fully endorsed Nehru's Objectives Resolution that set the agenda of the Assembly; it was his hope that Nehru would "stick to" that resolution "whatever be the criticism advanced or opinion held by others."[70] He was particularly happy that

---

[66] Chatterjee, *Nationalist Thought and the Colonial World*, p. 116.

[67] Elsewhere I have analyzed the four meanings of swaraj in Gandhi's philosophy and their relationship to each other. See A. J. Parel, (ed.) *Gandhi, Freedom and Self-Rule* (Lanham, MD: Lexington Books, 2000).

[68] Austin, *The Indian Constitution*, p. 31.   [69] CW, 86: 162.   [70] Ibid., p. 234.

B. R. Ambedkar "was good enough to attend the Assembly."[71] Though Gandhi did not directly participate in the Assembly debates, there was no doubt in anybody's mind that, as Nehru observed, he was not only "the father of the nation" but also "the architect" of the Assembly that produced the nation's constitution.[72]

---

[71] Ibid., p. 426.
[72] J. Nehru, in *Constituent Assembly Debates*, Official Report, vol. I, 2nd reprint (New Delhi: Lok Sabha Secretariat, 1989), p. 60.

4 The economy

("We must have industry, but of the right kind."[1]

Wealth, being part of artha, is a constitutive element of human well-being. Gandhi had a profound appreciation of this fact, despite the stereotype of him as an ascetic who glorified poverty. His poverty was entirely voluntary, and was meant to be a symbol of his protest against, and a critique of, the involuntary poverty of the Indian masses. He regarded involuntary poverty as a dehumanizing curse upon humanity. The mass poverty of India was as intolerable to him as was colonialism. It is a remarkable fact, but one often forgotten by critics, that his famous "Declaration of Independence" contained an important economic clause. Indeed, its opening sentence paired the inalienable right of people for political freedom with their right to economic freedom as well.[2]

Gandhi was not an economist in the accepted sense of that term. But he had deeply held ideas on the economy that constituted a coherent philosophy. They were the following:

1. Human beings have a right to the fruit of their labor just as they have an obligation to earn their livelihood by the sweat of their brow.

2. Human beings are each endowed with a soul, and because of this self-interest is not the only motivation at work in economic relations. Moderating self-interest and leading it to its legitimate ends is soul-force, the source of love, compassion, and natural justice (nyaya-buddhi). A sound economy, therefore, is not a violent economy.

3. The vice of greed is an ever-present threat to human well-being. Humans, therefore, have an obligation to cultivate the virtue of non-possessive individualism or aparigraha.

4. As every individual has a right to private property, so he or she has an obligation to abstain from theft. There is the further obligation to cultivate the virtue of "freedom from thieving" or astea.

---

[1] CW, 8: 374.   [2] CW, 42: 384.

5. As the universal human family is divided into distinct and sovereign political entities, each such entity has the first obligation to look after its economic well-being, without in any way harming the economic well-being of other units. This calls for the practice of the virtue of *swadeshi*, or "what pertains to one's own country."

6. To have a full and accurate understanding of wealth, it should be taken in two senses: as material possessions of exchangeable value and as human persons. Modern political economy gives primacy to the first sense. Gandhi, following Ruskin, corrects it, and gives priority to the second. The wealth of a nation, therefore, consists in the first instance in its people and in the second instance in material possessions of exchangeable value.

7. The first concern of a sound economy should be the welfare of the last and the least of society.

8. In a theological sense God, as the originator of everything, is the lord of the material universe. Humans, taken collectively and individually, are its trustees. Though the right to private property is a right, it is not absolute but conditional to meeting the needs of the political community; it ought to work in harmony with the principle of trusteeship.

9. The science of wealth, *artha-sastra*, though autonomous within its specific sphere, is still connected to the other sciences and arts necessary for life, and, therefore, ought to adapt its conclusions to the wider concerns of ethics, pleasure, and spirituality.

10. In particular, the enjoyment of wealth ought to harmonize with the enjoyment of aesthetic and artistic pleasure.

11. Technology has a place in the modern economy, its purpose being to lighten the burden of labor. However, it may not be allowed to replace human labor or to become antagonistic to it.

Gandhi's Indian sources

Gandhi derived his economic ideas from both Indian and Western sources. The Indian sources included, from among the ancients, the Ishopanishad, Patanjali's *Yoga Sutra*, and the *Bhagavad Gita*; and from among the moderns, the writings of Dadabhai Naoroji (1825–1917) and Romesh Chunder Dutt (1848–1909).

His extraordinary interest in the first verse of the Ishopanishad, one of the oldest of the Upanishads, may come as a surprise to some. The extravagant praise that he showered on it as containing the essence of Hinduism may surprise even more. He had memorized it, used it as part of his daily prayers, and had read the commentaries on it by such luminaries as Sankara and Sri Aurobindo.[3] He even considered the *Gita* to be an extended commentary on it. Living up to its teaching, he remarked, was like experiencing "the new birth" that the New Testament spoke of or the need for constant dedication to God that Hinduism taught.[4] The verse itself is terse, and reads as follows:

> By the Lord [*isa*] enveloped must all this be –
> Whatever moving thing there is in the moving world.
> With this renounced, thou mayst enjoy.
> Covet not the wealth of anyone at all.[5]

Gandhi's commentary on it amounts to being a theological analysis of the meaning of wealth and of the conditions under which it may be enjoyed.[6] Five ideas are involved: ownership, detachment, enjoyment, covetousness, and trusteeship. God, as originator of everything, is the owner, lord, and master of the whole material universe. Humans are only its trustees. They may appropriate by their labor what they need for their sustenance. "Enjoy the things of the earth by renouncing them," was a sovereign principle. They ought to enjoy them, not as proprietors but as trustees.[7] They ought not to claim absolute mastery of the resources of the earth. Absolute mastery belongs to God alone. They, therefore, have to renounce all pretensions to absolute ownership. On condition that they do so, they may enjoy the wealth that they create. At the same time, they ought not to covet what they do not need and what belongs to others. They should act as the trustees of their surplus wealth.

A theological approach to wealth such as this may sound "strange" to secular ears, both capitalist and socialist. But it was precisely its "strangeness" that he wanted others to hear. He was of the opinion that humans were not absolute masters of material nature and, therefore, they ought not to treat it as if they were. His philosophical anthropology included not only the body and its needs but also the immortal soul and God, and the love that linked them. He writes: "There must be recognition of the existence of the soul apart from the body, and of its permanent nature, and this recognition must amount to a living faith; and, in the last resort, non-violence does not avail those who do not possess a living faith in the God of love."[8]

---

[3] CW, 50: 263; CW, 64: 259.   [4] CW, 84: 327.

[5] R. E. Hume (trans.), *The Thirteen Principal Upanishads* (2nd rev. edn, Madras: Oxford University Press, 1954), p. 362.

[6] For his commentary see CW, 64: 258–59; 263–65.   [7] CW, 44: 115.

[8] Cited in E. F. Schumacher, *Small Is Beautiful: A Study of Economics as if People Mattered* (London: Abacus, 1978), p. 37.

Gandhi was by no means alone in taking the theological dimension of "global" economics seriously. St. Thomas Aquinas in the Western tradition had done something quite similar. He too had asserted that God alone had absolute dominion over material nature. Humans had only relative dominion, and that too limited to the *use* of material things. No one was entitled to manage the world's resources "merely for himself; he must do so in the interests of all, so that he is ready to share them with others in case of necessity."[9]

The movement away from being the trustees of material nature to being its masters started with Francis Bacon. It found its most famous expression in René Descartes. Through science humans should be able to treat material nature as if they were its "masters and possessors."[10] Descartes could not have foreseen the direction that modern economic science would take. Gandhi is perhaps the first modern of stature to defend explicitly the view that the application of modern science to the exploitation of the world's resources should be guided by the spirit of trusteeship and not by that of absolute ownership.

But here a word of caution is in order. Critics sometimes treat trusteeship as an alternative to the principle of the right to private property. Evidence cannot support this interpretation. Trusteeship for Gandhi was a moral, even a theological, principle, but not a political, much less a constitutional, principle. You enacted that principle through private ethical conduct, not through legislation.

Gandhi used both Patanjali and the *Gita* to reinforce his interpretation of the Upanishad cited above. He mentioned by name the two economic virtues of Patanjali – *astea* and *aparigraha*. Though he used them by name he changed their meaning rather significantly. In Patanjali they were meant to be private virtues leading to an ascetic ideal – to solitude, withdrawal from society, and from socially useful labor. Gandhi gave the two virtues a social and economic interpretation. Freedom from thieving was not only a negative virtue; for it had a positive content as well. It meant the exercise of the right to private property in an inclusive sense – inclusive in the sense that the right to private property involved the obligation not to exclude those in dire straits from benefiting from the fruit of your labor. Freedom from greed also had a negative as well as a positive meaning. Negatively it meant freedom from the limitless desire for things – in the modern idiom, consumerism. Positively it meant the enjoyment of things that one needed for maintaining a decent standard of life. Renunciation of

[9] St. Thomas Aquinas, *Summa Theologiae*, 2a 2ae, Question 66, Articles 1, 2.
[10] See E. Gilson (ed.), *René Descartes, Discours de la méthode* (Paris: Vrin, 1976), pp. 62, 446.

the superfluous was compatible with the enjoyment of what was needed.[11]

Dadabhai's *Poverty and Un-British Rule in India* (1901) and Dutt's two-volume *Economic History of India* (1901–2) were Gandhi's sources for his understanding of modern Indian economy. They were essentially critiques of the economic policies of the colonial government. Dutt had argued that, from the Indian point of view, foreign investment in irrigation made better sense than did investment in the railways. Yet foreign investment went to the railways because it was there that the investors would get a better return. Irrigation might have produced more food and averted famines. But such considerations did not dominate the thinking of the colonial system. Dadabhai Naoroji also used the example of the railways to illustrate his so-called "drain-theory" – the theory that under colonial regime foreign investments drained wealth out of India and contributed to India's growing poverty. Gandhi could not have found better source materials than these works to bolster his argument for including the economic virtue of *swadeshi* in his economic philosophy.

As for the economic virtue of *swadeshi*, it is important to ask in what exact sense it was an economic virtue, for, on the face of it, it appeared more like a vice than a virtue. Looking after one's own interest appeared selfish, not virtuous. However, this was not how Gandhi saw it. For him the principle underlying this virtue was that of neighborliness. "A man's first duty," he argued, was "to his neighbor." This did not mean hatred of the foreigner or partiality towards one's own. It meant that in serving one's neighbor one served the whole world. Whoever achieved one's own economic interests without hurting the economic interests of others would be serving the interest of everyone. As he put it succinctly, no one could serve others without serving oneself.[12]

Gandhi's sources: Ruskin

John Ruskin's influence on Gandhi's economic philosophy is universally recognized. Romesh Diwan and Mark Lutz in their *Essays on Gandhian Economics* have claimed that his "primary concepts" of economics come from *Unto This Last*, the title coming from the parable of the workers in

---

[11] CW, 79: 261.

[12] CW, 50: 217–21. Gandhi's much vaunted interest in *khadi*, or cloth produced by cottage industry, was prompted by the virtue of *swadeshi*. For a study of Gandhi's politics of the neighbor, see Ajay Skaria, "Revisting Secularism: Gandhi and the Politics of the Neighbor," an unpublished paper.

the vineyard in St. Matthew 20: 1–16.[13] Gandhi himself spoke of the "magic spell" that that work had exerted on him, and "the instantaneous and practical transformation" that it had brought about in his life.[14] While critics focus their attention on this work, they ignore, unaccountably, a second work of Ruskin that had also influenced him. I refer to *"A Joy Forever": And Its Price in the Market*, published in 1857 under the original title *The Political Economy of Art*. This is also listed in the Appendix to *Hind Swaraj*, calling for special attention. I shall analyze this work in detail in chapter 9. Here it is sufficient to mention that Ruskin helped Gandhi to see economics not only as a specialized modern discipline but also as one that had a bearing on other disciplines such as ethics and aesthetics. Modern political economy, without the influence of aesthetic values ennobling it, was in danger of becoming not only a "dismal science" but also a barbarous one.

Here our attention is focused only on *Unto This Last* (1862). Ruskin himself had thought of this work "the best and most valuable of all his works."[15] Kenneth Clark, the art historian, counted this book among the "prophetic books" of the nineteenth century, which included the *Communist Manifesto* (1848) and *On the Origin of Species by Means of Natural Selection* (1859). According to Clement Attlee, the Labour MPs first elected to the House of Commons in 1906 were of the opinion that *Unto This Last* was the book that had influenced them the most.[16] According to Clyde Wilmer, Ruskin had been a major influence on "much of twentieth century" British social legislation, notably on that introduced by the Attlee Government.[17] What Wilmer did not mention was perhaps the most important legislation that the Attlee Government passed: the Indian Independence Bill, passed on 17 July 1947, bringing the Raj to a close. There is then an intellectual chain that links Ruskin, Gandhi, Attlee, Gandhian political economy and Indian Independence.

There are two formal statements by Gandhi on *Unto This Last* that deserve attention. The first is brief and appears in the autobiography.[18] It states that he had learned three things from that book. The first was that the good of the individual was contained in the good of all. The second was that human beings had a right and a duty to engage in socially useful work. And the third was that the "lowly" work of the peasants and the handicraftsmen was worthy of high respect.

[13] R. Diwan and M. Lutz (eds.), *Essays on Gandhian Economics* (New Delhi: Gandhi Peace Foundation, 1985), pp. 11–12.

[14] CW, 39: 129.

[15] See John Ruskin, *Unto This Last and Other Writings*, edited by C. Wilmer (London: Penguin, 1985), p. 29.

[16] Ibid., p. 30.   [17] Ibid.   [18] CW, 39: 239.

The second statement was much longer. In fact it took the form of a paraphrase of the whole book, published in 1908 in a nine-part series in *Indian Opinion* (Durban, South Africa). Later it was published in book form under the title *Sarvodaya*, which was also the name that he gave to his economic philosophy.[19]

Reflective and philosophic in tone and substance, *Sarvodaya* focused on the nature of economic motivations, the meaning of wealth, and the place of honesty, truth, and natural justice in its acquisition, distribution, and enjoyment. *Unto This Last* was a critique of, not an alternative to, capitalism – a friendly critique with a view to improve it, and not a hostile critique with a view to overthrow it, as was the case with the negative critique of Karl Marx, a contemporary of Ruskin.

The truth about modern economics, according to Ruskin, was that two kinds of motivation were at work in economic activities – self-interest and social affections. This was because humans were body–soul composites. Modern political economy focused on humans as bodily creatures: "man as a mere body, a machine," a money-making machine.[20] Avarice and self-interest were the "constants" and social affections the "accidental" elements of economic behavior.[21] The truth, however, according to Ruskin and Gandhi, was that the soul was the "predominant" unit of human nature. It was the source of social affections and natural justice (*nyaya buddhi*).[22] The soul-force, therefore, was an active force operating in economic relations, and in so far as this was the case, natural justice should be allowed to moderate the working of the law of the market or that of supply and demand.[23]

A key question arose as to whether wealth – the object of the science of economics – could be acquired under conditions of natural justice, truth, and honesty.[24] This led Ruskin to a careful analysis of the meaning of wealth, and of the concept of "value" of an economic good. John Stuart Mill had defined wealth as the possession of agreeable and useful things of exchangeable value.[25] Ruskin subjected this definition to a stern criticism, focusing on the concepts of "use" and "value." "Every material utility," he pointed out, depended on its "relative human capacity," and the agreeableness of a thing depended on its "relative human disposition." In so far as this was the case, political economy should be seen as a

---

[19] Regarding Ruskin's title, Gandhi wrote the following: "We do not even explain what the title of the book means, for it can be understood only by a person who has read the Bible in English. But, since the object which the book works towards is the welfare of all – that is, the advancement of all and not merely of the greatest number – we have entitled these articles 'Sarvodaya'" (CW, 8: 241).

[20] CW, 8: 257.   [21] Ibid., p. 241.   [22] Ibid., pp. 257–58.   [23] Ibid., p. 270.
[24] Ruskin, *Unto This Last*, pp. 161–63.   [25] Ibid., p. 206.

science "respecting human capacities and dispositions."[26] For an object to be useful in the economic sense it had to be "not only of an availing nature, but also in availing hands."[27] Thus a horse would be useful only in a country where people knew how to ride or harness it to a plow or cart. Briefly, an object to be economically significant had to take into account human capacities. Now the fundamental human capacity was life itself. Hence Ruskin's famous conclusion, "there is no wealth but life."[28]

Gandhi echoed these sentiments: we could not estimate a nation's wealth on the basis of "the quantity of cash" it possessed.[29] The people themselves constituted the wealth, "not gold and silver. We must search for wealth not in the bowels of the earth, but in the hearts of men ... the true law of economics [was] that men should be maintained in the best possible health, both of body and mind, and in the highest honor."[30] This could not come about unless natural justice came into play in economic activities. "True economics is the economics of justice. That people alone will be happy which learns how to do justice and be righteous under all conditions of life."[31] Money is only a means to life and "there is no wealth besides life."[32]

With Ruskin the meaning of wealth had begun to shift from being considered as possessions to being considered as people – people who had the appropriate "capacities" and "dispositions." Gandhi, in his turn, re-emphasized this meaning: a sound economy is one that empowered the last and the least of society, and helped create and develop in them the necessary capacities and moral dispositions. A century later, Amartya Sen would come up with the idea that the promotion of "capabilities" and "freedoms" should be the marks of a good economy.[33]

The conclusions that Gandhi reached from paraphrasing Ruskin were striking. If the latter's ideas were applicable to Great Britain, in the throes of the Industrial Revolution, they were "a thousand times more applicable" to India in thrall to colonialism.[34] Indians were pining for *swarajya* (independence). Independence should mean, Gandhi reminded his readers, a desire not only for political freedom but also for economic freedom. The dispute was not whether India needed industries, but whether it needed the sort of industries that produced imperialism. For Gandhi was not slow to lament the fact that modern liberal economics worked hand in hand with the imperial instincts of the Europeans. "Let it be remembered," he reminded the Indians, "that Western civilization [is]

---

[26] Ibid., pp. 206–7.   [27] Ibid., p. 211.   [28] Ibid., p. 222.   [29] CW, 8: 304.
[30] Ibid., p. 325.   [31] Ibid., p. 339.   [32] Ibid., p. 372.
[33] See A. Sen, *Development as Freedom* (New York: Knopf, 1999).   [34] CW, 8: 373.

only a hundred years old, or to be more precise, fifty."[35] He was thinking, of course, of the new industrial civilization emerging in the West. In that "short span," he observed, the Western people appeared to have been reduced to "a state of cultural anarchy." Western nations were falling on each other in the arms race and the race for conquering colonies. He saw a connection between European liberalism and imperial colonization, and hoped that India's industrialization would avoid this particular path.[36] The industries that India needed must reflect the nature of true wealth and the conditions under which it should be acquired and shared, viz., truth, justice, and non-violence. India, therefore, ought not to industrialize itself on the Western model. If it attempted to do so, it would have to become imperialistic itself. "We cannot industrialize ourselves, unless we make up our minds to enslave humanity."[37]

The last paragraph of *Sarvodaya* reads like a prelude to *Hind Swaraj*: "We must have industry, but of the right kind. India was once looked upon as a golden land, because Indians then were people of sterling worth. The land is the same but the people have changed and that is why it has become arid. To transform it into a golden land again we must transmute ourselves into gold by leading a life of virtue." And the secret to that national self-transmutation is truth (*satya*). "If, therefore, every Indian makes it a point to follow truth always, India will achieve *swarajya* as a matter of course. This is the substance of Ruskin's work."[38]

The work ethic

"Bread labor" is one of the four "economic virtues" of Gandhi's ethical system. His immediate source of the idea of this virtue was Timofei Bondaref, a nineteenth-century Russian thinker, now all but forgotten.[39] Bread labor, called also "physical labor" or "body labor" or "manual labor," was the labor essential for meeting the basic needs of human life.[40] It was the labor that humans had to engage in by virtue of their being bodily creatures, and no one was exempt from it, whether prince or pauper. While the poor had to do it out of necessity, others had to do it out of choice, whether in the form of housework or some form of voluntary work. Most religions had recognized its importance. The Book of Genesis spoke of the obligation to earn one's bread by the sweat of one's brow.[41] *Gita* III: 3–12 spoke in a similar vein. "Work and body are inseparable" – to use R. C. Zaehner's comment on these *Gita* verses.[42] Gandhi had also

---

[35] CW, 8: 374.   [36] Ibid.   [37] CW, 58: 400.   [38] Ibid., pp. 374–75.
[39] CW, 44: 149.   [40] CW, 50: 215.   [41] CW, 32: 156.
[42] R. C. Zaehner (trans.), *The Bhagavad-Gita*, p. 161.

taken note of the Benedictine dictum that work was worship – *laborare est orare*.[43] In Sabarmati Ashram bread labor was part of daily routine – three-and-a-half hours of manual work in the field and three hours of work in the kitchen and dining hall.[44]

Despite the injunction of the *Gita*, manual work was looked down upon by Indian culture, taken as a whole.[45] Gandhi spent his entire active life fighting this prejudice. The promotion of the cottage industry producing *khadi*, homespun cloth, formed part of that campaign. For the poor and the seasonally unemployed, it was meant to be a source of income. For others it was meant to be a *yagna*, a sacrifice. A plea for the spinning wheel, he wrote, was a plea for the dignity of labor.[46] He urged even the great poet Tagore to spin half an hour a day and set an example to Indian intelligentsia. "I do indeed ask the Poet and the page to spin the wheel as a sacrament."[47] "If the Poet spun half an hour daily his poetry would gain in richness."[48]

Critics have questioned the economic value of the cottage industry producing *khadi*. Whatever its economic merit, Gandhi's approach to it was guided by his concern for the plight of the poor and the cultural prejudice against manual labor. He believed that engaging in *khadi* work would enable the poor to acquire "capabilities" and "dispositions" such as economic self-discipline, the art of cooperation, and punctuality. The lessons learned from *khadi* could be transferred to "hundreds of other beneficial activities."[49] This did not mean that he considered *khadi* to be the magic solution to India's poverty; nor did he see it as an alternative to other modes of industrial production. He saw it as marking "a transitional stage" in the economic improvement of those who participated in it.[50] The important thing was that India needed a work ethic that would apply to the poor and the rich alike, and would break down the cultural and psychological distance between them.

Gandhi, the Buddha, and the work ethic

There is an important issue in Gandhi's economic thought that has not caught the attention of critics. It has to do with his criticism of the attitude of historical Buddhist monasticism towards manual labor. A very delicate

---

[43] CW, 32: 164.   [44] CW, 13: 97.
[45] See A. L. Basham, "Traditional Influences on the Thought of Mahatma Gandhi," in R. Kumar (ed.), *Essays on Gandhian Politics* (Oxford: Clarendon Press, 1971), p. 40.
[46] CW, 21: 289.   [47] Gandhi, pleading with Tagore, CW, 21: 288.
[48] Gandhi, urging Tagore to set an example, CW, 28: 427.   [49] Ibid., p. 249.
[50] CW, 21: 290.

question, given the reverence with which he had held the Buddha, "one of the greatest teachers of mankind."[51] However, he had certain concerns which he expressed in the following three questions.

First, why did the Buddha not teach the ethic of manual work instead of that of contemplation? In his own words, "if I had the good fortune to be face to face with one like him [the Buddha], I should not hesitate to ask him why he did not teach the gospel of work, in preference to one of contemplation." Then to make clear that there was no sectarian edge to the question, he added that he would do "the same thing" if he were to meet Hindu saints such as Tukaram and Jnanadev.[52]

Second, had the Buddha done any manual work before he attained enlightenment, considering that Jesus had worked as a carpenter before the start of his ministry? Again the question was posed with the utmost delicacy. "We do not know how much manual work [the] Buddha did before he attained wisdom. Yes, we know this much, that he did not propagate religion for securing his livelihood. He lived on charity. That could not militate against the duty of labor. A roving ascetic has to do a lot of manual work."[53]

The third question concerned the responsibility of the Buddha for the rise of an anti-work ethic within Buddhist monasticism. Did he foresee the course that Buddhist monasticism would take? Again, the question was raised with the utmost respect and reverence.

Who am I to criticize a great soul like the Buddha? Besides, I love and revere him. But did he himself set up the organizations [of monasteries] or did his followers do so? Whoever did it, the monasteries which were established became, in obedience to this universal law, stagnant and by-and-by acquired a reputation as dens of sloth. Even today we find Buddhist monks in Ceylon, Burma, and Tibet sunk in ignorance and the veritable images of sloth.

Then, again, to remove any sectarian animus, he alluded to the state of Hindu monasticism as well. "In India, too, the monks known as *sannyasis* are not found to be shining specimens of humanity."[54]

To understand Gandhi's attitude towards the Buddha, it is important to bear in mind that he considered him to be one of his own, "a Hindu of Hindus," and "the greatest among Hindu reformers."[55] He did not give the world "a new religion" but only a "new interpretation" – of Hinduism. He was "the prophet" who fought "the priest" within Hinduism. "He taught us to defy appearances and trust in the final triumph of Truth and Love."[56] In particular, he taught that Hindus should drop animal

---

[51] CW, 40: 160.   [52] CW, 62: 85.   [53] CW, 42: 489.   [54] CW, 50: 410.
[55] CW, 35: 310, 324.   [56] CW, 24: 85.

sacrifice and the caste system. He showed that "God was not a God who [could] be appeased by sacrificing innocent animals."[57]

At the same time, he felt it necessary to criticize the imbalance between work and the spiritual life. The theory that begging was holy and that living off the labor of others legitimate, provided it was done by mendicants (*bhikhus*), also came for criticism. He made it clear that his criticisms did not spring from any sectarian bias. They sprang from the insight that the work ethic was mandatory on all, mendicants as well as lay people. The work ethic was part of any real solution to the problem of suffering in the world.

Given the differences between Gandhi and the Buddha it is difficult to comprehend a recent trend to interpret Gandhi through the Buddha. R. Iyer has asserted that Gandhi interpreted Hindu values "in the light of the message of the Buddha."[58] Pankaj Mishra's *An End to Suffering: The Buddha in the World*, has argued recently that Gandhi "consistently applied Buddhist principles to the murky world of politics."[59] With his "Buddhist insight" into suffering as the universal problem, Gandhi made "compassion the basis of political action."[60]

However, according to Mishra's own analysis, the Buddha applied his solution only to the individual, not to society. He did not apply it to "the external world." Nor did he seek to cure human suffering if the means used called for a "large-scale restructuring of state and society." This "indifference to ambitious political projects was part of his belief in individually achieved, rather than collectively organized redemption."[61] He did not seek to transform the external world through science and politics; rather he sought to solve suffering by deconstructing the notions of God, the soul, the mind, and eternity.[62]

What is especially fascinating is Mishra's analysis of the institution of Buddhist mendicants (the *bhikhus*). He informs us that it was instituted by the Buddha himself. Like the Lama in Rudyard Kipling's *Kim*, the *bhikus* in Mishra enjoy a privileged status. They live off "the common wealth of society," remarks Mishra – approvingly. They renounce private property, which *entitles* them, he adds, to "an exalted position in society." They are "fed and clothed by the general population." In

---

[57] CW, 35: 335.

[58] This hardly applies to the value of work. Nor does it apply to the ideas of *atman*, Brahman, and God. See Iyer, *The Moral and Political Thought of Mahatma Gandhi*, p. 235. T. Weber, *Gandhi as Disciple and Mentor* (Cambridge: Cambridge University Press, 2004), pp. 203–16, has drawn our attention to Johan Galtung's attempt to see Gandhi through Buddhist eyes.

[59] P. Mishra, *An End to Suffering: The Buddha in the World* (London: Picador, 2004), p. 337.

[60] Ibid., p. 340.   [61] Ibid., pp. 29, 399.   [62] Ibid., pp. 186–90.

exchange, they offer themselves to society as models of virtue and self-awareness.[63]

It was precisely this life style of the *bhikhus*, and its underlying assumptions, that Gandhi found unacceptable. He was all for ending suffering by means of mental discipline. But for him, mental discipline was not enough; it could only be the beginning, not the end, of the process of ending suffering. The solution had to embrace the economic and political transformation of society as a whole. Compassion (*karuna*) was necessary, but its basis had to be truth (*satya*). He was convinced that the alienation between economics and politics on the one hand and the pursuit of nirvana on the other was precisely one of the historic causes of not only sloth but also much material suffering in the Indic world. The alienation between the work ethic and the spiritual life, between spiritual freedom and civic freedom had to be brought to an end. The transformation had to begin with the individual, but it had to extend itself to society as well. The need to change both the individual and society was at the heart of Gandhi's economic philosophy. It was incomprehensible to him how the *bhikhus* could remain indifferent to mass poverty. His famous "talisman" was addressed to them as much as to anyone else:

Whenever you are in doubt or when the self becomes too much with you, apply the following test. Recall the face of the poorest and the weakest man whom you have seen, and ask yourself if the step you contemplate is going to be of any use to him. Will he gain anything by it? Will it restore him to a control over his own life and destiny? In other words, will it lead to swaraj for the hungry and the spiritually starving millions?

Then you will find your doubts and yourself melting away.[64]

The work ethic was the key to the alleviation of poverty. The voluntary poverty of the mendicants did not absolve them from the duty to engage in socially beneficial labor. This was Gandhi's firm conviction.

Appropriate technology

Gandhi's attitude towards modern technology evolved over the decades. In his South Africa days, 1893–1914, under the influence of Ruskinian and Tolstoyan ideas, he remained highly skeptical of the benefits of rapid industrialization. The Phoenix Settlement and the Tolstoy Farm were laboratories for conducting experiments to test the virtues of life not dependent on modern technology.

[63] Ibid., pp. 194–213; 23–24.   [64] CW, 89: 125.

The terminology that he used for "technology" belonged to the nineteenth century – "machinery." *Hind Swaraj* devoted a whole chapter to "Machinery." It was the symbol of modern civilization. It was an "evil," a "sin," and, despite its initial success, was bound to harm humanity. The metaphors that he used spoke for themselves. It was a snake-hole containing hundreds of snakes.[65] It was the poisonous Upas tree that killed all the vegetation nearby.[66] It was a whirlwind that caused vast destruction, and a drift net that destroyed indiscriminately.[67]

From 1920 onward, however, his attitude began to change. He came to realize that the connection between modern economy and modern technology could not be broken. The question was under what conditions the connection could be made beneficial to humanity. For "machinery" was both a "grand" and an "awful" invention.[68] It was grand when it could "help and ease human effort,"[69] and awful when it created permanent unemployment or underemployment.[70] Mass production was the wrong policy where the masses were unemployed. What the masses needed was not "mass production," but "production by the masses."[71]

Gandhi's analysis of "machinery" made three main points. The first was that it had a tendency to displace human labor, rather than supplement it or increase its efficiency. The second was that it had no internal principle of self-limit and, therefore, its potential for growth was limitless. The third was that it displaced human labor, not because it was desirable but because it was its law.[72] He could visualize a stage when "machinery" would "engulf civilization." Instead of humans controlling it, it would control humans.[73] Instead of saving labor, which was good, it could lead to the atrophying of human limbs. He was not aiming at the eradication of "machinery" but at limiting its role in the economy.[74]

Taking into account both its strength and weakness, Gandhi identified three dangers in the unrestrained alignment of modern technology to modern economics. The first was the economic exploitation of the less technically advanced nations by the technically more advanced nations. This was a problem of justice. The second was the negative impact that an economy driven by modern technology and profit motive had on the

---

[65] *Hind Swaraj*, p. 110.   [66] Ibid., p. 62.
[67] Gandhi uses the same term "craze" to translate the Gujarati words *wayaro* (whirlwind) on p. 108, and *sanchani jal* (drift net) on p. 111.
[68] CW, 48: 353.   [69] CW, 61: 416.   [70] CW, 47: 89–90.
[71] E. F. Schumacher built his theory of "Technology with a Human Face" on the basis of this dictum of Gandhi. "The technology of mass production," he wrote, was "inherently violent, ecologically damaging, self-defeating in terms of non-renewable resources and stultifying for the human person." Schumacher, *Small is Beautiful*, p. 149.
[72] CW, 85: 95.   [73] CW, 48: 353.   [74] CW, 25: 251.

natural environment, affecting the quality of the water, soil, air, and atmosphere. This was an ecological problem. The third was the potential threat to human freedom, especially to the freedom of choice of consumer goods. Instead of promoting real freedom of choice, it was promoting compulsive consumption of unnecessary things.

One way to avoid these dangers was to adopt only appropriate technology. An appropriate technology was one that was guided by the principles of justice, ecology, and human freedom. E. F. Schumacher, D. R. Gadgil, and others had originally thought of appropriate technology as something that only developing nations needed.[75] Now everyone realizes that appropriate technology is what the whole world needs, regardless of standard of life. The modern economy has to become more person-centered than technology-centered.

Economic development and spiritual development

An idea running through this book is that Gandhi attempted to establish and maintain a dynamic relationship between the different human strivings. It is, therefore, appropriate to conclude this chapter with a consideration of his explanation of the relationship of economic development to spiritual development.

Of all his writings there is one that deals with this precise problem with great clarity and rhetorical brilliance. It is his 1916 lecture to the Muir Central College Economic Society, Allahabad. The topic was "Does Economic Progress Clash with Real Progress?" By economic progress he meant "material advancement without limit," and by real progress he meant "moral progress" or progress of "the permanent element [the spirit] in us."[76] The question was really whether spiritual progress increased in "the same proportion" as material progress. Some thinkers in the West had maintained that the two advanced in the same proportion, that spiritual development was a byproduct of economic development, and that therefore people in the developed world were spiritually more advanced than were the people in the developing world. It was this modern misunderstanding of the nature of spirituality that Gandhi met head on.

Such evidence as he had was against the modern Western theory noted above. In South Africa, for example, he had found rich Indians considerably less interested in spiritual and moral matters than were the poor Indians.[77] His hypothesis was that the desire for wealth that was not in

---

[75] See Schumacher, *Small is Beautiful*, pp. 142–85. On Gandhi's influence on him, see Weber, *Gandhi As Disciple and Mentor*, pp. 218–31.
[76] For the text of the lecture see CW, 13: 310–17.   [77] Ibid., p. 313.

harmony with the desire for transcendence was a hindrance to human development rather than a positive indicator of it.

The bulk of his analysis was taken up by a masterly analysis of the parable of the rich young man as found in the Gospel of St. Mark, 10: 17–31. The rich man in question was no ordinary rich man, for he had led a very ethical life. He never defrauded any one, committed adultery or murder. He had honored his father and mother. Still he felt an inner vacuum within his soul that the ethical life by itself could not fill.

Jesus intuited his problem: "One thing thou lackest. Go thy way, sell whatever thou hast and give to the poor, and thou shall have treasure in heaven – come take up the cross and follow me." At this the young man went away grieved, which prompted the saying that it was hard for those that trust in riches to enter the kingdom of God. "It is easier for a camel to go through the eye of a needle than for a rich man to enter the kingdom of God."[78]

Gandhi saw this parable as teaching "an eternal rule of life" – one that was also taught by other scriptures. The rule was that we should seek wealth without ignoring the injunction to seek the kingdom of God also. Otherwise the quest for wealth would produce the sort of inner emptiness that the rich young man had experienced. The idea of progress that concerned itself with only economic progress would not in his view qualify as real human progress. Real human progress therefore had to remove the historic antagonism between artha and moksha.

In his opinion, the modern attempt to combine the pursuit of wealth as the sovereign end and the pursuit of spiritual life as its subsidiary end – or as an option available to those who seek it, as some liberals would have it, was "foredoomed to failure." That one could not serve both God and Mammon was an "economic truth of the highest value."[79] To drive home the point he had recourse to Shakespeare. No one could harmonize radically opposed elements; no one could be "'wise, temperate, and furious' in a moment."[80]

There was a further point: economic pursuits, even when supported by ethics, could not fully satisfy the human spirit. The spiritual yearning could be fully satisfied only by spiritual means. The practice of dharma (ethics) in economic activities was of course necessary but not sufficient. One needed, in addition, the pursuit of moksa. The pursuit of artha and dharma had to be complemented by the pursuit of moksha.

---

[78] Ibid.   [79] Ibid., p. 314.
[80] Ibid., p. 315. Gandhi is paraphrasing *Macbeth* here: "Who can be wise, amazed, temperate and furious, loyal and neutral, in a moment? No man" (Act II, Scene 3, 90–91). Shakespeare was speaking of the impossibility of harmonizing in the same personality contrary humors of temperance and fury.

Part III

Dharma

Gandhi used the concept of dharma in three senses: as duty, religion, and ethics. Dharma directly relates human beings to one another, to the communities to which they belong, and indirectly to their transcendental destiny. Indirectly, because, when properly pursued, dharma has consequences not only for life in time, but also life outside time. Hence its bearing on religion.

Historically, a good deal of what went under the name of dharma had to do with caste (*varna*) and the stages of life (*ashrama*). However, since modernity has undermined the moral basis of both caste and the stages of life, an ethical vacuum has arisen. Gandhi filled this vacuum with the universal ethic of non-violence and human rights.

5   Dharma as duty

"With hands uplifted I cry:
(But none listens to me)
Dharma yields both artha and kama;
Why is that dharma not observed?"[1]

Dharma in the sense of duty was the foundation of classical Indian social philosophy. The stability of the social order depended on the sense of duty with which members of society carried out their activities. If the sense of duty were guaranteed by sources superior to human will, the stability of the social order would be even greater. And dharma had such a guarantee. It was guaranteed by the principle that sustained the cosmic order itself. Besides, revelation too had given it its stamp of approval.

The two famous social institutions that depended on dharma as duty were the four castes (*varna*) – *brahmin, kshatria, vaisya* and *shudra* (*sudra*) – and the four stages of life (*ashramas*) – those of the student, householder, retiree, and renouncer. The *purusa sukta* metaphor described in *Rig Veda* X: 90 gave the four *varnas* (castes) their scriptural sanction:

When they divided *purusa* how many portions did they make? What do they call his mouth, his arms? What do they call thighs and feet? The Brahmin was his mouth, of both his arms was *Rajanya* made. His thighs became *Vaisya*, from his feet the *Sudra* was produced.[2]

The *Bhagavad Gita*, in its turn, gave its approval of the four *varnas*. Krishna tells Arjuna: "The four-caste system did I generate with the categories of 'constituents' and works."[3] Our analysis of Gandhi's conception of dharma as duty focuses on his attitude towards the institutions

---

[1] These lines, from the "Swragarohan" section of the *Mahabharata*, were cited by Gandhi in CW, 72: 248, in an article entitled "A Cry in the Wilderness." The paradox of history is that dharma as duty is more often breached than observed.

[2] J. Pelican (ed.), *The Rig Veda, Sacred Writings, Hinduism*, translated by R. T. H. Griffith (New York: Book-of-the-Month Club, 1992), bk. X, hymn 90, 11–12, p. 603.

[3] Zaehner, *The Bhagavad-Gita*, 4: 13; the idea recurs in 17: 41–48.

of "caste" and the "stages of life." He had taken, at different times, three different positions on caste. The first was that the four castes, as sanctioned in the *Rig Veda* and the *Gita*, embodied an egalitarian ethic. In the beginning all the four castes were equal in dignity. They were based on the three natural qualities or *gunas* and the natural aptitude for work. These were the bases on which Krishna gave his approval to the caste system. According to the theory of natural qualities, human beings were divided into three types. Some possessed *sattva* or the quality causing virtue, others possessed *rajas*, the quality causing passion, and still others possessed *tamas*, the quality producing dullness. The first quality was present in those inclined towards truth, wisdom, beauty, and goodness; the second quality was present in those inclined towards action, energetic behavior, and violence; and the third quality was present in those inclined towards stupidity, gloom, and melancholy.[4] One was born with one or other of these three qualities. In addition, one had a natural aptitude for a particular occupation, but not for others. A combination of natural qualities and natural aptitudes determined one's caste, not birth or heredity. This, briefly, was Gandhi's initial understanding of the scriptural teaching of the caste system.[5]

Gandhi interpreted the organic metaphor of the *Rig Veda* X: 90 as teaching concord and egalitarianism: "no simile could be happier," was his comment. "If they [the four *varnas*] are members of one body, how can one be superior or inferior to another? If the members of the body had the power of expression and each of them were to say that it was higher and better than the rest, the body would go to pieces. Even so, our body politic, the body of humanity, would go to pieces, if it were to perpetuate the canker of superiority or inferiority."[6] The scriptures approved of a functional division of labor. No society could survive, much less prosper, unless there was a division of labor as well as harmony between the functional units of labor.

The *Rig Veda* was not alone in using the body metaphor. Livy, the Roman historian, had used the same to explain the concord between the patricians and the plebeians of ancient Rome. If the members of the body did not agree on the good of the whole body, the whole body would waste away to nothing.[7] The greatness of the Roman Republic depended on the

---

[4] See A. L. Basham, *The Wonder That Was India* (London: Sidgwick and Jackson, 1956), p. 325.
[5] See CW, 59: 61–67; p. V. Kane supports Gandhi's interpretation of the *Gita* IV: 13: see *History of Dharmasastra*, vol. V, part 2, p. 1635.
[6] CW, 59: 65–66.
[7] See Livy Titus, *The Early History of Rome*, bks. I–IV, translated by Aubery de Selincourt (London: Penguin, 1976), pp. 141–42.

concord between the two classes understood in organic terms. Machiavelli, during the Italian Renaissance, using a similar metaphor, reached a similar conclusion. What accounted for Rome's greatness was its regard for the principle of the concordance of the "humors" of the body politic, and what accounted for the decline of contemporary Florence was the disregard for the same principle. Indeed he thought that the organic metaphor best described the harmony between republican liberty and functional social divisions.[8] St. Paul also had used the metaphor of the body in a sustained way to describe the ideal of community that Christians ought to entertain. Just as the body was one and had many members, and all the members of the body, though many, were one body, so it was to be with the Christian community. "If the foot should say 'Because I am not a hand, I do not belong to the body,' that would not make it any less a part of the body." And so on with the other organs of the body. And apropos the present discussion, the ethical conclusion that St. Paul drew from the metaphor was very relevant. He argued that diversity of functions ought to increase the respect paid to the so-called less important organs, so that there might be no discord in the body, but that the members might have the same care for one another. "If one member suffers, all suffer together; if one member is honoured, all rejoice together."[9]

Gandhi's interpretation of the metaphor of the body organism accurately captured the intent of the *Rig Veda*, which was to convey the meaning of unity and concord in the diversity of functions. It is worth noting this, in the light of B. R. Ambedkar's different interpretation of the same metaphor. The latter, reading history backwards, interpreted the *Rig Veda* metaphor in the light of later history and contemporary preoccupations. Accordingly, he saw in the metaphor a justification for "an ascending scale of reverence and a descending scale of contempt." The metaphor, according to him, was unique inasmuch as it fixed a permanent warrant of precedence among different classes. The warrant of precedence was based on the principle of graded inequality among the four classes.[10] Gandhi did not claim that India had put into practice the ideal of harmony and equality proposed in the *Rig Veda* and the *Bhagavad*

[8] Machiavelli used the metaphor of the four humors and the human body, to illustrate the nature of liberty and concord in the body politic. See A. J. Parel, *The Machiavellian Cosmos* (New Haven: Yale University Press, 1992), pp. 101–13.

[9] I Corinthians, 12: 4–26.

[10] B. R. Ambedkar, cited in O. Herrenschmidt, "Ambedkar and the Hindu Social Order," in S. Jhondhale and J. Beltz (eds.), *Restructuring the World: B. R. Ambedkar and Buddhism in India* (Delhi: Oxford University Press, 2004), p. 42. Herrenschmidt mentions Livy, but only to dismiss his teaching as "the ideology of the dominant class" (ibid., p. 41).

Gita, but he did claim that they had proposed them as ideals to be pursued not only by Indians but all humanity.[11] The fact that later history did not live up to the ideal did not detract from the validity or the integrity of the ideal.

Gandhi's second position on caste was that in its present form it did not reflect the ideal envisaged in the scriptures at all. As it was practiced today, it was a "hideous travesty" of the original idea; it existed only "in a distorted form."[12] The law of the *ashrama* was "extinct alike in profession and observance," and "the law of *varna* [had] become a dead letter."[13] As for the law of the *ashrama*, it had become "a dead letter today."[14] In an age when everyone felt free to follow any calling, it was "an idle dream" and a "childish folly" to attempt to revive the *varna* system.[15] Briefly, he was not going to revive the institutions of caste and the stages of life, even though in the distant past they were intended to promote an egalitarian ethic.

His third position on caste was that the system as it existed today had to go. In 1935 he outlined his position, in eleven propositions, in an article under the title, "Caste Has to Go." The Vedas had taught egalitarianism. The *Shastras* are not part of revelation and, therefore, did not require the same moral assent that revelation required. The scriptures must be interpreted according to the needs of society as it evolved. What was contrary to "universal truth" could not be accepted, even if the *Shastras* had accepted them in the past. What in the *Shastras* were in conflict with reason could not be accepted. The *varnashrama* of the *Shastras* was non-existent today. The present caste system was "the antithesis" of the original idea. "The sooner public opinion [abolished] it the better." The present prohibitions regarding inter-caste marriage, inter-caste dining, and the free choice of labor was "doubly wrong." Untouchability, "the greatest blot on Hinduism," was unknown in the *Shastras*. The "most effective, the quickest, and the most unobtrusive way to destroy caste" was for reformers to practice what they preached in their lives and in their immediate family circles. "Reviling the orthodox" was not the best way to go about abolishing caste. The change had to be "gradual and imperceptible."[16]

The political context of Gandhi's attack on caste ought to be taken into account here. It was because of that context that he did not ask the colonial state, an alien institution, to intervene. He wanted instead public opinion to create an anti-caste outlook. Neither did he believe in a violent social revolution or a civil war within Hinduism. He would attack it

---

[11] CW, 59: 66.   [12] Ibid., pp. 63–64.   [13] Ibid., p. 62, 66.   [14] Ibid., p. 63.
[15] Ibid., p. 67.   [16] CW, 62: 121–22.

indirectly rather than confront it directly. By attacking Untouchability, he was attacking both Untouchability and the caste system. This was Jawaharlal Nehru's understanding of Gandhi's strategy.[17]

Another strategy that Gandhi used was to suggest that all the existing castes be reduced to one. The numbers attached to *varnas*, in his view, had no sanctity about them. Their value was due to the fact they defined "the duties of man." When once equal status was assigned to all castes the question of number took care of itself.[18] With one caste covering the entire Hindu community, "inter-caste" dining and "inter-caste" marriage would become the norm.[19]

Gandhi attempted to make the Sabarmati Ashram a model of a caste-free society. Its 1915 Constitution stated that the Ashram did not follow the *varnashrama* dharma and that its members considered themselves as belonging to just one *ashrama*, the *sannyasa ashrama*.[20] Though the ethic of *varnashrama* dharma was rejected, the notion of dharma itself was not. The members of the Ashram carried out their various responsibilities from a sense of duty, regardless of their original caste background. In this regard the Ashram appeared like a tiny island in the vast ocean of caste society. Gandhi was aware of the enormity of the task involved in reforming the entire caste system. It would be, he said, like "Dame Partington with her mop, trying to push back the Atlantic Ocean."[21]

In this regard it is worth remarking that Sarvepalli Radhakrishnan also had toyed with the idea of a one-caste society as the solution to the caste system. "In the beginning there was only one caste," he wrote. "We were all Brahmins or all Sudras."[22] In his commentary on the *Gita* he identified the source for the concept of one-caste society as the *Mahabharata*, according to which "the whole world" was originally one caste. The emphasis of the *Gita*, he stated, was not on birth or heredity, but on temperament and vocation.[23]

---

[17] Gandhi told Nehru that the following was his strategy: "If Untouchability goes ... the caste system goes. So I am concentrating on that." Cited by R. Gandhi, *The Good Boatman* (Delhi: Viking, 1995), p. 241.

[18] CW, 50: 227.

[19] For rhetorical reasons, he called the one universal caste the Harijan caste (CW, 82: 86). In CW, 84: 389, he called it the Bhangi caste.

[20] CW, 13: 94. The Sabarmati Ashram was an experiment in his idea of re-creating a caste-less society. It would retain the old ethic of duty, but not recognize the current institution of caste.

[21] CW, 50: 227.

[22] S. Radhakrishnan, *Religion and Society* (2nd edn, London: Allen and Unwin, 1956), p. 129.

[23] S. Radhakrishnan, *The Bhagavad Gita* (2nd edn, London: Allen and Unwin, 1976), p. 161.

Gandhi's final position, briefly, was that Hindus should become a modern, egalitarian society. Civic nationalism should replace casteism.

Can dharma survive without the *varnashrama dharma*?

The concept of dharma extended to spheres beyond caste and stages of life. The *Shastras* themselves had recognized this. In addition to the concept of *svadharma* – the dharma of the individual derived from his or her caste and stage of life – there was the general or universal dharma, called *sadharana dharma*. Manu, among others, mentions it. It included specific duties: the duty to be non-violent (*ahimsa*), truthful (*satya*), to refrain from theft (*astea*), and to exercise control over the senses.[24] These were duties that applied to human beings as human beings, regardless of the caste they belonged to.

In his Introduction to a biography of Rajchandbhai, his spiritual advisor, Gandhi gave a remarkable description of the concept of universal dharma that he shared with him. There was a dharma that was distinct from the dharma taught by revelation and tradition. This dharma, he wrote, was a "quality of the soul" and was to be found in all human beings. Through this dharma human beings came to know two things: what their fundamental duties were, and how they ought to behave towards one another. The text is important enough to warrant full citation:

Dharma does not mean any particular creed or dogma. Nor does it mean reading or learning by rote books known as *Shastras* or even believing all that they say.

Dharma is a quality of the soul and is present, visibly or invisibly, in every human being. Through it we know our duty in human life and our true relation with other souls.[25]

What is implicit in the above passage is that there are two kinds of dharma: the dharma that is found in positive sources such as revelation and tradition, and the dharma that is found in the quality of the soul, or the dharma that is discovered by the faculty of *buddhi* (intelligence and will). The first we may call "positive" dharma, and the second, "natural" dharma. Every human being that exercises his or her *buddhi* in the right way can *ipso facto* know the first principles of natural duty (dharma). The first principles are that there is a distinction between good and bad, and that therefore there is a duty to do and pursue what is good and a duty to shun what is bad. One does not learn these principles from revelation or

---

[24] Doniger and Smith, *The Laws of Manu*, 10: 63. See also Lipner, *Hindus*, pp. 223–29.
[25] CW, 32: 11.

tradition. Indeed one can understand what revelation and tradition teach only on the assumption that the *buddhi* has the innate capacity to understand the first principles of natural duty. This is implied in Gandhi's statement that dharma is a quality of the soul. Elsewhere we find him linking dharma to atman: "only dharma abides; it is imperishable because it is related to the atman."[26]

The centrality of the role of *buddhi* for discovering the idea of duty is generally recognized in the tradition. *Gita* II. 63, for example, speaks to this point, albeit in a negative way. It says that humans lose their moral compass when they lose their *buddhi*, i.e., when they act against its dictates:

From anger comes bewilderment, from bewilderment wandering of the mind, from wandering of the mind destruction of the soul [*buddhi*]: once the soul is destroyed the man is lost.[27]

In this context it is useful to recall Radhakrishnan's comment that *buddhi* is the root of the ability to distinguish between right and wrong.[28] Lipner's remarks on the meaning of *dur-buddhi* (being "stupid" or "evilminded") also point to the pivotal role that *buddhi* plays in grasping natural dharma. Only those whose *buddhi* is perverted act both stupidly and immorally.[29] The requirements of universal dharma, noted above, flow from the first principles of the ethical life grasped by *buddhi*. By exercising their *buddhi* in the proper way humans perceive that they are morally obliged to be non-violent and truthful.

Though the rejection of the ethical basis of caste did not mean the rejection of the idea of dharma altogether, it nevertheless created a moral vacuum. The presence of this moral vacuum is a major crisis currently faced by Indian civilization. Rightly or wrongly, that vacuum is being filled by the modern idea of rights. For all practical purposes, by 1894, i.e., from the very beginning of his public life, Gandhi had mentally rejected the ethic of caste and had replaced it with the ethic of rights.

His training in Western jurisprudence had given him a deep insight into the role that human rights play in modern life. Though dharma was the foundation of the ethical life, humans could not live by dharma alone. Without rights supplementing dharma, civilized life became virtually impossible in the modern world. Gandhi was fully convinced of this. His activities in South Africa were devoted entirely to the defense of the civil rights of the Indian immigrants there. The idea of rights was the thread that connected his legal practice and political activities. It

---

[26] CW, 65: 57.   [27] Radhakrishnan, *The Bhagavad Gita*, II: 63, p. 154.
[28] Ibid., p. 126.   [29] Lipner, *Hindus*, pp. 214–15.

explained his interest in the Natal Franchise Law of 1894, the Immigration Amendment Law of 1895, the Immigration Restriction Law and Dealers Law of 1897, the Smuts (anti-Indian) Laws of 1911, 1912, and 1913. The concessions he won would appear trivial by today's standards. They included the right of Indians to use the sidewalks of Pretoria and Johannesburg, their right to acquire, keep and dispose of private property, to vote in local elections, to establish homes in locations, to travel without pass laws and curfew, and to contract valid marriage according to the rites of the Hindu, Muslim, and Zoroastrian religions.

On his return to India in 1915, he continued his campaigns on behalf of the rights of different groups. In Champaran (1917) he defended the rights of the indigo workers; in Ahmedabad (1918), it was the rights of the textile workers that he defended. In the Rowlatt agitation, it was the right to free speech that was involved. At Vykom (1924–25) it was the right of the Untouchables against the Brahmins, and in Bardoli (1928) it was the rights of the peasants against the revenue department that were at issue. And the focus of the famous salt march of 1930 was the right of Indians to pick salt from open beaches. This impressive record was capped in 1931 by the successful passing, as mentioned, of the Resolution on Fundamental Rights. Nowhere, in his entire political career, do we find him attempting to restore the dharma of the discredited *varnashrama*. Even the case of the Untouchables was approached not in terms of caste dharma but in terms of modern rights.

Satyagraha: a new way of securing rights

It is important to remind ourselves here that the original definition of satyagraha was made in terms of rights. It was a way of defending human rights by soul-force, and not brute force.[30] Later developments have made satyagraha look as if it were a method of conflict resolution. Certainly, it is a method of resolving conflicts in a non-violent way. But the underlying issue was human rights.

Though Gandhi derived the notion of rights from Western sources, he did not accept the philosophical premises on which the Western notion rested. Those premises, going back to Hobbes, were that humans were possessive individualists[31] in conflict with one another – in a condition of the war of all against all. As Leo Strauss has reminded us, "the ultimate reason of the state" for Hobbes was the protection of life, life that was

---

[30] *Hind Swaraj*, p. 90.
[31] On possessive individualism, see Macpherson, *The Political Theory of Possessive Individualism*.

threatened by insecurity, with no effective sense of natural duty restraining humans from behaving violently. Right was the original fact; the sense of duty, in Hobbes' account, arose only after the establishment of the state. And the state could rely only on the conditional obedience of the citizen, the condition being the securing of their rights against those who violently threatened them. The only kind of duty that was recognized in this philosophy was the legal duty to obey the state, once it came into existence.[32] Moral duty, in this view, had no effective role to play in the modern state.

Gandhi's philosophy of right started with natural dharma, which, as we saw, was a dictate of *buddhi*. Conflicts had to be solved non-violently, not because it was expedient to do so, not because the state existed, but because it was a requirement of dharma. Human beings are fundamentally social beings. The obligation to be non-violent arose from this prior obligation. The original moral experience was to pursue good and avoid evil and the recognition that there was an obligation to be non-violent towards others.

However, just as I have a duty to be non-violent, to be truthful, not to cheat, and to keep my emotions under control, so I have a right not to be attacked, not to be lied to, not to be cheated, and not to be a victim of someone else's emotional outbursts. A right in this account is the capacity that I have by virtue of being endowed with the faculty of *buddhi*. The state exists to protect these rights by the use, if necessary, of legitimate force. Gandhi's philosophy of rights does not invoke a Hobbesean theory of human nature to justify it. The main difference between his theory of rights and the modern theory that traces its origin in Hobbes is that it comes as a package: it comes together with duties, with universal dharma (*sadharana dharma*), which a human being never abandons. Humans start with duties (dharma); rights are added later in order to protect them from those who do not act according to dharma.

In Gandhi's view, the Western manner of securing rights depended, ultimately, on the use of violence. He took the example of the Reform Act of 1832 to make his point. Violence was used in order to extend the right to vote. "Real rights" according to him could only be the result of performance of duty. The modern Western philosophy of rights did not begin with the idea of duty. That was why the rights gained by the French Revolution or the American War of Independence or even by the

---

[32] See L. Strauss, "Comments on Carl Schmitt's *Der Begriff des Politischen*" in G. Schwab (ed. and trans.), *Carl Schmitt: The Concept of the Political* (New Brunswick, NJ: Rutgers University Press, 1976), p. 88; and *Natural Rights and History* (The University of Chicago Press, 1971).

Glorious Revolution in Great Britain were preceded by violence in one form or another. And that was why it still required fresh exercise of violence to make further advances in human rights. That was why, according to him, rights secured in these ways remained a burden.[33]

Gandhi sought to secure rights in a non-violent way. That is the theoretical significance of satyagraha. Today the old idea of dharma survives in the new practice of satyagraha. The soul-force, with which dharma is linked, becomes active as citizens begin to exercise their rights. That is to say, it manifests itself as the force that promotes adherence to duty. This force can sustain itself only if certain virtues are practiced. *Hind Swaraj* mentions several of them: among them, the virtue of non-violence, truthfulness, abstention from theft, and control over the passions[34] – all of which, as noted before, were part of universal dharma. Modern Western philosophy of civil rights relies on enlightened self-interest rather than on virtue. It encourages citizens and interest groups to make as many claims as they wish. It does not encourage citizens to be moderate in their desires. There is a reason for this. It is that it is reluctant to promote the claims of natural duties. Until there is a change in this attitude, the disregard for dharma as a foundation of human rights will continue.

Gandhi never wavered in his conviction that dharma and rights had to work in tandem. The emphasis in modern culture was to over-emphasize the role of rights and to under-emphasize or even ignore that of duty. This explains why he refused to sign a "Charter of Rights" that H. G. Wells, the British writer, was sponsoring. Begin with a "Charter of Duties of Man," Gandhi wrote back, "and I promise right will follow as spring follows winter."[35] His response to the United Nations Human Rights Commission, charged with the responsibility of drafting the Universal Declaration of Human Rights (1948), expressed a similar sentiment: "all rights to be deserved and preserved came from a duty well done." From this fundamental principle he wanted to define "the duties of man and woman and correlate every right to some corresponding duty to be first performed."[36]

It may be pointed out here that not all who subscribe to modern Western political philosophy prefer rights to duties. For there are modern Western thinkers who do not subscribe to what is basically a Hobbesean position. Mazzini, one of Gandhi's sources on rights,[37] is one of them.

---

[33] *Hind Swaraj*, pp. 80–82.   [34] Ibid., pp. 93–99.   [35] CW, 71: 430.
[36] CW, 89: 346–47.
[37] Gandhi had placed Mazzini's *The Duties of Man* in the Appendix to *Hind Swaraj*, as a book to be read by those who wanted to go deeper into his (Gandhi's) philosophy.

According to him, knowledge of rights was not enough to enable human beings to effect any appreciable or lasting improvement in human affairs. In order to achieve that goal they had to look upon rights "as a consequence of duties fulfilled, and one must begin with the latter in order to arrive at the former."[38] Similarly, "you cannot obtain your *rights* except by obeying the commands of *Duty.*"[39]

Jacques Maritain, an admirer of Gandhi's philosophy of satyagraha, had also recognized that rights and duties went together. The ancient and medieval theory of natural law, he pointed out, had paid more attention to obligations than to rights. However the eighteenth century brought out in full light that rights were also needed by natural law. He regretted, however, that in more recent times a shift had occurred from obligations to rights only. "A genuine and comprehensive view would pay attention *both* to the obligations and the rights involved in the requirements of natural law."[40]

Simone Weil likewise was emphatic in defending the priority of duty over rights. "The notion of obligation," she writes, "comes before that of rights, which is subordinated to the former. A right is not effectual by itself, but only in relation to the obligation to which it corresponds."[41] Adhering to almost a Gandhian pattern of thought, Weil writes that a genuine moral obligation originates in the soul. It does not (and it cannot) originate in any convention, for conventions are liable to be modified according to the wishes of the parties to them. But a moral obligation is an eternal one. "It is coextensive with the eternal destiny of human beings. Only human beings have an eternal destiny." Positive rights that are in contradiction to moral obligations are *pro tanto* illegitimate.[42] As Gandhi had written, "Man-made laws are not necessarily binding" on a *satyagrahi.* "That we should obey laws whether good or bad is a new-fangled notion."[43]

Dharma as social duty in India today

Gandhi did not participate in the drafting of the new Indian constitution. It is, therefore, idle to speculate on what difference it would have made,

---

[38] G. Mazzini, *The Duties of Man* (London: J. M. Dent, 1907), p. 16.

[39] Ibid., p. 54. The Italics are Mazzini's.

[40] J. Maritain, *Man and the State* (Chicago: University of Chicago Press, 1951), p. 94. The Italics are Maritain's. His favorable comments on Gandhi's philosophy of satyagraha appear in ibid., pp. 69–70.

[41] S. Weil, *The Need for Roots: Prelude to a Declaration of Duties Towards Mankind* (London: Routledge, 1997), p. 3.

[42] Ibid., p. 5.   [43] *Hind Swaraj*, pp. 91–92.

had he participated. P. V. Kane has observed that the new Indian con-stitution ignores the dharma of *varna* and *ashrama*.[44] This, as noted before, would have been consistent with Gandhi's view on the matter. He had followed two principles in dealing with what was viable in the *Dharmasastras*. The first was that nothing in them that was contrary to "universal truths and morals" should stand. And the second was that nothing in them that was "capable of being reasoned" should stand, if it was in conflict with reason.[45] It would have been his position, then, that legislative reason and judicial reason should approach the *Dharmasastras* in the light of these two principles.

The obsolescence of the dharma of caste and stages of life does not undermine the continuing validity of universal dharma (*sadharana dharma*). It is therefore the duty of individuals and social sub-groups, acting in and through civil society, to give effect to the latter. His *Constructive Programme* was grounded on the principles of universal dharma.

However, there is a strong element of realism in Gandhi's philosophy of dharma as duty. The verse from the *Mahabharata*, cited at the beginning of this chapter, reflects this. It recognizes the fact that history in signifi-cant part involves a struggle between duty and interest. The chances of duty gaining ascendancy over interest depend on virtue. Modern society, by contrast, has placed its bets on rights rather than on virtue, which to Gandhi was a matter of deep concern. He wanted modern society to place equal emphasis on rights, duties, and virtue.

---

[44] Kane, *History of Dharmasastra*, vol. V, part 2, p. 1664.   [45] CW, 62: 121.

6 Dharma as religion

"A religion has to be judged not by its worst specimens but by the best it might have produced."[1]

Being religious, according to Gandhi, is a means of achieving the supreme purushartha. It bridges the gap between the spheres of the ethical and the spiritual, without being fully identified with either. As an inner movement that originates in the soul, religion seeks to establish the soul's rightful relationship to God.

Margaret Chatterjee's *Gandhi's Religious Thought* gives an excellent overview of the Mahatma's position.[2] Here we approach his religious thought from the perspective of the theory of the purusharthas. A key that is helpful here is his distinction between religion as idea, as timeless, and religion as institution, as time-bound. A good deal of what he had to say on religion as institution concerned his own religion, Hinduism. How its scriptures should be interpreted became a major issue since the social institutions of caste and Untouchability were justified in terms of the scriptures. The question of religious pluralism also received his most serious attention, especially because of the recurrent, and apparently unending, conflict between Hindus and Muslims. While he adhered to the view that religion was necessary for the achievement of our purushartha, he also adhered to the view that the state should be neutral in religious matters. The state, being rooted in artha, had its own immediate ends, which were not the same as those of moksha. Though the two – artha and moksha – belonged to the same system of ends, they were to retain their distinct spheres of concern. To this extent secularism and religiosity co-exist – and are meant to coexist – in his philosophy. Finally, prayer, being a religious activity *par excellence*, occupied a prominent place in his philosophy. While some look upon secularism as a sign of progress, he adhered to the view that even secular progress that is truly

[1] Gandhi's response to B. R. Ambedkar, CW, 63: 154.
[2] M. Chatterjee, *Gandhi's Religious Thought* (London: Macmillan, 1983).

beneficial to human beings needed the spiritual benefits derived from the habit of prayer.

The idea of religion

The ability to conceive of the idea of religion, according to Gandhi, was a distinguishing mark of normal human beings. From the religious point of view humans were engaged in a twofold relationship: that of the temporal ego to the permanent self, and of the latter to God or Supreme Reality. Religion helped to purify and transform the ego and to unite the self to God. Religion as idea transcended religion as institution. The *telos* of the latter was to realize the idea in time, place, and culture. These were Gandhi's basic religious ideas, and of the many statements that he made on their behalf, the following was perhaps the most representative:

Let me explain what I mean by religion. It is not the Hindu religion, which I certainly prize above all other religions, but the religion which transcends Hinduism, which changes one's very nature, which binds one indissolubly to the truth within and which ever purifies. It is the permanent element in human nature which counts no cost too great in order to find full expression and which leaves the soul utterly restless until it has found itself, known its Maker and appreciated the true correspondence between the Maker and itself.[3]

This Gandhian manifesto on religion contains five main points: religion transforms our nature, it binds us to Truth, it purifies us, it establishes the "correspondence" between us and our "Maker," and it transcends all historical religions.

The change that the idea of religion can bring about is that from an ego-centred way of being to a "self"-oriented way of being. Being composites of body and soul means that there are two centres of activity in human beings, the ego and the self. The ego is the guardian of our material interests and the self that of our spiritual awareness. There is an initial struggle between the two centres of action. Unless this struggle is managed properly, there is the likelihood of its ending in the victory of the ego over the self. In which case, ego satisfaction becomes the ultimate goal of life. However, religion helps us to resolve the struggle in favor of the self, so that ego satisfaction can take place in a manner consistent with the requirements of the spiritual self. What the idea of religion helps us to achieve is not the elimination of the ego and its material interests – for that is impossible in the embodied existence – but their harmonization with the self and its goal, which is ultimate liberation or moksha. The

---

[3] CW, 17: 406.

harmonization is made possible through various spiritual self-disciplines, notably the virtues. Such is the nature of the self-transformation that religion can bring about.

The second function of religion is to bind us to the truth within. The truth within is the image of the self-subsistent, eternal Truth. Gandhi had famously defined Truth as God. The claim here is that the self in us has the innate capacity to know truth, and that this capacity when actualized unites us with the self-subsistent Truth. Religion, therefore, has always to be attentive to the question of truth: it can in that way spare us from superstitions, delusions, and all manner of self-deception that otherwise go under the name of religion. The notion that anything goes if it bears the sign of religion is rejected here. One is reminded of William James' famous definition of religion as *"the feelings, acts, and experiences of individual men in their solitude, so far as they apprehend themselves to stand in relation to whatever they may consider the divine."*[4] Gandhi would have difficulty with the phrase "whatever they may consider the divine." In his view, the idea of religion cannot be properly satisfied with any idea of the divine. It has to be the right idea of the divine. The right idea of religion and of the divine is within the reach of the seeker. True, the search for truth is difficult, and experimental. It is not surprising that he should entitle his autobiography *The Story of My Experiments with Truth*. Life for him was a series of experiments with truth, which, when properly conducted, would lead to Truth-realization.

This takes us to the third function of religion – its capacity to purify the ego. The purification of the ego is both a psychological and spiritual process. Psychologically, it calls for the proper management of the passions that are at work in the human psyche – greed, anger, lust, envy, vanity, and the like. Spiritually, it helps the ego to function in harmony with the inner self. Not that the ego would be transformed into the self – that would be impossible, given our constitution – but that the ego would no longer pose as an obstacle to our spiritual development. We cannot live without the ego. Yet too much of it causes conflicts and sufferings. The process of purification can refine the passions of the ego and make them the positive elements of an integrated life. For example, the passion for wealth, when left to itself, can become greed, but, when purified, can become a means of establishing the appropriate material conditions of human life. And so on with the other passions of the ego.

The process of purification removes only the false claims that the ego makes for itself. The removal of such claims results in the awareness of the

---

[4] W. James, *The Varieties of Religious Experience: A Study in Human Nature* (London: Fontana, 1960), p. 50. Italics James'.

true nature of the self in us. It enables the ego to integrate its interests with those of the self. Such integration does not result in emptiness (*sunyata*) as some would have it, but in fulfillment or the realization of purushartha. To become aware of the true inner self is to become aware of God too, and of the truth of the adage *tat tvam asi* ("that thou art").

The fourth function of religion as idea is the establishment of "the true correspondence" between the self and its "Maker." The use of the term "Maker" indicates the theistic orientation of Gandhi's religious thought. And the use of the term "correspondence" refers to the mode of the self's relationship to its Maker. The "correspondence" implies that the self retains its identity. The awareness that there is a "correspondence" between the self and its Maker is the most profound spiritual experience that religion can provide. It is an experience that transcends sectarian boundaries, and one that cannot be conceptualized or verbalized. "The one Religion," writes Gandhi, "is beyond speech."[5]

The final attribute of religion as idea is that it transcends all historical, institutional religions. This claim is made not in order to disparage institutional religion. Rather it is made in order to provide a criterion for evaluating institutional religions. His description of religion as idea is remarkably free from any sectarian bias. Institutional religions are necessary for sociological and cultural reasons. Without them the idea of religion would not find actual expression in time and place. But without the idea of religion animating them, institutional religions would lack the specifically religious element in them.

The juxtaposition of the idea and the institution of religion raises an interesting methodological question. It would seem that to understand the phenomenon of religion fully we have to understand both the idea and the institution. The one without the other would give only a distorted picture of the reality. For, as he says in *Hind Swaraj*, there is a religion that underlies all religions.[6]

Hinduism as an institutional religion

The institutional religion that Gandhi was most familiar with was of course Hinduism. His interest in it was not that of a neutral observer but that of a believer. His knowledge of it was knowledge through identity – the intuition of a thing that was one with the knowing subject, to use the words of Hilaire Belloc.[7]

---

[5] CW, 44: 167.   [6] *Hind Swaraj*, p. 42.
[7] See H. Belloc, *Europe and the Faith* (London: Constable, 1920), p. 3.

His interest in Hinduism was twofold. First, he wanted to see to what extent Hinduism had realized the idea of religion and contributed to the attainment of the ultimate end of all religions, viz. moksha. Second, he wanted to know to what extent institutional Hinduism had become an obstacle to the realization of the idea of religion.

He believed that all institutional religions, including Hinduism, were "divinely inspired." At the same time they were imperfect in so far as the human mind was involved in their historical evolution.[8] And, if human agency accounts for their imperfections, it also can contribute to their reform. The removal of such imperfections of Hinduism as he could observe became one of the major purposes of his interpretation of institutional Hinduism.

His reflections on Hinduism extended over a period of at least fifty years, beginning from 1894. In that year he wrote a letter to Rajchandbhai, his spiritual advisor, in which he raised twenty-seven questions. The questions touched on such subjects as the nature of the soul, God, moksha, *bhakti* (devotion to God), the Vedas, the *Gita*, the status of Rama and Krishna as avatars, and the role of Brahma, Vishnu, and Shiva in the Hindu pantheon. Hinduism's status in relation to Christianity was also raised.[9]

He came back to these topics throughout his life in lectures, articles, commentaries, and declarations. He considered himself to be an orthodox (*sanatani*) Hindu. The basic beliefs of Hinduism, according to him, were concerned with the soul and its relationship to God. The doctrines of karma and transmigration formed part of the Hindu belief system. The Hindu scriptures were made up of the Vedas, the Upanishads, the Epics, and the *Puranas*, with the *Gita* occupying a prominent place.

Though the letter to Rajchandbhai did not raise the issue of the imperfections of institutional Hinduism, *Hind Swaraj* did.[10] Only relatively late did the question of caste and Untouchability begin to preoccupy him. But once he understood the scope of the damage that they had inflicted on institutional Hinduism he set his mind to combat them. The history of his fight against Untouchability is too well known to require elaboration here. It was his firm belief, however, that a purified Hinduism would be a force for good in the modern world. A reformed Hinduism would also be ecumenical in outlook, recognizing the *de jure* legitimacy of all religions and the right to exist and to flourish side by side with Hinduism. Such an

---

[8] CW, 44: 167.
[9] For Gandhi's questions and Rajchandbhai's answers, see CW, 32: 593–602.
[10] *Hind Swaraj*, p. 70–71.

open Hinduism, instead of the closed Hinduism of the *Hindutva* propo-
nents, would be the Hinduism of the future.

Nowhere did he express his hopes for an open, modernized Hinduism
more clearly and deliberately than he did in a letter that he wrote in 1935
to Sarvepalli Radhakrishnan. In the secondary literature this letter has not
received the sort of attention that it deserves. Surely it deserves greater
attention than does the other famous letter that he wrote in 1894 to
Rajchandbhai.[11]

Apart from what the content of this letter says, it deserves our attention
for two main reasons. The first is the eminence of its recipient, arguably
the twentieth century's foremost Hindu philosopher. The second reason
is the time and care that went into its preparation. He had been mulling
it over ever since Radhakrishnan had invited him to contribute a chapter
for the volume (*Contemporary Indian Philosophy*) that he was editing.
Gandhi at first hesitated, pleading incompetence in philosophy,[12] where-
upon Radhakrishnan sent him three questions the answers to which, it was
agreed, would constitute the substance of the contribution that he had
asked for.[13] The three questions were:
1. What is your religion?
2. How are you led to it?
3. What is its bearing on social life?[14]

Gandhi's replies were very short. His religion, he said, was Hinduism,
which for him was the "religion of humanity." He saw it as being an open
religion, absorbing the best elements from all religions known to him. He
did not elaborate on what exactly he had taken from the other religions,
but the syncretic approach was readily admitted.

The substance of the second answer was that the quest for Truth was
the essence of modern Hinduism. His formula "Truth is God," was
designed to accommodate theists as well as atheists. Denial of the idea
of God was not uncommon. But not even those who denied the idea of
God would deny the existence of Truth. The reason was that there was a
"spark" of Truth in every human being, and if one allowed that spark to
become active, it would ultimately lead one to Truth.

The third answer emphasized that the service of fellow human beings
ought to be the outward expression of modern Hinduism as he

[11] For the text of the letter of 23 January 1935, see CW, 60: 106–7. J. T. F. Jordens'
Gandhi's Religion: A Homespun Shawl (London: Macmillan, 1998), does not mention
this letter in its otherwise good survey of Gandhi's thoughts on Hinduism.
[12] See Gandhi's letter to Radhakrishnan, of 16 September 1934, cited in chapter 1.
[13] In his letter to Radhakrishnan dated 22 November 1934, Gandhi agreed to send the three
answers. See CW, 59: 385.
[14] CW, 60: 106.

interpreted it. The reason was simple enough: the realization of Truth was impossible without the loving service of one's neighbor. This was fully in keeping with the emphasis that he placed on the virtues of truth and non-violence, or "love in the broadest sense."

It is remarkable that his answers make no mention of rituals or the social structure of Hinduism. Nor do they make any mention of such doctrines as karma and transmigration. Not that they were unimportant, but that the quest for Truth and the disinterested service of fellow human beings were to be the hallmark of modern Hinduism.

The interpretation of the Hindu scriptures

The question of how to interpret the scriptures had become an urgent issue for Gandhi. Since he believed that Hinduism was a revealed religion, a reliable way of interpreting the texts that contained the revelation was of supreme interest to him. Obviously, he had no difficulty in accepting the broad principle of scriptural authority. At the same time he was not a dogmatist who refused to see the need for new interpretations of the old scriptural truths. What was needed was a judicious balancing of the authority of the scriptures and the exercise of personal freedom.

The first question that he addressed in this regard concerned the content of the body of revealed truths. Given that the Hindu scriptures consisted of a very vast corpus, gathered over many centuries and mixed with all manner of accretions, the question made good sense. The following was his position: "The scriptures properly so called can only be concerned with eternal verities and must appeal to any conscience, i.e., any heart whose eyes of understanding are opened. Nothing can be accepted as the word of God which cannot be tested by reason or capable of being spiritually experienced."[15] Every claim made on behalf of revelation should be capable of being tested "on the anvil of truth with the hammer of compassion."[16]

The task of separating eternal verities from the temporal ones was indeed a daunting one. Even more daunting was the application of the criterion of "spiritually experiencing" the truth that needed interpretation. He attached great importance to this criterion, however. His interpretation of the *Bhagavad Gita*, for example, used this criterion. At the back of his reading of this work, he wrote, there was the claim of an endeavor to enforce its meaning in his own conduct "for an unbroken period of 40 years."[17] The right understanding of the meaning of any

[15] CW, 63: 153.   [16] CW, 24: 320.   [17] CW, 44: 92.

revealed truth required "a well-cultivated moral sensibility and experience in the practice of their truths."[18]

Remarkably, he did not think that the modern-day Shakaracharyas (successors to the original Sankara) and *shastris* – the traditional interpreters of the Hindu scriptures – were meeting the criterion of "experiencing the truth" that they were interpreting. For this reason, he "most emphatically" repudiated their claim to be the authentic interpreters of the Hindu scriptures.[19] They did not practice the necessary virtues – truth, non-violence, celibacy, and detachment – in sufficient degree. Their status as gurus therefore could no longer be recognized. It was a rare thing today, he remarked, to find in them a combination of purity of life and depth of learning. The "millions" therefore have to go without their help.[20]

Gandhi next took up the question of the role of learning in the interpretation of the scriptures. His comments are likely to shock scripture scholars everywhere, not just in India. Learning, he said, was necessary but not sufficient. What was equally necessary was the scholar's holiness of life. "Learning there must be. But religion does not live by it. It lives in the experiences of its saints and seers, in their lives and sayings. When all the most learned commentaries of the scriptures are utterly forgotten, the accumulated experience of the sages and saints will abide and be an inspiration for ages to come."[21]

Gandhi was responding to Ambedkar's criticism: because the caste system had the sanction of the scriptures, the scriptures themselves had to be thrown out together with the caste system.[22] It was easy for him to say this because already in the 1930s he had mentally rejected Hinduism as a system of personal belief. Unfortunately, his solution did not address the issue of how the scriptures should be interpreted and how later accretions should be expurgated. Gandhi's point was that the whole should not be condemned because of the defects of some of its parts. The Hindu scriptures taken as a whole had the power to lead humans to genuine holiness of life. This was the point that the saints had made. And it is this inherent power of the scriptures that should not be forgotten.

Gandhi's response has relevance beyond the borders of Hinduism. The scriptures of every religion, not just those of Hinduism, are more than just literature. They are vehicles that take those who believe in them to holiness of life. As such they should be interpreted differently from

---

[18] CW, 28: 316.   [19] CW, 21: 246.   [20] Ibid.   [21] CW, 63: 153.
[22] B. R. Ambedkar, "A Vindication of Caste by 'Mahatma' Gandhi," *Dr. Ambedkar Birth Centenary Souvenir* vol. III (London: Ambedkar Centenary Celebration Committee, 1991), p. 54.

secular literature. The activity of interpreting the scriptures is not a secular activity even when secular methods are used in the process of interpretation. It is an activity that is closer to being a spiritual exercise than to being a secular academic activity. Learning without holiness of life tended to secularize the scriptures – to denature them. But learning informed by holiness of life helped to unearth the religious truth that lay buried underneath.

There was a second principle that Gandhi used in his interpretation of the scriptures. It had to do with the phenomenon of the historical evolution of the meaning of concepts found in them. On examining the history of languages, he wrote, it became evident that the meaning of important concepts had changed or expanded over a period of time. The meaning of great writings often underwent historical evolution.[23] In the case of the *Bhagavad Gita*, he had noticed this phenomenon with respect to several terms, including words such as "sacrifice" (*yagna*) and "asceticism" (*sannyasa*). The term sacrifice before the time of the *Gita* meant mostly animal sacrifice, a meaning totally absent from it. In the *Gita*, according to Gandhi, it meant "continuous concentration on God," or "physical work."[24] Likewise, *sannyasa*, in the age before the *Gita*, had meant "complete cessation from work" and withdrawal from the active life. In the *Gita*, according to him, it meant "work, but without the desire for the fruit of work."[25] The author of the *Gita* was showing how to change the meaning of terms to fit the needs of his day. A present-day interpreter of this work would have to show the same creative spirit: he or she would have to interpret the concepts of the *Gita* in a manner intelligible in the present time. As Gandhi writes, "by expanding the meaning of words," the author of the *Gita* teaches us to imitate him.[26] Old terms would have to be given new meanings. In doing so the interpreter would be able to breathe a new life into Hinduism and enable it to become a "living faith speaking like a mother to her aching child."[27] Briefly, holiness of life, academic learning, and a historical understanding of the evolution of language – all these contributed to the activity of interpreting the scriptures.

Religious pluralism

Religious pluralism refers to a theory of religions that holds the *de jure* legitimacy of all institutional religions. The legitimacy in question, it is worth repeating, is *de jure*, and not merely *de facto*. Religious pluralism

---

[23] CW, 41: 99.   [24] Ibid., pp. 99–100.   [25] Ibid., p. 100.   [26] Ibid.   [27] CW, 63: 339.

does not pretend to invent a new religion. Its role is to examine the relationship of religions among themselves. Gandhi accepted religious pluralism wholeheartedly on the principle that all institutional religions had their origin in divine revelation.[28] The one true religion, he asserted, subsequently became many "as it passed through the human medium."[29] In other words, God had revealed himself (or herself) to the whole of humanity. At the same time, humanity expressed the meaning of the received revelation differently, depending on language and culture. The unity of religious truths was guaranteed because of their divine source, but their diversity became unavoidable because of culture, and the philosophical or theological systems that arose from them. Dogmas, cults, and codes reflect these cultural differences.

Indian culture, from its very beginning, had intimations of the twofold character – unity and diversity – of the religious experience. In *Rig Veda*, for example, we read: "To what is One, sages give many a title."[30] According to the *Bhagavad Gita* humans could approach God by different paths: "In whatsoever way any come to Me, in that same way I grant them favor."[31] Gandhi had a cultural predisposition to embrace the theory of religious pluralism. He also had an experiential basis for accepting it. Classical India had produced not only Hinduism, but also Buddhism and Jainism. Sixteenth-century India had produced Sikhism as well. India had welcomed Christians, Jews, Muslims, and Zoroastrians as they intermingled with an already religiously diverse population.

Gandhi used a number of metaphors to express his thoughts on religious pluralism. Institutional religions were *roads* that led to the same destination.[32] They were the *branches* of the same tree.[33] Or, they were the *rivers* that flowed into the same ocean.[34] Finally, there was a core and a periphery to all religions.[35] The experience of unity and diversity was intrinsic to deep religious experience. It reflected the eternal and the temporal dimensions of basic religious truths.

Gandhi saw two great values in the theory of religious pluralism. In the first place, it provided an objective basis for religious toleration within the state, and in the second place it supplied the foundation for the dialogue between religions.

Since all institutional religions had a divine origin, humans had a moral obligation to respect them. The Gujarati term he used for tolerance was

---

[28] CW, 44: 167.   [29] Ibid., p. 166.   [30] *Rig Veda* I: 164, 46.
[31] F. Edgerton (trans.), *The Bhagavad Gita* (Cambridge, MA: Harvard University Press, 1972), IV: 11.
[32] *Hind Swaraj*, p. 53.   [33] CW, 44: 166.
[34] CW, 7: 338. See *Gita* II: 70 for the source of this metaphor.   [35] *Hind Swaraj*, p. 56.

sahishnuta, which carried a more positive meaning than did the English term "tolerance." The latter implied, he felt, "a gratuitous assumption of the inferiority" of the other. The Gujarati term, by contrast, implied respect and sympathy for religions different from one's own.[36] Respect for religions other than one's own was one of the eleven civic virtues of his moral philosophy. As a virtue, tolerance went beyond mere political calculations or legal obligation. It appealed to the moral and religious conscience of the citizen.

Religious tolerance, according to Gandhi, was of crucial importance to a country like India. The harmony between its religious communities depended on it. His *Constructive Programme* made it the first step towards national reconstruction. That was why he appealed to every Indian, whatever his or her religion, to feel his or her identity with members of every religious denomination of the country. In order to realize this he exhorted every member of the Congress party to cultivate "personal friendship with persons representing faiths other than his own."[37] And non-violence was to be the master key of such friendship.[38]

Religious pluralism made the dialogue between religions a serious activity – his second reason for promoting it. The future of peace between religions lay, he was convinced, in the dialogue between them. Dialogue was a process, not of superimposing one's own religious views on the other, but of understanding the other as a different religious being. To have genuine dialogue, the participants had to maintain their own identities and beliefs. If the difference was not maintained and respected as difference, how could there be genuine dialogue in the first place? In a genuine dialogue, one spoke from one's position. One did not hope to discover what one's position would be at the end of the dialogue. One had to have a position grounded in truth before any genuine dialogue could commence. Otherwise the dialogue would lack both credibility and integrity. Dialogue would then become an exercise in the joint search for truth, tolerance being only a means to truth.

At the same time in a dialogue one had to be open to the other, not just to the ideas of the other, but to the other as a religious being. The outcome of such openness would not be the fusion or the uniting of the religions concerned. The outcome would enable, as he wrote, an orthodox Hindu to remain what he was, and yet to respect an orthodox Muslim for what he was.[39] Nor would the outcome be the creation of a third "neutral" religion. The outcome would rather be the assimilation, as much as possible, of the truths that were in the religion of the other.

---

[36] CW, 44: 166.   [37] CW, 75: 147.   [38] CW, 72: 254.   [39] CW, 19: 305.

The participants, being aware that all religions had an initial divine impulse, and that culture and language had created the actual differences, would endeavor to penetrate these cultural and linguistic barriers.

Gandhi believed that Hinduism was peculiarly equipped to promote this type of inter-religious dialogue. Though it had a revelation to start with, it developed a culture without a central religious authority formulating and continuously updating its beliefs and dogmas on such issues as karma and transmigration. "Not being an exclusive religion," he wrote, it enabled its followers not merely to respect other religions but also "to admire and assimilate" whatever was good in them.[40] Remarkably, he felt that Christianity also had such a potential. As he told the Rev. Joseph Doke, Baptist missionary and his first biographer, "the fullness of Christianity could only be found in its interpretation in the light and by the aid of Hinduism."[41] Given what is happening in Christian–Hindu dialogue today, these are indeed prophetic words.[42]

Gandhi himself was a model of conducting inter-religious dialogue. He remained, as we noted, a believing Hindu. Yet he assimilated as much as he could the ethics of other religions. For example, he had a deep appreciation of the art and music of Christianity. His experience of being moved to tears by the sight of a medieval Crucifix in the Vatican Museum[43] and his life-long appreciation for Cardinal Newman's hymn "Lead, Kindly Light" were examples of this. As Joseph Doke noted in his biography of Gandhi, his religious views were too closely allied to Christianity to be entirely Hindu, and too deeply saturated with Hinduism to be called Christian. His sympathies were so wide and catholic that the formulae of sects appeared meaningless.[44]

The one thing in this regard that grieved him most was the conflict between Hindus and Muslims, which continued unabated despite his best effort to resolve it. He was right, however, in thinking that genuine acceptance of the *de jure* legitimacy of all religions would be the first step in the direction of peace between them. The second step would be the abjuration of the use of violence as a legitimate means of religious expression. Until *jihadist Islam* came to accept these two principles – the *de jure* legitimacy of all religions and the abjuration of jihad as a means of

---

[40] CW, 35: 166–67.   [41] CW, 12: 176.

[42] For the growing literature on Christian–Hindu dialogue see B. Griffiths, *The Cosmic Revelation: The Hindu Way to God* (London: Collins, 1983) and J. Dupuis, S. J., *Toward a Christian Theology of Religious Pluralism* (Maryknoll, NY: Orbis Books, 1997).

[43] Noted in R. Rolland's Diary: see *Romain Rolland and Gandhi Correspondence* (Delhi: Government of India Publications Division), 1976, p. 235.

[44] J. J. Doke, *M. K. Gandhi: An Indian Patriot in South Africa* (Varanasi: Sarva Seva Sangh Prakashan, 1959), p. 142.

religious expression – Gandhi's hope for peace between religions would remain unrealized.

Prayer

Prayer (*prarthana*), according to Gandhi, is a spiritual exercise that puts the soul in communion with the divine. What food is for bodily life, prayer is for spiritual life. To be spiritually active, one has to have a habit of prayer. The presupposition underlying a prayerful life is that human beings are ultimately dependent on God.

Prayer, according to him, fulfils three main functions: worship, meditation, and inner purification.[45] The essence of worship is the acknowledgement of our dependency on God. Dependency of this sort does not detract from human dignity or autonomy. It is a consequence of the realization that free human beings are also contingent beings. Our contingent existence comes to an end only with the attainment of moksha. The latter is not a way of asserting self-sufficiency, but of achieving the union with the source of Being. Genuine prayer recalls to our consciousness the existential truth about ourselves.

The forms of worship depend on imagination, aesthetic feelings, art, and imagery. Music, poetry, sacraments, and symbols are also involved in worship. This is true, more or less, of all religions. Gandhi is of the opinion that we mortals must of necessity depend upon the faculty of imagination.[46] That is why the liturgy depicts God as possessing certain attributes, even though intellectually we know that God is formless and without attributes (*nirguna*). "I am intellectually conscious of this," Gandhi writes, "and still I cannot help dwelling upon the attributes of God. My intellect can exercise no influence over my heart."[47] In prayer as worship the role of imagination cannot be totally set aside, no matter how puritanical we wish to be. Humans have a need to express their deep spiritual perceptions through representations, whether in language or art forms. Such representations are false and yet not false. They are false in that God is beyond representation. They are not false because it is only through them that we can initiate worship.

According to Gandhi, human imagination is at work in articulating the notion of avatar. What humans imagine Krishna to be is more important to them than what the real historical Krishna was. "Krishna of the *Gita* is perfection and right knowledge personified, but the picture is imaginary. That does not mean that Krishna, the adored of his people, never lived.

---

[45] CW, 50: 203.   [46] Ibid., p. 200.   [47] Ibid., p. 201.

But perfection is imagined. The idea of a perfect incarnation is an aftergrowth."[48]

Meditation is the second function of prayer. Here there is no dependency on imagination. In meditation it is the spiritual faculty (*buddhi*) that is at work. The theory underlying meditation is that God is not an alien being, indifferent to human beings. As Gandhi writes, "God is not some person outside ourselves or away from the universe ... He abides in our hearts and is nearer to us than the nails are to the fingers."[49]

There have been many different schools of meditation within Hinduism, not to mention the other religious traditions. Some thought of meditation as being the activity of focusing on the inner self, others as an activity of emptying the mind of the thirst for material pleasures, and still others viewed it as the process by which the mind sought to understand itself. Gandhian meditation was not preoccupied with one's inner self as isolated from God. Meditation for him was the spiritual effort to experience the relationship of the inner self to the formless and quality-less God. The concept here was not that of emptying, but of enriching the inner self.

Meditation that was concerned only with the mind, one that did not conceive of its relationship to the Absolute, was not Gandhian. As he explained to his Buddhist friend, Dr. Charles Fabri, Buddhism would not have survived as a religion had it not adopted the practice of prayer. A merely rational conception of life was not adequate to meet the realities that lay outside the reach of human reason. There was a yearning in humans that sought after union with the Absolute. There was something infinitely higher than human reason that ruled over the universe.[50] And it was in meditation that humans really understood the nature of their being and the meaning of their existence in time.

Purification is the third function of prayer. The exercise of imagination and meditation makes one realize the need for inner purification. For the disorderly state of the passions introduces "impurity" into our lives. Passions such as anger, greed, lust, and hatred disturb not only the inner life of the individual, they also pollute the purity of social relations. The worshipper and the contemplative come to realize that union with the Absolute is possible only if the passions are purified.

In his autobiography Gandhi spoke of the difficulties involved in conquering what he called "subtle passions," and "dormant passions."[51] Even if the overt manifestations of the passions were brought under control, these other manifestations of the passions also had to be brought

[48] CW, 41: 94.   [49] CW, 50: 203.   [50] CW, 70: 29.   [51] CW, 39: 402.

under control. Prayer, in the form of self-examination or self-analysis, was one way of accomplishing this. What was needed was what he called "the triple purity" – purity in thoughts, words, and deeds.

Prayer as self-purification makes one aware of the fragility of the spiritual life. Human beings are spiritually fragile because of the pressure arising from the passions. In prayer of this sort, human beings recognize the need for humility if they are to make progress in spiritual life. As he wrote in the conclusion to his autobiography, "So long as a man does not of his own free will put himself last among his fellow creatures, there is no salvation for him."[52]

Gandhi had kept a detailed schedule of this prayer life.[53] He prayed twice daily – half an hour in the morning from 4:15 to 4:45, and half an hour in the evening from 7:00 to 7:30. The morning prayer consisted of verses from the *Ashram Hymnal*, a hymn in praise of Ram (the *Ramdhun*), and a reading from the *Gita*. The whole of the *Gita* was recited in a seven-day cycle. The evening prayer consisted of a hymn, the *Ramdhun*, reading from some sacred book, and the recitation of the last nineteen verses of the second chapter of the *Gita*. Though these items were taken for the most part from the Hindu sources, items from other religions were also included, such as the hymn "Lead, Kindly Light."

What was noteworthy in his prayer schedule was the role that institutional religion had played in it. His preference for Ram, instead of Krishna, was also noteworthy. On the other hand, the dominant role that the *Gita* played in his prayer-life reflected his commitment to philosophic meditation. The daily recitation of the last nineteen verses of its second chapter, which describe the attributes of a person of "stable wisdom," indicated that the pursuit of wisdom was the concrete goal of his prayer-life. Meditation seemed to energize him spiritually. What William James said of the power of prayer to set free energy that "but for prayer would be bound" applied exactly to Gandhi's case.[54] Prayer no doubt was a major source of the prodigious energy that he was able to spend in so many different fields of activity.

Finally, Gandhi's prayer-life reveals how deeply aware he was of his own inadequacies and of the continuous need for self-improvement and self-purification. To his credit, he never considered himself to be a mahatma.[55] He was embarrassed rather than honored by the title of

---

[52] Ibid.   [53] See CW, 50: 197–205.
[54] James, *The Varieties of Religious Experience*, p. 446.
[55] On the meaning of the concept of mahatma see Dieter Conrad, "Gandhi as Mahatma: Political Semantics in an Age of Cultural Ambiguity," in V. Dalmia, A. Malinar, and M. Christof (eds.), *Charisma and Canon: Essays in the Religious History of the Indian Subcontinent* (New Delhi: Oxford University Press, 2001), pp. 223–49, at 242.

mahatma popularly given to him. To suggest that he wore the mask of divinity, as a recent scurrilous book has done, is to display not only crude bias but also deplorable ignorance of the significance of his prayer-life.[56]

Religion and secularism

Secularism is a modern theory of religion and politics according to which the state should remain neutral towards all religions. The ethical basis of the state in this view is not derived from any particular religion, but from the common agreement on what constitutes the rights and duties of the citizens who compose it. Secularism promotes a positive value in as much as its emphasis is on democracy and equal citizenship.[57]

Modern secularism had its origin in the West – in the intellectual changes brought about by the Enlightenment. As Owen Chadwick has pointed out these changes resulted in the freeing of science, the arts, and learning in general from their theological origins or bias. He defined secularism as "the relation" in which modern Western civilization and society stood to the Christian elements of its past and continuing Christian elements in its present.[58] In its moderate form it stood for the equal treatment of all citizens regardless of the religion they professed or did not profess. In its extreme form it stood for an open warfare against religion as such, as in France in the decades following the French Revolution, or in Russia and China following the Marxist Revolution, or in Germany following the Nazi coup.

Gandhi's secularism was different from all these. Though he integrated the idea of a limited constitutional state into his political philosophy, he did not endorse, on that account, any hostility towards religion, as both idea and institution. This was because his secularism was grounded in the theory of the purusharthas. According to that theory, as we have been arguing in this book, artha was compatible with both dharma and the pursuit of moksha. And dharma in the sense of religion meant all religions, not just Hinduism. Respect for all religions (*sarva dharma sama bhava*) was a requirement of Gandhi's theory of the purusharthas.

There have been some misgivings, notably among the promoters of the ideology of *Hindutva*, that Gandhian secularism was alien to India and that it was likely to impede the growth of a strong national sentiment in

---

[56] See G. B. Singh, *Gandhi: Behind the Mask of Divinity* (Amherst, NY: Prometheus Books, 2004).

[57] On the question of secularism in India, see Bhargava, *Secularism and Its Critics*.

[58] O. Chadwick, *The Secularization of the European Mind in the 19th Century* (Cambridge: Cambridge University Press, 1993), p. 264.

the country. They are based on a profound misunderstanding of Gandhi's position. For nothing is more fundamentally Indian than is the theory of the purusharthas.

T. N. Madan has argued that the type of secularism that modern India has adopted is not suited to India's cultural temper. Eastern religions – Hinduism, Buddhism, Jainism, Islam, and Sikhism – he asserts, are "totalizing in character, claiming all of a follower's life."[59] From the historical perspective, Madan is right. From the perspective of theory, however, he appears to be on shaky grounds, as far as classical Hindu thought is concerned. True, in Buddhism the value of artha is either eliminated or collapsed into that of dharma. In traditional Islam, of course, religion and state are also collapsed into one. But in classical Hindu thought, thanks to the theory of the purusharthas, artha is conceived of as being distinct from dharma and moksha, but not opposed to them. Historically, however, under the influence of the ascetic tradition, as we have been arguing, the idea of moksha tended to marginalize artha.

It is precisely this historical marginalization that Gandhi was fighting against. He wanted to restore artha to its rightful place, and, in attempting to do so, he further clarified its secular character. He freed it not only from its submergence by the ascetic tradition, but also from its historic association with sacred monarchy. The rajahs and maharajahs had to give way to civic nationalism, and its secular principle of the political community.

Madan, however, is right in expressing the hope that India needs someone like Gandhi to teach "the proper relation between religion and politics, values and interests."[60] That was exactly what he (Gandhi) was teaching through the theory of the purusharthas. He was against any one purushartha totalizing the whole person and the entire culture. If medieval Indian culture erred in permitting moksha to totalize Indian culture, modern Western culture is permitting artha to totalize modern culture. Gandhi was opposed to all forms of totalizing.

In this regard it is worth noting that his stand is similar to that taken by St. Thomas Aquinas in the West in the late Middle Ages. The latter had drawn a distinction between "the faithful" (*fidelis*) and the citizen (*civis*), which was of crucial importance to the development of political philosophy in the West. The member of a religious community and the member of a political community derived their legitimacy from distinct sources. As he argued, a human being did not belong to the political community "entirely in his whole person, and with all that he was." Therefore, it was not required that each of his actions should be judged with reference to

---

[59] See Bhargava, *Secularism and Its Critics*, p. 302.   [60] Ibid., p. 314.

the political community alone.[61] In other words, he was against religion or politics totalizing the whole person – exactly Gandhi's position.

Gandhi was rightly apprehensive of the tendency of modern secularism to totalize the individual and civilization itself. He regretted that "bodily welfare" was the only purushartha that modern civilization cared for.[62] He was not impressed that some Western thinkers would regard religion as a "superstitious growth."[63] When they had nothing good to say about religion, they would accuse it of being the source of wars and hatred in the world.[64] His "first complaint," therefore, about modern Western civilization was that it might turn India into a secular state on the Western pattern. He was afraid that if India adopted that pattern, it would undermine not just Hinduism, but the very idea of religion itself.[65]

Given Gandhi's balanced approach to religion and politics, it would not be possible to evaluate correctly his achievements as a religious thinker without keeping in mind his achievements as a political thinker. Equally inadequate would be the attempt to evaluate his political achievements without paying due attention to his achievements as a religious thinker. Yet such imbalance can be found all too easily in the Gandhi literature.

A particularly striking example is found in George Orwell. He faulted Gandhi for his saintliness. Saints he asserted were guilty until proven innocent. Gandhi's "basic aims were anti-human and reactionary." His teachings could not be squared with the humanistic belief that Man was the measure of all things. And there was no way that the humanistic and the religious positions could be reconciled. One had to choose between God and Man, and all progressives had chosen Man. Orwell was prepared to applaud what he regarded as Gandhi's main political achievement (the peaceful ending of the Raj) only on condition that his religious thought was discounted.[66] The tendency to isolate Gandhi's political philosophy from his religious philosophy is a tendency not uncommon among secularists.

The religious fundamentalism of *Hindutva* and jihadism is not the only intellectual force that Gandhi's moderate secularism has to resist. It has also to resist the hyper-secularism of the sort that Orwell represents.

---

[61] St. Thomas Aquinas, *Summa Theologiae*, 1a 2ae, Question 21, Article 4, ad. 3.
[62] *Hind Swaraj*, p. 35.   [63] Ibid., p. 37.   [64] Ibid., p. 43.   [65] Ibid., p. 42.
[66] G. Orwell, "Reflections on Gandhi," *Partisan Review*, 16 (1949), pp. 88–92.

7   Dharma as ethics

"There cannot be an ideal higher than truth and there cannot be any duty higher than non-violence."[1]

Gandhi's name is universally associated with the ethic of non-violence. He conceived of non-violence in two distinct ways – as in itself and as a derivative of truth. In itself, it is one of the eleven moral virtues listed in his moral philosophy. As a derivative of truth, it is foundational to the other moral virtues.[2] He writes: "*Ahimsa* [non-violence] may be deduced from Truth or may be paired with Truth. Truth and *ahimsa* are one and the same thing ... Truth is the end, *ahimsa* is the means thereto."[3] Truth is the ultimate criterion of judging whether non-violence is the right ethic for a given context. Not paying attention to this distinction has led many commentators to make exaggerated claims on behalf of non-violence. In itself non-violence is a virtue that opposes inflicting harm on others; however, truth may require that non-violence be applied differently in different situations. For instance, the truth of artha may require that coercion be used in self-defense. Such exercise of coercion would be consistent with Gandhi's notion of non-violence.

Gandhi's Sources

Gandhi's ideas on non-violence were drawn from a number of different sources. The *Mahabharata* was certainly one of them. The pairing of truth and non-violence came from there.[4]

---

[1] CW, 62: 224.
[2] The eleven moral virtues of Gandhi's philosophy are: truth, non-violence, courage, celibacy, non-stealing, freedom from greed, control of the palate, manual labor, *swadeshi* (regard for one's own country), opposition to Untouchability, and equal respect for all religions.
[3] CW, 44: 90.
[4] "There is no dharma higher than truth" (*satyanasti paro dharma*) comes from *Adi Parva*, XI: 13; and "there is no dharma higher than the duty of non-violence" (*ahimsa paramo dharma*) comes from *Shanti Parva*, CLXII: 24.

Patanjali's *Yoga Sutra* was another important source. The thirty-fifth aphorism of Book II of this work, "When one is well grounded in non-violence, there is abandonment of violence in one's presence," was a favorite of Gandhi. He used to repeat it like a mantra in times of personal crisis. He was convinced that perfect non-violence was "self-acting." "I literally believe in Patanjali's aphorism that violence ceases in the presence of non-violence"[5]

The influence of the *Bhagavad Gita* on Gandhi's theory of non-violence is well known. His contention was that the *Gita* was not about the ethic of war, but about the ethic of right action, action that would lead to moksha. That ethic was the ethic of the renunciation of the fruit of action, which it was impossible to put into practice without the exercise of the virtue of non-violence.[6] The war setting of the book had only a tangential relevance to its argument. The real *Kuru-kshetra* (the name of the battle-field mentioned in the *Gita*) was the human heart, which was also the *dharma-kshetra* (the field of the ethical life).[7]

Of his Western sources Plato's *Apology* had exerted an early influence on him. The Socratic principle that it was better to suffer harm than to inflict it on others had "the qualities of an elixir."[8] In 1908 he published a paraphrase of the *Apology* under the title *Story of a Soldier of Truth*. Already here we see how Gandhi tended to pair truth and non-violence.

By far the most extensive Western influence came from Leo Tolstoy's *The Kingdom of God is Within You* (1893). This book, as he wrote in his autobiography, had "overwhelmed" him. It was his *vade mecum* during his South African days. It was a mandatory reading for members of both Phoenix Settlement and Tolstoy Farm. He had it translated into Gujarati, with him suggesting a Gujarati title for it, *Khudano Darbar Tara Antermen Chhe*.[9]

The book was a fierce critique of the international relations of European powers at the end of the nineteenth century. The criticism was based on the ethic of the Sermon on the Mount. The case for non-violence was stated as follows:

How to settle the conflicts between people who now consider a thing evil that others consider good, and vice versa. To say that evil is what I consider evil although my adversary considers it good, is not a solution to the difficulty. There can be but two solutions: either to find an absolute and indubitable

---

[5] Patanjali's *Yoga Sutra*, cited in CW, 71: 225; CW, 42: 480; CW, 83: 324; and CW, 86: 279.
[6] CW, 41: 100.   [7] CW, 49: 113.   [8] CW, 8: 174.
[9] CW, 9: 240. He took this book to the Volksrust jail; on leaving the jail he presented it to the warden, Mr. G. Nelson, with the inscription: "For his many kindnesses, within the law, during my incarceration at Volksrust" (ibid., p. 115).

criterion of evil, or not to resist evil by violence. The first course has been tried since the beginning of history, and as we all know has so far led to no satisfactory results. The second course – not to resist with violence what we consider evil, until we have found some universal criterion – is the solution proposed by Christ.[10]

The authentic ethic of Christianity, according to Tolstoy, was a non-violent ethic. Christ's non-violence was active, not passive. It was not enough to abstain from harming others; it was equally necessary to resist violence by non-violent means, to return good for evil, and to love one's adversaries. The motive came from the consciousness that humans, whatever their acquired attitude towards one another, were brothers and sisters in Christ, whose perfection they were called upon to approximate. If you took the Sermon on the Mount seriously, you had to reject the state as an inherently unethical institution. You had to withdraw from political society and live in small self-governing communes.

Another of Tolstoy's writings, *Letter to a Hindu* (1908), also had a profound influence on him. It forced him to rethink the historical role that violence had played in Indian society. It pointed out that the British were able to hold India by violence because Indians themselves seemed to accept violence as the basis of society. That was why they submitted themselves to the tyranny of their rajahs and maharajahs. That was why they mistreated the Dalits so cruelly. The Brahmins could teach Nietzsche a lesson or two in what it was to behave like supermen. That being the case, the complaints of Indians against the British seemed like the complaints of alcoholics against liquor vendors. If the Indians were serious about ending the violence of colonialism, they had first to be serious about ending violence in their own society. Gandhi was so impressed that he translated the *Letter* into Gujarati and published it, together with an English translation, in the columns of his weekly newspaper, *Indian Opinion*.

Though Gandhi had gathered his ideas from different sources, it was Indian philosophy that gave them their unity and coherence. Human beings were composites of body and soul, nature and spirit (atman). Both body-force (*sharir bal*) and soul-force (*atma bal*) were at work in society. The body-force tended to serve the interests of the ego – the "I sense" of the unenlightened person – while the soul force tended to serve the interests of the enlightened person or persons and society. The passions and the calculating mind tended to side with the ego, unless the soul-force, with the help of intelligence and will (*buddhi*), succeeded in directing them to socially beneficial ends. Violence, which was a fact of

[10] L. Tolstoy, *The Kingdom of God and Peace Essays*, translated by Aylmer Maude (London: Oxford University Press, 1935), p. 58.

life, had its source in the needs of the body, or our material existence. Though a fact of life, Gandhi never accepted violence as its norm, for he believed that humans "by nature" were non-violent.[11] This was because of the constitutive presence of the spirit (atman) in us. That presence made us not only non-violent but also sociable by nature. Our humanity was tied to our capacity for non-violence. The presence of the spirit in us, "the mystery of soul-force"[12] and the natural sociability that followed from that presence constituted the philosophical basis of his ethic of non-violence.

When Gandhi made non-violence the new universal norm of human conduct, he was doing so in full view of the factual reality of violence within and between individuals. He was quite explicit in acknowledging the reality of violence in the human world. "Perfect *ahimsa* [non-violence]," he writes, "is possible only in the atman in its disembodied state. But when the atman takes on a body, *ahimsa* manifests itself in one as a feeling of compassion."[13] "All life in the flesh exists by some *himsa* [violence] ... The world is bound in a chain of destruction. In other words *himsa* is an inherent necessity for life in the body ... None, while in the flesh, can thus be entirely free from *himsa* because one never completely renounces the will to live."[14] "No doubt destruction in some form or other of some life is inevitable. Life lives upon life."[15] "I cannot become wholly free of violence so long as I have the feeling that this body is mine."[16] "Possession of a body like every other possession necessitates some violence, be it ever so little. The fact is that the path of duty [dharma] is not always easy to discern amidst claims seeming to conflict one with the other."[17] These are aspects of his theory of non-violence that his radically pacifist interpreters tend to ignore.[18] For what he has done (and here he follows the teaching of the *Gita*) is to integrate justifiable violence into the new ethic of non-violence.

The factual presence of violence in social life forced Gandhi to adjust the scope of his ethics to that reality. Hence the goal of Gandhian non-violence was not the total elimination of violence from social life, for that was impossible – given the body–spirit constitution of human beings – but the gradual reduction of its intensity and frequency. It would be utopian to think of the total elimination of violence. But to think of reducing its volume and extent would be realistic. What it sought was the freedom from moral culpability for the sort of necessary violence that embodied

---

[11] CW, 66: 421.   [12] Ibid.   [13] CW, 49: 430.   [14] CW, 37: 314.   [15] CW, 34: 130.
[16] CW, 36: 165.   [17] Ibid., 109.
[18] See for example J. Dear, S. J., *Mohandas Gandhi: Essential Writings* (Maryknoll, NY: Orbis Books, 2002); B. Gruzalski, *On Gandhi* (Belmont, CA: Wadsworth, 2001).

existence entailed.[19] And the normative force of non-violence arose from the social and the spiritual elements of the human personality. Given his spiritual vision, the "other" was not an enemy but a friend requiring respect, collaboration and love. The fact that conflict arose in one's relationship to the other was owing to the predominance of the ego, which refused to be guided by the spirit. As Gandhi had observed, most instances of human violence arose from disputes on what was "mine" and what was "thine."[20] Briefly, human nature had the capacity both to generate and to regulate violence – depending on the effectiveness of the soul-force. For it was the role of soul-force to activate sociability and to make non-violence the new universal dharma of modern times.

Definition and distinctions

In the light of the foregoing discussion we are in a position to define Gandhian non-violence. It is a moral virtue that habitually disposes individuals, social groups and constituted authority, (a) to resist violence through non-violent means, and (b) to take active steps to resolve conflicts by peaceful techniques. The mandate to resist violence by non-violent means is a general mandate, and, like all general mandates, it admits of exceptions depending on persons, circumstances, time, and place. The mandate to take active steps to resolve conflicts through non-violent means requires not only moral commitment but also inventiveness on the part of those who practice this virtue. If the existing means are not adequate, new means would have to be invented. This was exactly what happened with Gandhi when he invented satyagraha. The latter was only the beginning, not the end of the search for the techniques of resolving conflicts.

The virtue of non-violence has a long history behind it. In Buddhism and Jainism, as in ascetical Hinduism, it had occupied an honorable place in the list of *yamas* (virtues).[21] However, in these traditions it was treated as a passive virtue, i.e., a virtue that required you only to abstain from inflicting pain on sentient creatures. They did not impose an obligation on you to intervene actively to stop violence. In Patanjali for example, non-violence was considered as the personal virtue of the yogi. Its ultimate aim was to encourage him to withdraw from society and polity into the solitude of spiritual life. The state of society or polity did not concern him. The non-violent *jivanmukta* (the renouncer who had attained

---

[19] I have discussed this point in further detail in *Hind Swaraj*, p. lv ff.
[20] CW, 49: 113.
[21] For example, Patanjali's *Yoga Sutra* II: 30, and *The Kautiliya Arthasastra*, I: 3, 13.

liberation in the embodied state) too had no obligation to engage actively in social and political affairs, being content to radiate his moral influence on those around him.

Gandhian non-violence, by contrast, is an active, creative virtue. It is the virtue of the citizen, as distinguished from the yogi. It is an active virtue that requires civic engagement with the world and not the withdrawal from it. Taking active steps to reform social and political *institutions* is one of its major concerns. A purely mental approach to violence and suffering which neglects institutional changes is rejected as being quite inadequate.[22]

Gandhi drew a distinction between non-violence as creed and non-violence as policy. Non-violence as creed prohibited always and everywhere the use of violent means to resist violence. Such non-violence might be called heroic non-violence, for it might demand from its practitioner every manner of personal inconveniences, including the ultimate sacrifice. For Gandhi this form of non-violence is an option available only to exceptional individuals; he neither expects nor demands it from the average citizen.

Non-violence as policy or civic non-violence is what he expects from the average citizen. Like heroic non-violence, civic non-violence too is committed to strict principles. It is not correct to see it as being grounded in mere expediency.[23] There is of course a difference between heroic non-violence and civic non-violence. The latter permits the lawful use of violence for the sake of the public good, such as the maintenance of public order and the exercise of the right to self-defense. Legitimate self-defense here includes self-defense by the minimum permitted use of military force. Satyagraha is concerned with civic non-violence rather than with the heroic variety, its aim being to secure the good of society rather than the private good of the citizen.

What Gandhi has done is to introduce a new mode of non-violence, one that did not exist in the Indian tradition. Civic non-violence now is available side by side with the heroic one. In introducing a new category of non-violence he has gone beyond the Buddha and the ascetical tradition generally.

What is noteworthy is the humanism – the Gandhian humanism – that underlies civic non-violence. He articulated its basic features in a remarkable eight-part series entitled "Is This Humanity?"[24] In it he defended the

---

[22] For a recent restatement of the purely "mental" solution to poverty and suffering in the world, see Mishra, *An End to Suffering: The Buddha in the World*, p. 399.

[23] For a contrary interpretation see Gruzalski, *On Gandhi*, p. 23.

[24] For this series, see CW, 31; CW, 32.

view that ultimately *human welfare* was to be the basic criterion of non-violence as a civic virtue. There was the troublesome question of the ill-treatment of domestic animals in Indian society. Dogs, for example, were not properly cared for. As his research revealed, in 1926 in Gujarat alone there were 990 reported cases of hydrophobia caused by roaming mad dogs.[25] There was no enabling legislation prohibiting owners of dogs to abandon them or let them roam. The question arose as to what one should do under these circumstances when animals, through no fault of their own, posed a danger to society. Ideally a non-violent society would not allow such a danger to arise in the first place. But since India had not yet become such a non-violent society, what principle would his non-violence suggest that could deal with the immediate problem? The answer of the traditional notion of non-violence was clear enough. There was, for instance, the bizarre example of Rajchandbhai advising him that "rather than kill the serpent" that threatened to kill him, he should allow himself to be killed by it.[26] He did not obviously follow this dreadful advice. On the other hand he did not want to approach the issue of disposing of deadly animals "in a purely utilitarian spirit." It was his view that humans did not have "the right of disposal over the lower animals."[27] At the same time his civic non-violence was obliged to reject the view that the sub-human species had the same rights as had human beings. When their rights clashed with those of the humans, the latter had to prevail. He therefore had no compunction in arguing for the disposal of mad dogs, stray dogs, harmful monkeys, snakes, mosquitoes, and the like whenever they proved to be a threat to human welfare.[28] As late as 25 April 1946 we find him writing the following:

My *ahimsa* [non-violence] is my own. I am not able to accept in its entirety the doctrine of non-killing of animals. I have no feeling in me to save the lives of animals which devour or cause hurt to man. I consider it wrong to help in the increase of their progeny. Therefore, I will not feed ants, monkeys or dogs. I will never sacrifice a man's life in order to save theirs.

Thinking along these lines I have come to the conclusion that to do away with monkeys where they have become a menace to the well-being of man is pardonable. Such killing becomes a duty.[29]

Predictably the application of the principles of his civic non-violence to the treatment of animals brought him into sharp conflict with the defenders of the traditional notion of non-violence that made no distinction

---

[25] Ibid., p. 15.
[26] Ibid., p. 72. See his famous letter of 1894 (CW, 1: 91), in which he had sought Rajchandbhai's advice on this matter.
[27] Ibid., p. 72.   [28] CW, 31: 487–88; 524; 544–46.   [29] CW, 84: 62.

whatsoever between humans and beasts. He remained adamant in defending the violence involved in the exercise of civic non-violence. He permitted the use of legitimate violence not only in the treatment of animals that threatened human welfare, but also in reducing unnecessary and unjustifiable human suffering.[30]

Fields of non-violence

One of the original contributions that Gandhi had made to the analysis of non-violence was the introduction of the distinction between the various "fields" of non-violence. By "field" he meant the "community" in which non-violence was to be practiced. Four such fields were identified – the family, the political community, religions, and the international community.[31] The basic point of the distinctions was simple enough: though non-violence was a universal norm, it worked differently in different communities. It was not a monolithic ethic that applied the same way to each of the four fields. It did not work as an ethical force apart from the other forces at work in the various fields. Reform of these fields was a condition for the success of non-violence. This was the deep insight of his *Constructive Programme*. In other words, without the help of the necessary social reforms it was futile to hope to make society as a whole non-violent.

The family, he held, was "the best field" for practicing non-violence, and family included "family-like" institutions such as ashrams. It was in these intimate communities that "the alphabet" of non-violence was first learned – lessons in the meaning of unconditional love, the habit of abiding by basic rules, patience, forgiveness, cooperation, and the like.[32]

There was no suggestion here that family life was conflict-free. He knew from his own experience that this was not the case, and that the family produced its own brand of tensions and conflicts. His wife for example did not always agree with his social philosophy, especially that relating to caste – at least in the early years of their marriage. His eldest son, Harilal, was a rebel. It was by facing up to these realities of family life that he trained himself to behave non-violently. The integration of the family into the broader system of communities that included the political community, the religious community, and the community of states gave new depth to his theory of non-violence.

---

[30] On Gandhi's thoughts on dealing with unnecessary human suffering, see Ronald Terchek, *Gandhi: Struggling for Autonomy* (Lanham, MD: Rowman and Littlefield, 1998), pp. 206–09.

[31] CW, 72: 248–50; 271–72; 281–82.   [32] CW, 72: 271.

The second field was the political community. It was in this field that civic non-violence in the form of satyagraha had its greatest success.[33] The account of the non-violent techniques that Gandhi developed is so readily available in the secondary literature that there is no need to rehearse them here.[34]

What is worth reiterating, however, is the fact that civic non-violence succeeds best in some political communities rather than others. It works well in liberal democratic polities, but not in totalitarian or fascist or theocratic states. It succeeded in colonial South Africa and colonial India because they were governed under the general supervision of a basically liberal metropolitan state, viz., Great Britain. It succeeded in the United States under the leadership of Martin Luther King Jr., because America was a liberal democracy. However, it failed in independent Pakistan. The reason for the failure is worthy of attention. For under the colonial regime non-violence did succeed in the Northwest Frontier Province, a predominantly Muslim region. But the Khudai Khidmagar movement, the standard-bearer of civic non-violence, disappeared without trace soon after it came under the new Pakistani regime. It could not survive in an Islamic political culture. Even a colonial state under liberal supervision was more conducive to the practice of non-violence than was the newly independent Muslim state.

The example of Nazi Germany was even more telling. The question of Jews and Nazism came up in the famous debate that Gandhi had with Martin Buber, the Jewish philosopher, and Judah Magnes, the first chancellor of the Hebrew University of Jerusalem. The debate was occasioned by an article that Gandhi had written in November 1938 on "The Jews."[35] He compared the situation of the Jews in Nazi Germany with that of Indians in South Africa. The solution would be the same for both groups: satyagraha. Since the Jews believed in Jehovah, they should trust in Him and refuse to be expelled from Germany. They should accept the sufferings that would follow in the knowledge that they would give them moral superiority over the Germans. Refusal to be expelled might result in "general massacre," which to the God-fearing should hold no terror. It would be "a joyful sleep to be followed by a waking that would be all the more refreshing for the long sleep." Moreover, it would enable the Jews to score "a lasting victory" over the Germans and to convert them to humanity.[36]

---

[33] For an account of the origin and early development of satyagraha, see CW, 29: 1–272.

[34] On the technique of conducting satyagraha see Bondurant, *Conquest of Violence*, and M. Juergensmeyer, *Gandhi's Way: A Handbook of Conflict Resolution* (Berkeley: University of California Press, 1984).

[35] Gandhi, "The Jews," CW, 68: 137–41.   [36] Ibid.

In April 1939, both Buber and Magnes responded to Gandhi in "Two Letters to Gandhi," which appeared in *The Bond*, a publication of a group called "The Bond."[37] Buber strongly denied that any parallel existed between Indians under colonialism and Jews under Nazism. "Thousands on thousands" of Jewish shops had been destroyed and many synagogues with the sacred scrolls in them had been burned to the ground. Besides, there were the concentration camps. There were no parallels to any of these in either South Africa or India. Buber's most telling point was that satyagraha had no chance of being organized in a fascist state. For satyagraha required, he pointed out, mutual recognition, which it was impossible to have under Nazism. The word "satyagraha" signified testimony. But testimony without acknowledgment would be unobserved martyrdom, a martyrdom cast to the winds.[38]

Magnes also pointed out the utter impossibility of organizing civic non-violence under Nazism. The slightest sign of resistance, he remarked, meant death or concentration camps. This was in sharp contrast to the attention that Gandhi received in India. "Contrast this with one of your fasts, or with your salt march to the sea, or a visit to the Viceroy, when the whole world is permitted to hang upon your words and be witness to your acts." This was possible largely because "despite all the excesses of its imperialism," England was a democracy with a parliament and a considerable measure of free speech. Magnes wondered if Gandhi would have been able to win public opinion in Nazi Germany, where life was snuffed out like a candle, and no one saw or knew that the light was out.[39] As the *Jewish Frontier* of New York City wrote in this connection, a Jewish Gandhi in Nazi Germany, even supposing one could be found, would have lasted for about five minutes.[40]

What we can learn from this debate is the need to be consistent with the principles of non-violence. Gandhi had broken two of them. The first was that he did not do enough research to find out what exactly was the condition of the Jews in Germany. This was against his well-known principle of ascertaining the facts before proposing policies. The implementation of this principle was part of the secret of the success of his satyagraha campaigns. The second mistake was to demand heroic non-violence from the masses, which by his definition was capable only of civic non-violence. By demanding voluntary "general massacre" from the mass of German Jews, Gandhi was violating his own principle. Only the

---

[37] M. Buber and J. L. Magnes, "Two Letters to Gandhi," *The Bond, Pamphlets of the Group "The Bond"* (Jerusalem: Rubin Mass, 1939).
[38] Ibid., p. 5.   [39] Ibid., p. 25.   [40] CW, 69: 290.

exceptional *individual* could be expected to practice non-violence in the heroic degree.

All the same, this debate had great significance. It confirmed, though in a negative way, the validity of Gandhi's distinction between fields of non-violence. What applied to one case would not necessarily apply to another.

Turning now to non-violence applied to the field of religion, ironically it was in this field, by his own admission, that it had the least success.[41] The context of his analysis was the relations between Hindus and Muslims in India in the 1930s. He tried sincerely to apply his theory to pacify Hindu–Muslim relations. He supported the Muslim campaign to preserve the moribund institution of the caliphate then located in Turkey. It came to nothing as Turkey in 1924 abolished the institution itself. He supported the Muslim demand for a separate electorate. This too came to naught as the two-nation theory of the separatists and fundamentalists overtook it. He was willing to drop his support for the campaign to make *Vande Mataram* India's national song. Muslims had objected to it for being anti-Muslim in tone and context. Though Gandhi was personally fond of this song (he occasionally used to sign his letters with "*Vande Mataram* from Mohandas" instead of the usual "Yours sincerely") he urged Hindus not to use it in mixed gatherings.[42]

The "institution" that he designed specifically to deal with Hindu–Muslim violence was the "peace brigade" (*shanti sena*).[43] It was to be a small "army" of those capable of heroic non-violence as distinct from civic non-violence. They had to have "a living faith in non-violence," "a living faith in God," and they had to rely on divine grace. They should be able to lay down their lives, should the need arise, "without anger, without fear, and without retaliation."[44] They had to supplement heroic non-violence with another of the eleven virtues, viz., "the equal respect for all religions" (*sarva dharma sama bhavana*).[45]

None of the steps that Gandhi took to conciliate separatist Muslims seemed to work. Not because they were somehow defective in themselves, but because of two premises underlying Muslim separatism. The first was the theory of "outer jihad" or jihad as holy war. It had the

[41] CW, 72: 249.

[42] On Gandhi's esteem of this song, see CW, 69: 380–81; on his habit of using the title of this song for signing off letters see, for example, CW, 17: 439 and CW, 32: 66; for his request that this song be not imposed on the unwilling, see CW, 75: 164.

[43] For his idea of the peace brigade see CW, 67: 125–27.   [44] CW, 67: 126.

[45] CW, 75: 147. The idea of laying down one's life for the sake of defending religious harmony is mentioned in CW, 72: 249 also.

Koranic sanction: if Muslims felt threatened, they had the Koranic duty to declare a jihad. The second premise was what Abul Hasan Ali Nadvi, a leading moderate Muslim fundamentalist, called "the methodology" of the Prophet. According to this methodology, conflicts between religions had to be settled by accepting the Message that the Prophet had for humanity. In straightforward language it meant settling them on Muslim terms. It also implied a denial of the legitimacy of *de jure* religious pluralism. Islam, and no other religion, had the right solution to the problem of religious conflict.[46]

Nadvi reinforced his argument by an analysis of Gandhi's theory of non-violence. Gandhi's theory, he asserted, was bound to fail, because he was only a leader of his people, and not a prophet of all humanity. That is to say, a fundamentalist Muslim could not accept a theory of Gandhi because he or she had a "superior" theory coming from the Prophet. Being different from the Prophet, he "could not produce that fundamental change in the minds of his people" which was essential to the success of any moral movement. The Prophet's methodology was "the only sure and successful way of bringing about a radical change for the better in the religious and social affairs of humanity at large."[47]

It was not by accident that South Asian Islamic separatism and fundamentalism had its origin, in part, in response to Gandhi's civic nationalism and theory of non-violence. The revival of the idea of jihad began with Maulana Maududi, who was also the founder of modern militant Islamic fundamentalism in South Asia. However, as Seyyed Vali Reza Nasr has pointed out, it was M. A. Jinnah, a moderate liberal Muslim, who was urging Maududi to politicize Islam.[48] He did not object to the idea that the aim of Pakistan was nothing less than the realization of God's will on earth. "What was the *raison d'être* of Pakistan?" the popular slogan ran. It was to proclaim "there was no god but God." (*Pakistan ka matlab kya hai? La ilaha ila'llah*).[49] And, Jinnah was not averse to invoking jihad, if the Pakistan project were to be delayed.[50]

So long as jihad remained a legitimate weapon of settling religious conflicts, and so long as *de jure* religious pluralism was not recognized, there was no chance of Gandhi's non-violence succeeding in reconciling Hindus and separatist Muslims.

---

[46] A. H. A. Nadvi, *Islam and the World* (7th English edn, Lucknow: Academy of Islamic Research and Publications, 1982), pp. 48–49.

[47] Ibid., p. 49, n. 1.

[48] S. V. R. Nasr, *The Vanguard of the Islamic Revolution: The Jamaat-e Islamia of Pakistan* (Berkeley: University of California Press, 1994), p. 106.

[49] Ibid.   [50] Mirza, *From Plassey to Pakistan*, pp. 150–51.

Non-violence and the international field

Gandhian non-violence operated in the field of international relations in its own way. As a political thinker, he saw the legitimacy of the military means of securing national self-defense. The possibility of the reconciliation between Gandhian non-violence and the use of military means of self-defense may appear inconsistent at first sight. But it need not surprise us if we pay attention to his interactive theory of the purusharthas. According to that theory, as we have seen, dharma, in the political realm, does not operate in isolation from the requirements of artha. It takes into account the *truth* of politics, which is that under certain circumstances the use of military means is necessary for national self-defense. Gandhi accepted the interactive relationship of the dharma of non-violence to the politics of international relations. That is why he was neither a radical pacifist nor a conscientious objector. In accepting the state as a legitimate institution, he also accepted the means that the state needed to maintain itself.

The principle that states had the right to self-defense through military means was formally defended by him, as we have seen, at the 1931 Second Round Table Conference. His participation in the Boer War (1899–1902) and the Zulu Rebellion (1906) was based on the principle of the duty of citizens to come to the aid of the state. His active recruitment for the Indian Army during the First World War was also consistent with his theory of non-violence. The two pamphlets that he wrote in 1918 justifying this campaign are worth reading today, not only for their historical value but also for their doctrinal content.[51] No state could act responsibly and maturely in the international community if unable to defend itself. It was the inability to defend itself that had led India into colonial subjugation. One is not surprised, then, to see Gandhi regretting the absence of military science in the Indian curriculum. Though he was opposed to war personally, he was not opposed to those wanting to acquire military training.[52] In the same vein, one is not surprised that he should list the compulsory disarming of India by the Raj as one of the four disasters that it had visited on the country.[53] "The right to keep and bear arms in accordance with regulations and reservations made in that behalf" was one of the nine fundamental rights recognized by the famous Resolution on Fundamental Rights and Economic Changes that he had co-drafted with Nehru.[54]

[51] For the text see CW, 14: 439–43; 493–96.
[52] CW, 14: 29–30; see his lecture to the Gujarat Educational Conference.
[53] See CW, 42: 385.   [54] For the text see CW, 45: 371.

In his correspondence with his friend C. F. Andrews, the radical Christian pacifist, Gandhi had to remind him that war was an unavoidable phenomenon of embodied existence. Humans were not angels, but embodied beings whose material interests often collided. If you accepted bodily existence, you had to accept all that came with it. Classical Indian literature was very clear on this. The *Mahabharata* and the *Ramayana*, he pointed out, depicted even the incarnations as "bloodthirsty, revengeful, and merciless to the enemy." They were credited with having resorted to tricks for the sake of overcoming their enemies. "The finest hymn composed by Tulsidas in praise of Rama" gave the first place to his ability to strike down the enemy. "Buddhism conceived as a doctrine of universal forbearance [had] signally failed, and if the legends [were] true the great Shakaracharya did not hesitate to use unspeakable cruelty in banishing Buddhism out of India."[55] Not that war should be encouraged, but that its root causes had to be understood.

Even though he objected to India being drawn into the Second World War on the Viceroy's initiative, his sympathies were with the Allies. And he was in favor of India contributing to the war effort, provided India was granted independence and could act as a responsible member of the international community. As he wrote to President Franklin D. Roosevelt, he had no objection to the Allied troops being stationed in India, not to keep internal order, but "for preventing Japanese aggression and defending China." A treaty between an independent India and the Allied powers would have guaranteed this.[56]

Gandhi understood the nature of "military necessity" that Great Britain was facing in India during the war. He was, therefore, prepared to tolerate the presence of the British army in India even after India was granted independence: Britain would remain "not as rulers but as allies of free India."[57] This was yet another example of his desire to harmonize the principle of non-violence with the necessities of international relations. India as member of the international community, he confessed, had never been, and had never claimed to be, a non-violent nation.[58] The non-violence that applied to the relation between the state and its citizens did not apply to the relation of the states among themselves. In their external relations, states had the obligation to adapt non-violence to the needs of national security.

However, the horrors of the Second World War made Gandhi rethink the ethic of self-defense by military means. Rethinking did not mean the

---

[55] Desai, *Day to Day with Gandhi*, vol. I, p. 174.
[56] Gandhi's Letter to President F. D. Roosevelt, 1 July 1942, CW, 76: 265.
[57] Ibid., p. 215.   [58] Ibid., p. 291.

rejection of that ethic altogether. What it did mean was the addition of another obligation to the state – the obligation to develop new, non-military means of self-defense. This led him to speculate on the need to experiment with such ideas as self-defense through "a non-violent army."[59] Should such an army come into existence, states would have at their disposal two modes of self-defense – one through the usual violent army and the other through the new non-violent army.

He speculated on the options available to a non-violent army. He could not think of anything more than offering "non-violent non-cooperation" by specially trained masses of civilians. This would of course prove to be very costly, not least in human lives. A non-violent civilian army could become "fodder for the aggressor's cannons." In statistical terms, the loss of lives would probably not be greater. In moral terms, however, the death of innocent victims might raise the moral conscience of humanity. "The unexpected spectacle of endless rows upon rows of men and women dying rather than surrendering to the will of an aggressor must ultimately melt him [the aggressor] and his soldiery. Practically speaking, there will be probably no greater loss in men than if forcible resistance was offered."[60] These were of course musings on his part, not serious speculation on policy or doctrine. He knew very well that they were such, and that no one could translate them into state policy. Still he indulged in them, as if prompted by some unconscious inner frustration. The problem of violence in modern international relations had reached a pass that only speculations that made no practical sense seemed to make sense. We find him doing this again in his appeal "To Every Briton."[61] He wondered which was the more effective way of defeating Nazism, war with weapons or war without them.

The evolution of modern weaponry, culminating in nuclear weapons, only deepened his moral frustration. Nuclear weapons, in his view, had succeeded in deadening the finest moral feeling that had sustained humanity for ages. It also changed the rules of war. "Now we know the naked truth," he wrote, viz., that modern wars knew no law except that of might.[62] The weapons of mass destruction were for him the symbols of the modern disregard for the laws of war. Far from producing security, they would only deepen insecurity. The more we relied on them, the more anxious we became. Being products of science and technology, they would be available, sooner or later, to anyone who had the means. It was impossible to stop their spread, and, being products of modern science, they brought with them no special moral insights. The imagery of the death of "endless rows upon rows of men and women" fitted their

---

[59] CW, 72: 250.   [60] CW, 71: 407.   [61] CW, 72: 229–31.   [62] CW, 84: 393–94.

inherent amorality (*adhrama*). With such weapons becoming the decisive weapons of international relations, no one could rely on military science to protect the nation. A new science of non-violence had to emerge if nations were to be safe. According to Gandhi, "counter bombs" could not make the world safe from the atom bombs. Only non-violent weapons could save humanity from violence.[63]

The vast majority principle

Gandhi did not leave the role of non-violence in international relations to mere speculation. His positive vision of international relations led him to think in terms of the "vast majority" principle. The idea is simple enough: "a state can be administered non-violently, if the vast majority of the people are non-violent."[64] And, if there were a circle of such states, the relations between them would also become non-violent. Then and only then would a mixture of civilian and military means of self-defense work. Disarmament by the states that belong to such a circle would become a practical reality.

The vast majority principle placed the burden of war and peace equally on the shoulders of the ordinary citizens and their leaders. The leaders could secure peace only to the extent that the citizens were willing to become non-violent. They could become non-violent only if they eliminated, on their own initiative, the structures of violence prevalent in civil society. These structures often had economic or political or religious or racial or ethnic bases. Whatever they were, they had to be dismantled by the actions of ordinary citizens acting in concert with the appropriate institutions and their leaders.

Here we get a profound Gandhian insight into the sociology of non-violence applied to international relations. It is this: one may not blame the political leaders and the political institutions unless, in doing so, one is prepared to blame oneself. The ordinary citizen is as much implicated in the violence in the world as are the states and their leaders. The ordinary citizens, therefore, have to examine their pattern of life and engage in the reform of civil society. Unfortunately today's political culture of rights does not oblige the ordinary citizens to do this. Its emphasis is all too often on rights, not duties. Gandhi's theory of non-violence calls for a balance between rights and duties. The vast majority of a country can become non-violent only if there is such a balance, and only if the existing structures of violence are gradually dismantled.

---

[63] Ibid., p. 394. For G. Sharp's extension of Gandhi's position, see Weber, *Gandhi as Disciple and Mentor*, pp. 232–46.

[64] CW, 71: 407.

In practical terms, the vast majority principle means three things. First, violence in international relations can be reduced if more and more states become democratic. Second, violence can be reduced if religions abandon violence as a means of securing religious conformity and religions grant each other the *de jure* right to exist. Third, violence can be reduced if international economic institutions dismantle the violent structures under which they thrive.

I think that Gandhi's vast majority principle is comparable to Immanuel Kant's republican principle. Kant in the eighteenth century had argued that if there were a circle of republican states the relations between them would likely become peaceful. Gandhi goes one step beyond Kant. In Kant the focus was on the constitution. In Gandhi it was on both the constitution and the ordinary people. It was not enough for constitutions to recognize the need for non-violence. The vast majority of the population also had to enact non-violence in their daily pattern of life.

The vast majority principle seems to be working in recent history. The formation of the European Community may be considered as an example. After relying for centuries on the military means of self-defense, the European states now seem to rely on non-military means. The fall of Communism in Eastern Europe is another example of the vast majority principle. Communism fell not because the communist regimes were prepared to let it go, but because the vast majority of the people under it wanted it to go. One can only imagine what would happen if the vast majority of the people in Muslim societies were to become fed up with *jihadism*. Or, what would happen if the vast majority of consumers in industrialized societies were to object to what the international corporations are doing to the world community.

Gandhi's philosophy of international relations was realistic, not utopian. His goal was not the elimination of violence, for that would be impossible, given our bodily existence. Rather, his goal was to reduce the horrors, the frequency, and the intensity of wars, by giving non-military means of self-defense a greater role than to the military means. He believed that there was a chance of this dual path to self-defense becoming a reality. In his philosophy humans by nature were social beings, and it was their sociability that required them to look for non-violent ways of securing self-defense. Heroic non-violence did not apply to the field of international relations. What applied to that field was non-violence as policy – non-violence that recognized the right to self-defense.

We conclude by noting that the new dharma of civic non-violence stays clear of both the radical pacifism of the yogi and the crude realism of the moderns. It places the burden of non-violence on the shoulders of the rulers and the ruled, on the state as well as civil society.

Part IV

Pleasure

Gandhi's treatment of the value of pleasure is considered under the headings of "Celibacy and sexuality," and "Art and society." His approach to sexuality was so dominated by his concern for the pursuit of spiritual liberation that sexual pleasure did not receive the positive evaluation that the theory of the purusharthas had accorded it. This undervaluing is inconsistent with his otherwise consistent treatment of pleasure (*kama*).

In the Indian tradition aesthetic pleasures were also subsumed under the value of kama. Gandhi was keenly aware of the fact that human self-improvement, both at the personal and the social levels, was virtually impossible without the cultivation and the experience of the arts. This truth applied particularly to those who lived in the villages. His views on the role that the arts should play in society are examined in chapter 9.

8   Celibacy and sexuality

"Man is man because he is capable of, and only in so far as he exercises, self-control."[1]

Celibacy (*brahmacharya*) is one of the eleven virtues recognized by Gandhi's moral philosophy. It does not play a foundational role in his ethics as do the virtues of truth and non-violence. All the same, it is considered to be one of the major virtues by his moral lexicon. The reason is that the sexual instinct according to him is powerful enough either to enhance or retard an individual's overall development, depending on the way he or she manages to satisfy it. Without the proper harnessing of this force the other forces that make up human life cannot easily be harnessed either. Of course he approached celibacy as the counterpart of kama, a purushartha, an instinct whose operations necessarily related themselves to the striving for power, wealth, ethics, and spirituality. He did not therefore treat kama merely as instinct operating in isolation from these other forces. Its enjoyment therefore had to occur within the context of the other human pursuits, and therefore always with some degree of restraint. And restraint in this case meant nothing more and nothing less than paying attention to the legitimate requirements of these other equally valid human strivings.

Definitions and distinctions

Before we go into the definitions of celibacy, it is important to bear in mind that, according to Gandhi, not everyone was qualified to embark upon celibacy as his or her vocation. One had to have certain prior moral aptitudes before one could enter upon this path. To begin with, the passions, notably those of greed, anger and lust, had to be brought under control. One also had to have a reasonable control over one's imagination. A habit of prayer and meditation was a necessary

[1] CW, 39: 253.

requirement of anyone who thought seriously of a celibate life. Likewise one had to have a good reading habit that included serious literature. Idleness being incompatible with the celibate life, one also needed to develop the habit of hard work. The need for freedom from gluttony went without saying. He seemed to place particular emphasis on control over one's thought. In this regard, we find this puzzling statement about a celibate being above the vulgar male–female difference: "When one achieves complete control over one's thoughts," he writes, " 'man' and 'woman' include each other."[2] For those who did not have these qualifications or were unwilling to attempt to acquire them, celibacy was not a realistic option. Obviously only a small minority of humans could ever hope to meet these standards. For the rest of humankind the alternative path to moksha lay in chastity or control over the sexual instinct through the discipline of self-restraint.

As for the definition of celibacy, we find a short one as well as a long one. The short definition is that it is "a course of conduct ... adapted to the search of Brahman, i.e., Truth."[3] This, as we can see, is shockingly asexual, placed as it is within the exalted context of the ultimate end of human existence, viz., the attainment of moksha. There is hardly a reference here to sexual pleasure. Sexual pleasure is of course implied, but only within the broader context of one's pursuit of the ultimate spiritual goal. It already alerts us to his tendency to look upon sexuality not from the exclusive perspective of sexual pleasure. For one who takes kama to be a purushartha it is impossible to view sexuality from that limited point of view.

The long definition, given in 1947, almost towards the end of his life, is sexually more explicit. But here again, the sexual element is overshadowed by the spiritual element:

My meaning of *brahmacharya* is this: One who never has any lustful intention, who by constant attendance upon God has become proof against conscious or unconscious emissions, who is capable of lying naked with naked women, however beautiful they may be, without being in any manner whatsoever sexually excited. Such a person should be incapable of lying, incapable of intending or doing harm to a single man or woman in the whole world, is free from anger and malice and detached in the sense of the *Bhagavad Gita*. Such a person is a full *brahmachari* [celibate].[4]

Here again celibacy is presented as being concerned not only with sexuality but also with other aspects of life, such as spirituality, non-violence, self-restraint, anger management, and the like. There is no

---

[2] For the full account of the qualifications see CW, 70: 287–89.
[3] CW, 44: 70.   [4] CW, 87: 108.

mention here of marriage: whether celibacy was compatible with it or whether the celibate had to abstain from it. Unusual as it may sound, his kind of celibacy was compatible with marriage. The married couples who took the vow of celibacy did not have to break up their marriage in order to become celibates. However, they had to abstain from sexual relations and live as if they were not married. Needless to say this marriage-cum-celibacy sort of celibacy was quite different from the traditional Indian idea of celibacy, which by definition was not possible within marriage. The yogi was the exemplar par excellence of the traditional Indian celibate.

Gandhi's attention was focused mainly on celibacy as an Ashram virtue practiced by the members of the Sabarmati Ashram. The Ashram celibacy itself was of two kinds: the perpetual celibacy observed by the permanent members, such as Vinoba Bhave, and the temporary celibacy observed by the temporary members. Married couples were also permitted to become members of the Ashram and take the vow of celibacy provided they were prepared to live as brother and sister. Ashram celibacy, whether perpetual or temporary, was the celibacy of a *political* elite. This was its special attribute. Though the ultimate goal of Ashram celibacy was moksha, the path along which it was approached was that of politics. Its immediate object therefore was to prepare its practitioners for life in the social and the political arena. Another feature of Ashram celibacy was that it was women-friendly, and this by deliberate design. Gandhi had carefully planned it that way in "a deliberate imitation of life in the West."[5] The celibacy of a member of the Gandhian Ashram was therefore different from the celibacy of the traditional yogi. The latter was forbidden by the most stringent rules to have any contact with women. Besides, the yogi's celibacy had no dynamic relationship with the political and economic field, with artha. The celibacy of the Ashram celibates by contrast was specifically geared to life in the field of artha.

The "celibacy" that Gandhi's philosophy expected of those living outside the Ashram – and this meant the rest of society – was a civic virtue of self-restraint – mostly in the form of chastity within the bonds of marriage. Civic "celibacy" permitted sexual relations between married couples for the purpose of procreation. It did not seek, and apparently did not need, the support of any special vow. All it needed was fidelity to the marriage vow, and abstention from such vices as adultery. As far as the ordinary citizen was concerned, perfect celibacy, as the autobiography mentions, was only an ideal (*adarsiya*),[6] something to be aspired to.

---

[5] CW, 50: 210–11.   [6] CW, 39: 170.

Self-restraint within marriage was to the ordinary citizen what perfect celibacy was to the elite members of the Ashram. Ashram celibacy was heroic celibacy, while chastity within marriage was a civic virtue. However, even the practitioners of this civic virtue were expected to purify their imagination, mind and thinking from the noxious influences of the vestigial remnants of the sexual impulse. They too would have to sublimate their sexual energies into politically and socially beneficial activities. Though self-restraint within marriage was different from Ashram celibacy, it was thought to be capable of leading its practitioners to moksha itself.

Briefly, Gandhi approached sexuality in two different ways, each conducive to the attainment of moksha in its own way. The first was the strict, heroic celibacy of the political elite who lived in the Ashram but operated in the political community. And the second was "celibacy" in the form of chastity or self-restraint within marriage practiced by the ordinary citizen. It was never Gandhi's intention to impose Ashram celibacy on those outside it. He never imagined or wanted India to be the Sabarmati Ashram writ large. At the same time he wanted new India to develop a healthy attitude towards sexual matters, one that would permit every Indian to attain his or her other goals in life as well.

The question arises: why did he bother with the virtues of celibacy at all, given that it was the most private and the most personal of virtues? The answer lies in his insight into the theory of the purusharthas. Kama had an impact on society in general and public life in particular. Kama, according to the theory of the purusharthas, was relational even though it was a private matter. It had the ability to affect the quality of the operations in other fields of life such as artha, dharma, and of course moksha. A healthy approach to sexuality was a necessary condition of attaining the good life as Gandhi conceived of it. And he on a personal level chose to practice celibacy as part of his heroic approach to life.

Modern civilization and sexuality

There were two major issues with which his ideas on celibacy and to some extent of chastity were mostly concerned. The first was modern civilization and its attitude towards sexuality, and the second was the attitude of Indian civilization towards the same. These two issues impinged on his main concern in life, which was the renewal and regeneration of India as a political community.

Though critical of Western civilization, he did not condemn it in its entirety. Some Western sexual mores he appreciated as being very healthy. The easy mingling of men and women in his Ashram, as mentioned, was an example of the healthy Western mores that he endorsed.

So was the recognition of the social and political equality of women in society at large. But there were some unhealthy elements in the Western mores that he did not appreciate. Perhaps the most significant of these was the notion of the autonomy of the sexual instinct. The phenomenon of sexuality in humans was interpreted by some in the West as being the foundation of the ethical, aesthetic, and even religious values. These values, it was claimed, were the conscious or subconscious expressions of the sexual instinct. As can be imagined, such a notion of autonomy went against the basic insight of the theory of the purusharthas. Kama had no doubt its limited autonomy, but *ex hypothesi* it was relational in its nature and operations. There was no question of dharma and moksha being considered as expressions of unfulfilled sexual fantasies.

Gandhi's writings are replete with expressions of his disapproval of these unhealthy developments in Western thought. Perhaps none is more significant than the eight-part series that he published in 1926 in *Young India* under the title "Towards Moral Bankruptcy." Interestingly, it was based on *L'Indiscipline des mœurs* ("the indiscipline of morals" – Gandhi's translation), a work by Paul Bureau, a contemporary French writer (published in English under the title *Towards Moral Bankruptcy*).[7] As students of Gandhi know, whenever he found a book important enough, he had the habit of summarizing its main arguments and publishing them in his weekly newspapers. This was the case with Plato's *Apology*, which he abridged in 1908 and published in a six-part series. The same was true of Ruskin's *Unto This Last*, which was abridged under the title *Sarvodaya* and published in an eight-part series in the same year. The fact that he found time even in the 1920s to read and digest Bureau's massive volume (it was over 500 pages) shows how highly he regarded its arguments. Not only did he take time to read Bureau, but also did extensive research on the broad subject of sexuality before he started the series. As he informs us, he read "the standard literature" on the subject by borrowing books from the Servants of India Library in Poona.[8] Among the authors he read in this connection were such radical thinkers on sexual ethics as Bertrand Russell (the author of *Marriage and Morals*), Havelock Ellis (the author of *Sexual Inversion*), and Sir John Woodroffe (the author of *Shakti and Shakta* on Tantra).[9]

In his view, the "one single fundamental error" of modern Western civilization regarding sexual matters was the notion that "sexual indulgence for its own sake" was a human necessity and that without it neither man nor woman could achieve their full development.[10] The idea of the

---

[7] For the whole series see CW, 31, under the title "Towards Moral Bankruptcy."
[8] CW, 31: 77.   [9] CW, 87: 90–91.   [10] CW, 31: 104.

autonomy of the sexual instinct implied here was reinforced by the modern liberal notion that to impose restraint on sexual desires was contrary to the dictates of human freedom, the freedom to dispose of one's body as one pleased.[11] These ideas were further reinforced by the Neo-Malthusian theory concerning the dangers of overpopulation. The Neo-Malthusians had been arguing that those dangers should be forestalled by resort to chemical and mechanical means of birth control. The *coup de grâce* to the need for self-restraint was given by modern commercial capitalism, which saw great opportunities for making money in a culture that was becoming more and more sexually permissive. Like the Neo-Malthusians, Bureau and Gandhi also saw the need to control the growth of population; but they disagreed with them and the commercial capitalists that chemical and mechanical means were the best means to meet it. On this issue Gandhi sided with Malthus, who had himself recommended, as the Mahatma was careful to point out, continence and self-restraint.[12] The general conclusion that the series on Bureau reached was that "restraint on individual freedom" in sexual matters was a "sociological and psychological necessity"[13] – not a very popular position to take in contemporary culture, even in the India of the 1920s. Yet that precisely was the position that Gandhi took.

That human sexuality is not an autonomous faculty but one surrounded by other human faculties was not an oppressively moralistic notion. For psychologists themselves had recognized the need for some in-built safeguards against unrestricted sex. Even the *Kamasutra*, as Sudhir Kakar has pointed out, was opposed to "the ferocity of unchecked sexual desire." That Indian classic was aware of "the destructive aggression" and "the possessive violence" that went with sex without self-restraint.[14] *Kamasutra*'s "most valuable insight," Kakar reminds us, was that "in the realm of sex nature [required] culture."[15] To add to this, Sigmund Freud himself had come to realize the need for restraint if civilization was to make any progress. As he had argued, "many of the highly valued assets of our civilization were acquired at the cost of sexuality and by the restriction of sexual motive forces."[16]

But what happens if civilization itself becomes an agent of license and an opponent of restraint? This was the basic problem that Gandhi was facing with respect to modern civilization. Who will guard the guardians?

---

[11] Ibid., p. 218.   [12] Ibid., p. 309.   [13] Ibid., p. 218.
[14] See S. Kakar's Introduction to Doniger and Kakas, *Vatsyayana Kamasutra*, pp. xl–xli.
[15] Ibid., p. xlii.
[16] S. Freud, *An Outline of Psycho-Analysis*, translated and edited by J. Strachey (New York: W. W. Norton, 1969), p. 58.

Economic forces within modern civilization were aiding and abetting the idea of the autonomy of the sexual instinct. Gandhi's defense of celibacy and chastity is best seen within these doctrinal debates and cultural contexts.

Sexuality and the Indian traditions

Gandhi's attitude towards Indian approaches to celibacy and sexuality was a mixed one. On the one hand he wanted to reform certain aspects of the traditional approach to celibacy, while on the other hand he wanted to retain some other aspects. The most significant change that he sought to introduce in the traditional observance of celibacy was to remove its implied misogyny. He thoroughly repudiated the ascetic notion that woman was the "door keeper of hell."[17] Indeed, he wanted to make celibacy thoroughly woman-friendly. No moral progress was possible, he argued, unless the celibates were prepared "to get out of the rut of orthodox tradition." They should not allow themselves "to be cribbed by cast-iron convention."[18] He saw himself in the role of a reformer of the ancient institution of celibacy, one who wanted "to test, enlarge and revise the current definition of *brahmachrya*" and to free it "from the fetters that have been put upon it."[19] The key to the reform was giving equal access to women in the Ashram, and removing the negative image of women from the whole ascetic tradition. His own cultivation of the virtue of celibacy knew "nothing of the orthodox laws governing its observance." He framed his own rules "as occasion necessitated."[20]

He saw in the new celibacy that he was developing one of the powerful means of liberating men from their dominating or predatory attitude towards women, and women from accepting the submissive role assigned to them by society. Celibacy or chastity, as the case may be, could do more to foster gender equality than could the modern liberal notion of sexuality, which did not recognize the inherent need for self-restraint. Celibacy or chastity could enable men who practiced it to see women neither as sex objects nor as threats to their virtue, but instead as friends and collaborators. Drawing on his own experience he often remarked that his relationship with his wife became more friendly after he had taken the vow of celibacy than it was before he did so.

The second change that Gandhi wanted to see in Indian society concerned the custom of child marriage. One may wonder what the connection was between celibacy and child marriage. As he saw it, a link existed

---

[17] CW, 50: 210.   [18] CW, 87: 90.   [19] Ibid., pp. 91–92.   [20] CW, 70: 314.

between this terrible custom and the lack of sexual self-restraint in popular culture. Rather than give children sex education and training in self-control, parents took the easy way out by marrying them off. And this happened in a society whose high culture had recognized celibacy as the first of the four stages (*ashrama*) of life. In popular culture celibacy and self-restraint were regarded as the exalted virtues that only yogis and mahatmas needed to bother with. The others, including very young children, were seemingly exempt from the rules of self-restraint in sexual matters.

One of the consequences of child marriage was the problem of child widows. Child widows were forbidden to remarry and were obliged to practice compulsory celibacy – though as Gandhi pointed out, there was no warrant for it in the *Shastras*.[21] The colonial state was reluctant to intervene as the custom had its roots in popular culture. As Gandhi recognized, in the absence of a legitimate state, public opinion was the best hope against this evil.[22] *Young India* had the habit of publishing articles calculated to arouse public opinion in this regard as in others. It noted, for example, that according to the 1921 Census there were a total of 329,076 child widows in India. Of these 11,892 were under the age of five; 85,037 were between ages five and ten; and 232,147 were between ages ten and fifteen.[23] And society took no effective remedies against this evil, prompting Gandhi to remark with some bitterness that it took more interest in protecting the cow than in protecting "the human cow in the shape of the girl widow."[24] Admittedly social reform and political intervention were necessary to eradicate this evil. But even more necessary was the cultivation of sexual self-restraint – in the young as well as in the married couples. And India's popular culture, he felt, was not up to the task.

What Gandhi retained from tradition

He was in favor of maintaining three elements that had their roots in the tradition. They were, first, the concept of sexual pleasure as poison and as distorting; second, the attitude towards conjugal love in relation to the love of the neighbor and humanity; and third, the need to sublimate the sexual desire.

In analyzing Gandhi's concept of sexuality, as Sudhir Kakar warns us, it is important to pay attention to his Gujarati vocabulary.[25] The latter has

---

[21] CW, 31: 263.   [22] Ibid., p. 310.   [23] Ibid., p. 263.   [24] Ibid.
[25] See S. Kakar, *Intimate Relations* (Chicago: University of Chicago Press, 1989), pp. 100–101.

its roots in Indian philosophical thought. Here three terms are of crucial importance: *vishay*, *vikar*, and *vasana*. *Vishay* means poison, and *vikar* means passion that distorts. Gandhi used these terms interchangeably for lust and sexual passion. *Vasana* is the residue that past sexual behavior leaves on the psyche, residue that continues to be influential on present behavior. As Patanjali's *Yoga Sutra* reminds us, the aim of the spiritual discipline of Yoga is to still the disturbances of the mind and root out the *vasanas*. Lust as *vishay* is noxious to the self and accelerates the process of spiritual death. *Vikar* as passion distorts the truth and hides the true nature of the purpose of life. The aim of celibacy is not only to counteract the noxious effects of the spiritual poison and to set straight the truth about life, but also to root out the vestiges of past sexual experiences.

In reading *Hind Swaraj* and Gandhi's autobiography the linguistic and philosophic nuances of his thought ought to be kept in mind. *Hind Swaraj* warns its readers that heroic political action is not possible without getting rid of the sexual poison from the psyche. "He whose mind is given over to animal passions [*vishay*] is not capable of any great effort." And marriage does not help to get rid of this poison. "When a husband and wife gratify the passions, it is no less animal indulgence." Therefore, sexual intercourse, except for perpetuating the species, is "strictly prohibited" to the heroic *satyagrahi*.[26]

In the autobiography all the three terms mentioned above come into use. *Vikar* is used for lust in describing his near fall as a law student from the vow of celibacy while visiting Portsmouth, England. He was tempted at a card game by his Portsmouth landlady and he was "about to go beyond limits," when, being reminded of the vow he had made to his mother, he was able to overcome the *vikar*.[27] The circumstance leading to taking the formal vow of celibacy in 1906 is analyzed in terms of the metaphor of the serpent and sexual poison. He took the vow "to flee from the serpent," which he knew would bite him and kill him. The idea of sexual pleasure as poison could not have been better conveyed than by the metaphor of the deadly snake. Without the antidote of celibacy, the snake was "bound" to kill him.[28] The sexual impulse that tied him to his wife was referred to as *vikar*, and "carnal relations" were *vikar-sambandi* relations.[29] The site of inner poison is the faculty of the mind. "The mind is at the root of all sensuality [*vishay*]."[30] It was, therefore, not enough to abstain physically from sex, it was also necessary to control "the passions [*vikar*] lingering in the innermost recesses" of the heart.[31] The perfect celibate would not even "dream" of satisfying "fleshly

---

[26] *Hind Swaraj*, p. 97.   [27] CW, 39: 63.   [28] Ibid., pp. 167–68.
[29] Ibid., p. 168.   [30] Ibid., p. 170.   [31] Ibid.

appetite" (*vikari vichar*); he or she would have to overcome *vikari* dreams and *vishay-vasana* also.[32]

These three terms appear in his letters as well. Thus, writing to Harjivan Kotak, he spoke of the presence of "impure desires" deep down in his psyche, which were unconsciously at work "like some hidden poison." He spoke of his marital relations with his wife as being "unclean" and its residues still afflicting him in later life.[33] In writing to Prema Kantak, a female disciple, he regretted how he was paying in later years for the latent effects of his sexual indulgences from age fifteen to thirty.[34]

The negative attitude towards sexual pleasure that *vishay* and *vikar* connote, is, no doubt, a legacy of the ascetic tradition, a legacy that Gandhi did not totally disown. In many of the Indian myths, as Wendy Doniger has pointed out, "Soma [the elixir of immortality] is closely related to poison." As the gods churned the ocean for Soma, a flaming poison emerged and threatened the whole universe. Siva, taking the form of a peacock, came to the rescue and held the poison in his throat.[35] His ascetic powers were such that he could neutralize the deadly effects of the poison. In other words, there is a longstanding ambivalence in the Indic traditions, taken as a whole, towards the positive and negative aspects of sexuality, which is reflected in Gandhi as well.

The undervaluing of marriage and procreation also had a long history in the Indian traditions. The ascetic tradition, as Patrick Olivelle has argued, had minimized the religious significance of marriage and children and promoted the values of celibacy. The celibate replaced the householder as the key person in society.[36] The Buddha's first step to escape from suffering, as everyone knows, was to say goodbye to his wife and child. The family, according to the Buddhist ideology, was seen as a hindrance to nirvana, making the pursuer of nirvana look like a bamboo tree that got entangled with other bamboo trees.[37] The *ashrama* system did not definitively resolve the debate on the relative merits of the stage of the householder *vis à vis* the other three stages: it favored the celibate stages by disadvantaging the householder. Purva Mimamsa, according to Olivelle, had opposed the overvaluing of celibacy and had upheld the Vedic values of marriage and procreation. Celibacy, it had claimed, was meant only for the handicapped, the blind, and the impotent, and not for normal people.[38]

---

[32] Ibid., pp. 253, 256.   [33] CW, 35: 379.   [34] CW, 62: 429.

[35] W. Doniger, *Asceticism and Eroticism in the Mythology of Siva* (London: Oxford University Press, 1973), p. 278–79.

[36] P. Olivelle, *The Asrama System: The History and Hermeneutics of a Religious Institution* (New York: Oxford University Press, 1993), pp. 64–65.

[37] Ibid., p. 66.   [38] Ibid., pp. 237–43.

Gandhi took a middle position in the historic debate between the supporters and the opponents of marriage. While he freed celibacy from its misogyny, he attempted to make chastity a goal of married life. This involved a lowering of the status of conjugal love relative to celibate love. This was evident from his account of how he was persuaded by Rajchandbhai to embrace celibacy. It started with a debate on the conjugal love of the famous British couple the Gladstones. Rajchandbhai pointed out to Gandhi that the devoted love of a sister or even a maid of Mr. Gladstone would have been superior to the conjugal love of Mrs. Gladstone. The wife's love, he reasoned, was "natural" and, therefore, could be taken for granted, whereas the love of a sister or a maid was "acquired" and, therefore, morally superior. Moreover, the wife's love was normally tainted with lust (*vishay* and *vikar*). It could become morally praiseworthy only when it became free of that taint, as in celibacy.[39]

Gandhi agreed. It now dawned on him that his love for his wife was indeed tainted with lust (*vishay*), and that he treated her as an instrument of lust (*vishay*), and that so long as he remained a slave of lust (*vishay vasana*), his fidelity to her would lack full moral significance. It acquired full moral significance only after he had taken the vow of celibacy.[40]

Based on his new understanding of the meaning of marriage, Gandhi made numerous statements arguing that only celibacy in the form of self-restraint could bring out the true significance of marriage. Perhaps none was more poignant than the statement that he made in a letter to Manilal, his second son. He had already been in trouble, having been involved in 1913, while living in Phoenix Settlement under Gandhi's very roof, in an affair with a married woman (Jeki, the daughter of his father's best friend, Dr. Pranjivan Mehta).[41] Now, in 1922, he wanted to marry a Muslim lady, causing a bad political and social headache to his father. It was against this background that Gandhi wrote to Manilal:

Take it from me that there is no happiness in marriage. To the extent that Ba [Mrs. Gandhi] is my friend, I derive happiness from her, no doubt. But I derive the same happiness from all of you and from the many men and women who love and serve me ... If, at this moment, I get enamoured of Ba and indulge in sexual gratification, I would fall the very instant ... My relation with Ba today is that of brother and sister, and the fame I have is due to it.

... I am simply painting before you the world as I find it from experience. I cannot imagine a thing as ugly as the intercourse of man and woman ... I do not at

---

[39] CW, 39: 166. The terms used for "lust" in this context are *vishay* and *vikar*.   [40] Ibid.
[41] For an account of Manilal's Jeki affair, see U. Dhupelia-Mesthrie, *Gandhi's Prisoner?: The Life of Gandhi's Son Manilal* (Delhi: Permanent Black, 2005), pp. 106–7.

all believe that procreation is a duty or that [the] world will come to grief without it ... Moksha is nothing but release from the cycle of births and deaths. This alone is believed to be the highest bliss, and rightly.

I see every day that all our physical enjoyments, without exception, are unclean. We take this very uncleanliness to be happiness. Such is the mysterious way of God. However, our purushartha lies in getting out of this delusion ...

... do what you wish, but not what I wish. If you simply cannot do without marrying, do think of marriage by all means.[42]

If the taint of lust (*vishay*) was the first difficulty that he had with the accepted concept of conjugal love, its limiting effect on universal love was his second difficulty. Here Gandhi was touching on a very important issue: how could conjugal love harmonize with love of the country and love of humanity? Did love mean the same thing in these instances? Classical Western thought had well understood the distinction between the household (*oikos*), the city (*polis*) and the world (*cosmopolis*). Love operated differently in these communities. Placing himself within the Indian context, he began to argue for the need to transcend conjugal love if he was ever able to love the nation and humanity. Such transcendence need not be regarded as the downgrading of conjugal love. More appropriately it could be regarded as sublimation rather than anything else.

It is in this context that we have to interpret his numerous statements on the relationship of conjugal love to universal love. It was celibacy that facilitated the transition from family to nation to humanity. During the days of the Zulu War he saw clearly "that one aspiring to serve humanity with his whole soul" could not do so without the help of celibacy. He would find himself unequal to the task of serving humanity if he were engaged in "the pleasure of family and in propagation and rearing of children." Without the observance of celibacy, service of the family would become incompatible with the service of the community. With celibacy, however, they would become consistent.[43] He asked if a man gave his love to one woman or a woman to one man, what was there left for the world? The answer did not lie in avoiding marriage, but in married couples practicing celibacy after they had raised a family.[44]

Gandhi was of course aware that his theory of the relationship of conjugal love to celibacy had its roots in the Indian tradition. He knew equally well that it did not comport with modern Western thought, as found in Western fiction and jurisprudence. Modern jurisprudence approached sexuality from the limited angle of the presumed right of the individual to act in sexual matters according to his or her individual preference. The attitude of modern fiction towards self-restraint and

[42] CW, 23: 102.   [43] CW, 39: 252–53.   [44] CW, 44: 68–69.

adultery was ambiguous to say the least. Modern jurisprudence and modern fiction had their limited appeal, but they could not be expected to give any reliable moral guidance in sexual matters.[45] Reliable guidance in sexual matters had to come, ultimately, from spiritual sources and sound moral theology.

In Gandhi's view, it was the traditional figure of Sita, the wife of Rama, who reconciled marriage and self-restraint. Of course he was idealizing the Sita figure. As he advised his son, Manilal, her historicity was not the key issue; the key issue was that she represented, or was thought to represent, the idea of self-restraint in marriage; she was "our ideal woman." "We do not worship the historical Rama and Sita. The Rama of history is no more now. But the Rama to whom we attribute perfect divinity, who is God directly perceived, lives to this day. Reciting the name of this Rama would save us; the Rama of history, who is qualified by attributes, good or bad, would not have the strength to save."[46] The idealized Sita was "the last word" in wifehood as well as maidenhood, and her conjugal love was free from passion (*vishay, vikar*).[47] She was "a model Hindu wife,"[48] and just as she was the ideal wife, Rama was the ideal husband. Their type of love reconciled conjugal love, love of the kingdom, and love of God.[49] Gandhi did not enter into a debate on which interpretation of the Rama-Sita story should be preferred, Valmiki's or Kalidasa's or Tulsidas's.[50] His interest was less scholarly and more pastoral: he wanted to tell his audience what that story should mean to people living and acting in today's society. It should mean that marriage was a key institution of society, safeguarding the interest of the species, the nation, the married couples, and moksha. It could serve these multiple ends only if sexuality was approached with restraint. Gandhi's preferred mode of restraint was celibacy within marriage, even though he tolerated chastity too.

The question of sublimation

According to Sudhir Kakar, "Indian spirituality is preeminently a theory of 'sublimation.'"[51] By sublimation he meant the conversion of "base

---

[45] CW, 88: 234.   [46] Gandhi to Manilal and Sushila, 19 May 1929, CW, 40: 405.
[47] Ibid., p. 404.   [48] CW, 28: 30.   [49] CW, 31: 511.
[50] For an excellent treatment of this question, see V. Das, "Kama in the Scheme of *Purusharthas*: The Story of Rama," in T.N. Madan (ed.), *Way of Life: King, Householder, Renouncer* (Delhi: Vikas, 1982), pp. 183–203. See also the excellent article of M. Kishwar, "Gandhi on Women," in *Economic and Political Weekly*, 20 (1985), pp. 1691–1702, 1753–58.
[51] Kakar, *Intimate Relations*, p. 118.

wishes into socially sanctioned aspirations."[52] He summarized the Indian version of sublimation as follows. The semen (*virya*), the source of sexual energy, was the key element in it. It could move either downward, as in sexual intercourse, or it could move upward through the spinal chord to the brain, as in Kundalini Yoga. In the first case, there is the loss or waste of the sexual energy. In the second case, there was conservation of the same and its subtle transformation into spiritual energy called *ojas*. *Ojas* was the source of heroic achievements in the spiritual life. When sublimated, the semen becomes, in Kakar's words, a "bestower of immortality," while without it, it remained "a giver of death."[53]

As far as we know, Gandhi did not specifically speak of *ojas*. But he did speak rather frequently of the need to conserve the semen. Already in *Hind Swaraj* we see him extolling the need for its conservation. "A man who is unchaste (*a-brahmachari*) loses stamina, becomes emasculated and cowardly."[54] The term used for "loses stamina" is *a-viryavan* – a loser of *virya*: an *a-viryavan* is an *a-brahmachari*. Only a *viryavan* could hope to practice satyagraha in the heroic degree.

Now *virya* could be lost in many ways. The one that Gandhi was most concerned with was its loss through wet dreams. He analyzed these phenomena, with sobriety and sophistication, in terms of the subconscious sexual desires lying buried in the psyche – in the Indian terminology, in terms of the *vasanas*. For example, in his letter of Harjivan Kotak of 11 December 1927 he blamed himself for his wet dreams because of the "impure desires deep down" in him, which were acting up like a "hidden poison."[55] In another letter he blamed himself for the fifteen years of the sexual gratification that he had had with his wife, in the early years of their marriage.[56]

Kakar saw Gandhi's effort to conserve his sexual energy as fitting into the general scheme of Indian spirituality.[57] We know that already in South Africa he had been reading the classics in Indian spirituality, such as Patanjali's *Yoga Sutra* and Vivekananda's *Raja Yoga*.[58] As early as 1923 he had read Sir John Woodroffe's *Shakti and Shakta* on Tantra.[59] Chapter 29 of the latter work was on Kundalini Yoga. Briefly, that control of sexual energy in its conscious and subconscious manifestations was necessary for a successful celibate life was a constant of his thought. Whether this control should be understood in terms of the theory of sublimation or not is a question immaterial to the present argument. Bhikhu Parekh believes that "the very idea of *ojas* or spiritual energy is

---

[52] Ibid., p. 103.   [53] Ibid., p. 118.   [54] *Hind Swaraj*, p. 97.   [55] CW, 35: 379.
[56] CW, 62: 429.   [57] Kakar, *Intimate Relations*, pp. 93, 118.   [58] CW, 39: 211.
[59] CW, 23: 187, and CW, 87: 91.

largely mystical and almost certainly false."[60] Kakar, with his knowledge of the history of Indian sexuality and spirituality, thinks that sublimation is a convenient theoretical construct that may be used to understand what Gandhi was attempting to do. His effort to turn sexual instinct into civic virtue was partly through procreation and partly, perhaps, through sublimation. With sublimation sexual energy could be turned into socially beneficial activities and prevented from becoming violent inclinations.

Granted that the theory of sublimation is a useful explanatory device, the fact still remains that Gandhi did not stop with it. He went beyond it. For he viewed celibacy as something intrinsically good, contributing to inner freedom. However, for celibacy to become this, he recognized the need for something more than sublimation – divine grace, something that psychoanalysis does not normally recognize.[61] He was firm on the question that it was impossible to maintain celibacy "by mere human effort." Those who sought it for the sake of "God realization" (*Ishwar sakshatkar*) had reason for hoping to be successful: only their faith in God had to be equal to their confidence in themselves.[62] For celibacy was not a matter of "mere body." It began with the body, but did not end with it. For it involved the subconscious too. It was here that God's grace (*prabhu prasad*) and an "unreserved surrender to His grace" became crucial.[63] "The concupiscence of the mind [could] not be rooted out except by intense self-examination, surrender to God, and, lastly, grace [*Ishwar prasad*]."[64] "God's name" (*Ram-nam*) and "grace" (Ram-*kripa*) were the "last resources" of those who wanted to see God "face to face."[65]

The resort to divine assistance was not a matter of personal preference. For in the divine plan for humanity grace had its allotted role to play. According to the *Gita*, even a fleeting vision of the divine can permanently purify the soul:

> For a man who is fasting his senses
> Outwardly, the sense-objects disappear,
> Leaving the yearning behind; but when
> He has seen the Highest,
> Even the yearning disappears.[66]

---

[60] B. Parekh, *Colonialism, Tradition and Reform: An Analysis of Gandhi's Political Discourse* (rev. edn, New Delhi: Sage, 1999), p. 203.

[61] On sublimation in Freud see P. Ricœur, *Freud and Philosophy: An Essay on Interpretation*, translated by Denis Savage (New Haven: Yale University Press, 1970), pp. 483–93. On "divine and/or psychic causality" in the lives of saints, see W. W. Meissner, *Ignatius of Loyola: The Psychology of a Saint* (New Haven: Yale University Press, 1992), pp. 346–58.

[62] CW, 39: 171.   [63] Ibid., p. 254.   [64] Ibid., p. 263.   [65] Ibid., p. 171.

[66] *Gita*, II: 59, cited in CW, 39: 266.

"When he has seen the Highest even the yearning disappears": Gandhi interprets this verse to mean that the grace of divine illumination can remove from the subconscious even the last vestiges of sensual cravings (*vasanas*). Therefore, those who desire to observe perfect celibacy with a view to "realizing God" need not despair.[67] The celibate has only to remain a friend, a *bhakta*, of God and the latter will do the rest. In the final analysis, to be a successful celibate one has to be both self-disciplined and devoted to God.

A critical appraisal

From the foregoing analysis of Gandhi's thoughts on celibacy and sexuality two issues have emerged as being critical. The first is that he viewed sexuality primarily from the point of view of humans as seekers of release from *samsara*, and only secondarily from the point of view of humans as creative, or rather procreative, contributors to the process of *samsara* itself. I do not think it is unfair to say that his first concern trumped the second. This happened, despite the fact that procreation was an indispensable link in the chain of birth, death and rebirth: without procreation *samsara* would come to a sudden stop. He refused to accept the possibility of procreation being a legitimate and even holy activity under certain conditions.

The second critical issue that emerges from our analysis is the depth of Gandhi's will to eradicate the desire for sexual pleasure even from the subconscious. This was for him more than an issue of psychological health. It was primarily an issue of release from *samsara*. The will to root out the *vasanas* became so strong that he refused to admit defeat even when he failed, inculpably, on particular occasions. This led him to embark upon his well-known experiments in celibacy, which included testing his virtue by sleeping in the same bed next to his niece. As Wendy Doniger has remarked, even such cases had precedents in Hindu mythology. Lord Siva, for example, had allowed Parvati to test his celibacy and prove that he was "truly beyond the power of women."[68]

At the same time, Gandhi knew very well that the sex craving would always remain with humans and that it could not be totally eradicated.[69] He also knew that human effort by itself was not enough to secure victory in the struggle for celibacy. God's help would be needed to supplement human effort. Had he been consistent with this theological insight, he would not have been as adamant as he seemed to be with his experiments. He could have left the final outcome to God's grace. But a certain degree

[67] CW, 39: 171.   [68] Doniger, *Asceticism and Eroticism in the Mythology of Siva*, p. 260.
[69] CW, 62: 430.

of Pelagianism seemed to creep into his spiritual life. That was why he went to the extent of postulating a *dharmic* (moral) imperative at work in his experiments. They became as it were part of his *svadharma*. To give them up for fear of public opinion would have been *adharma*, immoral.[70] The term, "experiment," he explained to Nirmal Kumar Bose, his secretary during 1946–47, was "ill-chosen." For experiments could be dropped anytime during the period of investigation for reasons external to them; but something that belonged to the sphere of duty (dharma) could not be dropped for reasons external to it.[71]

Inconsistency apart, there are theological considerations that should be taken into account in assessing Gandhi's sexual ethics. The association of impurity with procreation was by no means unique to him. He did not invent the idea. He very likely inherited it from the ascetic traditions of India. Even outside the Indian tradition we see sin being associated with the procreative act. In Psalm 51, for example, David laments over the fact that he was conceived in sin: "Behold, I was shaped in iniquity; and in sin did my mother conceive me."

The Bible, of course, understood this in terms of the Fall, the Original Sin, and Redemption. That was why David could rely on both repentance (the human effort) and on grace (God's help). Addressing God, he further remonstrated:

Behold, thou desirest truth in the inward parts; and in the hidden part thou shalt make me to know wisdom
Purge me with hyssop, and I shall be clean; wash me, and I shall be whiter than snow . . .
Create in me a clean heart, O God; and renew a right spirit in me . . .
Restore unto me the joy of thy salvation; and uphold me with thy free
Spirit . . .
For thou desirest not sacrifice; else I would give it . . .
The sacrifices of God are a broken spirit; a broken and contrite heart, O God, Thou wilt not despise.[72]

Gandhi would have agreed with David's sentiments here: their two theologies seemed to be able to speak to each other. There is little doubt that he was quite aware of the theological dimension of his celibacy. For he saw himself in the mode of Shukadeva of the *Bhagavata*, and also in the mode of God's eunuch of St. Matthew 19: 12. Shukadeva, the son of

---

[70] CW, 86: 476.   [71] CW, 87: 104.

[72] Psalm 51. The context of David's contrition was the rebuke that the Prophet Nathan had given him for his affair with Bathsheba. Erik Erikson does not refer to the Bathsheba affair, but does refer to Abishay, a Shunamite "fair damsel" who cherished David in his old age and ministered to him, though he "knew her not." I Kings 1: 1–4 (E. H. Erikson, *Gandhi's Truth* [New York: W. W. Norton, 1969], pp. 404–5).

Vyasa, was a successful celibate. Even Christ spoke approvingly of those who made themselves eunuchs "for the sake of the kingdom of heaven" – not by castration or by nature, but by choice, confirmed by grace.[73] But St. Matthew mentioned something that Gandhi only rarely, if at all, mentioned, viz., that in Christ's teaching fidelity or chastity in marriage was also a way to the kingdom of heaven. Gandhi could have given as much emphasis to chastity as to celibacy, but he did not. Sometimes he seemed to convey the impression that only perfect celibacy could lead one to moksha. Even though he recognized the sufficiency of chastity for the masses, his preoccupation – excessive preoccupation, one might add – was with celibacy. Why he was not satisfied with chastity remains an unresolved issue.

Limiting the present inquiry with his concern for celibacy, there is, of course, a theological way of interpreting it, supplementing the interpretations of modern positivist psychology. Gandhi had crossed several theological borders in an effort to explain his position. His interpreters would do well if they too could do the same.

This has not always been the case with modern psychologists, even the very sympathetic ones such as Nirmal Kumar Bose and Erik Erikson. Bose's interpretation is based on the shallow psychological theory of external projection. Gandhi's mission, according to Bose, was to show that progress of civilization consisted in introducing into individual and collective lives the influence of love and self-suffering, and these qualities were best exemplified by women. That was why Gandhi attempted "to conquer sex by becoming a woman." This he was able to achieve because of the "mother-cult" of his boyhood days. He learned from his mother the values of love and self-suffering, which he was then able to project onto the larger canvas of history. The origin of his "desire to purify and civilize mankind lay within the depths of his personal relationship with his mother."[74]

Bose's analysis can take us some way towards understanding Gandhi, but not the whole way. He (Bose) does not concern himself with difficulties involved in conquering "the subtle passions" (*vikar*) and "dormant passions" (*vikar*), and the need to become "passion free" (*nir-vikar*) that the autobiography very poignantly speaks of.[75] Nor does he take into account his concern for the need of God's grace to intervene in history and civilization if they are to become gentler and less violent.

Erikson's analysis fares better than does Bose's. But even he does not do full justice to what is truly special to Gandhi, viz., the concern for

---

[73] CW, 62: 429.
[74] N. K. Bose, *My Days With Gandhi* (New Delhi: Orient Longman, 1987), pp. 175–78.
[75] CW, 39: 402.

moksha. True, Erikson devotes some profound, though obscure, pages to Gandhi as a *homo religiosus*.[76] It is to his credit that he sees Gandhi in terms of attempting to bring about a balance between three distinct human strivings – the instinctual, the logical, and the ethical. By the ethical Erikson means the habit of giving "an insightful assent to human values." Opposed to it is "moralism" understood as the habit of demanding "blind obedience" to absolute interdicts. Also, Erikson is of the opinion that Gandhi often mistook moralism for ethics. This explained his attitude towards procreation and the concomitant fear of the instinctual. Without the satisfaction of the instinctual, however, humans would only "wither away" as sensual beings and in the process become highly destructive. Without an "alliance" with women, men would become moralistic rather than ethical in sexual matters. Gandhi saw the need for a balance between ethics, instinct and logic, but he did not always succeed in achieving it.[77]

What is missing from Erikson's equation is the one element that Gandhi cared about most – the spiritual, the desire to see God "face to face" (*Ishwar Sakshatkar*) or moksha. Gandhi's equation contained four, not three, elements – i.e., all the four purusharthas. True, he did not fully succeed in bringing kama and moksha into a proper relationship, even though his theory required it.

The question is, why did this happen? It happened, in our opinion, because of his overreaching concern for moksha. This made him see kama in the light of moksha, and not in itself. He was aware of the teaching of *Gita* VII: 11, which declared that Krishna was the source of power and kama consistent with dharma. In other words, so long as kama was in harmony with dharma it was conducive to a holy life. Had Gandhi understood kama in this way, his interpretation of the ethics of procreation would have been quite positive. But he chose not to, as is evident from his commentary on the above verse. The following is his commentary:

"Kama not contrary to dharma," means the desire for moksha, or the desire to end the suffering of creatures.

If we desire to end the suffering of others, our suffering, too, will end. This is true in the ordinary sense of the words. But in Sanskrit the desire to end the suffering of others is described as a *maha-swartha* [supreme interest]. It means interest in the moksha of all creatures. Anyone who feels such a desire would be striving hard for his own moksha.[78]

---

[76] Erikson, *Gandhi's Truth*, pp. 393–402.
[77] This is a summary of Erikson's analysis in *Gandhi's Truth*, pp. 251–54.
[78] CW, 32: 257.

Gandhi's attitude towards procreation is inconsistent with the general theory of the purusharthas. However, the inconsistency should be seen as a byproduct of his over-emphasis on a particular way of restraining the sexual instinct, viz., through celibacy. If he was not consistent with the application of his theory to kama – as he seems to be – it is up to his interpreters to correct the imbalance and see kama in its true light. One does not have to over-emphasize the need to exercise a particular mode of restraint on sexuality (in this case celibacy) in order to promote the valid idea that self-restraint in sexual matters is a necessary requirement of the theory of the purusharthas. The enduring legacy of Gandhi's teaching on celibacy, chastity, and sexuality is that to be a purushartha, kama had to operate within the rules of self-restraint required by dharma and the pursuit of moksha.

9   Art and society

"Industry without art is brutality."[1]

"He is with the great artists, though art was not his medium."[2]

Gandhi's contributions to the general field of the arts are not given the kind of attention that they deserve. There is a deafening silence on the part of his major interpreters on this score. Not a word from such figures as Raghavan Iyer or Joan Bondurant. Even those who mention in passing the subject of Gandhi and art are reluctant to go any further. Partha Mitter, the author of the magisterial *Art and Nationalism in Colonial India 1850–1922*, opines that "in Gandhi's programme there was no room for art with the possible exception of Nandalal Bose's decoration of the Haripura Congress venue," done at his behest.[3] Bhikhu Parekh, arguably the foremost interpreter of his political thought today, believes that "his moralistic vision" prevented him from seeing the significance of the other dimensions of human existence, including the aesthetic.[4]

How can this be, given the grand vision of human excellence that his theory of the purusharthas provides? Besides, who can ignore the fact that his wide culture had enabled him to discuss knowledgeably such figures as Oscar Wilde, Jonathan Swift, and Upton Sinclair, or for that matter, to give advice on how to translate a poem like Newman's "Lead, Kindly Light"? Regarding Oscar Wilde, he remarked that he could speak of him because "he was being much discussed and talked about" while he was in England (1888–91).[5] During his time in England several of Wilde's works were published. They included *The Decay of Lying* (1889), *Critic as Artist*

---

[1] John Ruskin, cited in Ananda K. Coomaraswamy, *Essays in National Idealism* (Campden, 1909), p. 202.

[2] E. M. Forster, "Mahatma Gandhi," in S. Radhakrishnan (ed.), *Mahatma Gandhi: Essays and Reflections on His Life and Work* (Bombay: Jaico, 1995), p. 315.

[3] P. Mitter, *Art and Nationalism in Colonial India 1850–1922: Occidental Orientations* (Cambridge: Cambridge University Press, 1994), p. 379.

[4] Parekh, *Gandhi*, p. 99.

[5] Gandhi in an interview with G. Ramachandran, CW, 25: 248.

(1890), *The Picture of Dorian Gray* (1890), and *The Soul of Man Under Socialism* (1891). How many of these he might have read we do not know; all we know is that he felt competent to discuss Wilde. But we know a little more about his interest in Swift. *Gulliver's Travels* was first mentioned in 1910 when he asked Maganlal Gandhi to read it.[6] He asked him again in the following year: "Please read *Gulliver's Travels* sometime if you have not already done so."[7] A few weeks later he gave the reason why. It was because it contained "so effective a condemnation, in an ironic vein, of modern civilization." The book deserved to be read "again and again."[8] Besides, there was its great artistry. "Children can read it with enjoyment, so simple it is; and the wise ones get dizzy trying to comprehend its hidden significance. In Brobdingnag, Gulliver tumbles as low as he had risen in Lilliput. Even in Lilliput, he has represented the tiny people as possessing a few powers which were superior to his own, that is to say, those of normal people."[9]

The matter did not end there. In 1927 he used the example of Swift in advising a Gujarati writer on how to use irony as a literary device. "If you follow *Gulliver's Travels* and conceive an imaginary country in which to apply your correctives, you could say all that you have said ..."[10] As for Upton Sinclair, he was not a writer to be despised.[11]

Gandhi had a deep interest in the visual arts too. The memories of his visit to the Vatican Museum in 1931 stayed with him for a long time. He wrote about them to friends in India. "I very much enjoyed seeing the paintings in Rome, but what opinion can I give after a visit of two hours? What is my competence to judge? ... If I could spend two or three months there, I would go and see the paintings and sculptures every day and study them attentively. I saw the sculpture of Jesus on the cross. I have already written and told you that it was this that attracted me most."[12]

In 1936 in an address delivered to the Gujarati Literature Society he spoke of the country's need for art and literature that could speak to the millions. To make his point he referred to what he saw in the Vatican Museum. There he saw art, he said, that could speak. "Why should I need an artist to explain a work of art to me? Why should it not speak out to me itself?" He explained what he meant. "I saw in the Vatican art collection a statue of Christ on the Cross which simply captured me and kept me spell bound. I saw it five years ago but it is still before me."[13] We have an account of this particular scene from Mirabehn (Madeleine Slade). Three decades later she wrote as follows.

---

[6] CW, 10: 357.   [7] CW, 11: 20.   [8] Ibid., p. 77.   [9] Ibid.
[10] CW, 33: 207.   [11] CW, 50: 110.
[12] Gandhi to Prema Kantak, 25 January 1932, CW, 49: 37.   [13] CW, 63: 416.

In the Vatican, Bapu's eyes fell on a very striking life size crucifix. He immediately went up to it and stood there in deep contemplation. Then he moved a little this way, and that way, so as to see it from various angles, and finally went around behind it and the wall, where there was hardly room to go, and looked up at it from the back. He remained perfectly silent, and it was only when he left that he spoke, and then as if still in contemplation – "That was a very wonderful crucifix" – and again silence. So deep an impression did that scene make on me that it stands out all alone in my mind, and I remember nothing else of the visit to the Vatican.[14]

There is no need to belabor the point: in assessing Gandhi's understanding and appreciation of the arts, there is one mistake that no one should make. No one should regard him as an ignoramus. He had settled views on art and aesthetics, although he did not write about them. The choice was deliberate, and the proffered reason was "ignorance" – i.e., Socratic ignorance. He could "never dream" of writing on art, he told an interviewer, "for the simple reason that it would be an impertinence on [his] part to hold forth on art . . . I do not speak or write about it, because I am conscious of my own limitations . . . My functions are different from the artist's and I should not go out of my way to assume his position."[15]

His reluctance to write on art reminds one of his reluctance to write on philosophy. Be that as it may, even though he professed to have no original contribution to make to art theory, he paradoxically wanted the readers of *Hind Swaraj* to read books on art theory. A deeper understanding of his philosophy, it was implied, would not be possible without an understanding of art theory. The point was made obliquely by putting works by two giants of art theory and art history in Appendix I of *Hind Swaraj*. I am referring to Leo Tolstoy's classic *What Is Art?* and John Ruskin's *"A Joy for Ever": And Its Place in the Market*. This is a clue missed by almost all his critics. Why would he ask his readers to read Tolstoy and Ruskin on art unless he placed a link between the arts and his own main project in life – the regeneration of Indian society?

The point is that he had a serious interest in the arts. But that interest lay in the practical side of things more than in the theoretical ones. It lay in what he wanted to do with and for the arts as a man of action. Not only did he inspire a generation of Indian writers, poets, novelists and playwrights, but he also managed to bring the arts to the masses. He did this in a variety of ways: through the political symbols that he invented, through the pioneering work that he did for the revival of religious music, through his well-known crusade on behalf of village crafts, and above all through the effort that he made to make people aware that art was a public good.

---

[14] M. Slade, *The Spirit's Pilgrimage* (New York: Coward-McCann, 1960), pp. 150–51.
[15] Gandhi in his interview with G. Ramachandran, CW, 25: 250.

Tolstoy, Ruskin and Coomaraswamy

These three writers contributed significantly to the evolution of his thought on the arts. Of their writings, Tolstoy's *What Is Art?* (1898), was undoubtedly the most important. One of Tolstoy's "greatest contributions to the welfare of mankind,"[16] it had taken the author fifteen years to complete.[17] The Mahatma had a deep and sustained interest in it. In 1916 we find him arranging for its translation into Gujarati. "If you translate Tolstoy's *What Is Art?* for publication and read the proofs you will get Rs 100," he wrote to his favorite translator, Valji Desai. "The work . . . will go on for two months at the rate of four hours a day . . . I shall get the work done through you."[18] A decade later, in 1927, we see him giving a brief disquisition on art criticism to Sushila, his daughter-in-law. She was to read Tolstoy on art. For in the realm of art there should be no distinction between the indigenous and the foreign. Art transcended national boundaries. Lovers of art, he reminded her, tended to take a superficial view of art and used it as a cover for many weaknesses.

We should, therefore, examine what we mean by art. Not everything which appeals to the eye is art. What is accepted as art by many experts may not be art. I have read conflicting opinions about many paintings and statues expressed by art-critics who have become famous in the world. We should, therefore, think what art means. The book *What Is Art?* [has] been translated. Sushila should read it.[19]

It would have been interesting to find out who those famous art critics that he mentioned in the letter were. Even without that information, however, it is not difficult to see that it was not a novice that was giving the advice.

Turning to *What Is Art?*, there is no way we can adequately summarize its contents here. For our present purpose it is perhaps sufficient if we identified the main points that Gandhi took from it. In the first place, there is its definition of art. Art is the expression, through appropriate symbols, of deeply experienced feelings that the artist has undergone, expression that can evoke similar feelings in those who come into contact with the art.[20] Secondly, there is the notion of art being "one of the conditions of human life."[21] It cannot therefore be expected to meet all

---

[16] Aylmer Maude, *The Life of Tolstoy: The Later Years* (London: Oxford University Press, 1910), p. 541.
[17] Tolstoy, *What Is Art? and Essays on Art*, translated by Aylmer Maude, (London: Oxford University Press, 1929), p. 278.
[18] Gandhi to Valji Desai, 24 January 1916, CW, supplementary volume 1: 103.
[19] CW, 35: 363.   [20] Tolstoy, *What Is Art?*, p. 123.   [21] Ibid., pp. 120–21.

the needs of life. The question of the autonomy of art, therefore, did not arise. The formula of art for art's sake was something that recent aesthetes had invented for their own private satisfaction. Thirdly, all great art attempts to express what it takes to be "the religious perception" of the meaning of life. That perception in "our times" (Tolstoy was writing in the 1890s) is that our well-being, both material and spiritual, individual and collective, temporal and eternal, lies in the growth of amity among humans. "Art should cause violence to be set aside." It should aim to promote the feeling now attained by only "the best members of society, the customary feeling and the instinct of all men."[22]

Turning to "A Joy for Ever", it was the second book by Ruskin that he had recommended to the readers of Hind Swaraj. It was an expanded version of two lectures given in 1857 in Manchester on the occasion of the Art Treasures Exhibition there. Originally published under the title The Political Economy of Art, it was in 1880 reissued under the new title of "A Joy for Ever". Keats' famous line "A thing of beauty is a joy for ever" was used by the Manchester Exhibition as its official motto. Ruskin used part of this line ironically to express his criticism of what was going on in British society. The Industrial Revolution was paying no real attention to Keats though it was using his name. It was more interested in creating wealth by whatever means than in respecting beauty. It was ravaging the environment and brutalizing the lives of the industrial workers. "A Joy for Ever" was therefore more about art policy than about art theory: about how art might be used to beautify life and lighten the burden of existence in an industrial society.

According to Ruskin, no matter under what economic system humans live, a good society should always try to make it possible that the material conditions of life strike a balance between utility and splendor. Unfortunately, early capitalism tended to pay more attention to utility than to splendor such that poverty and squalor became as much its outcome as the wealth of the new industrial class. One of the urgent tasks before the modern industrial society, therefore, was to strike a new balance between utility and splendor.[23]

But there was a catch. What happened if mass poverty persisted? In that case, argued Ruskin, providing for necessities should take precedence over providing for luxuries. So long as there was "cold and nakedness" in the land there could be no question at all but that splendor of dress be treated as a "crime" – a sentiment with which Gandhi was in full

---

[22] Ibid., pp. 287–88.
[23] Ruskin, "A Joy for Ever": And Its Place in the Market (London: George Allen, 1900), pp. 7–14.

agreement. So long as there were any that had no blankets for their beds and clothes for their bodies, blanket-making and cloth-making must have priority over lace-making.[24] It does not take much imagination to see how Gandhi made a mental connection between Ruskin's approach to mass poverty and his own.

Ananda K. Coomaraswamy was the third influence on Gandhi's aesthetic thought, especially as it concerned India. Not that he was unaware of developments in India in regard to the revival of interest in the arts. As the editor of *Indian Opinion*, he was quite familiar with the works of such figures as E. B. Havell, a pioneer in the revival of interest in Indian art. Sir George Birdwood, another pioneer in the same field, was a personal friend with whom he had kept up a rather substantial correspondence.[25] However, Coomaraswamy's *Essays on National Idealism*, published a month after *Hind Swaraj* was published, confirmed many ideas brewing in his own mind. Coomaraswamy's aim was to explain "the true significance" of the Indian nationalist movement. He did not believe that the national regeneration of the Indian people could take place without the support of the arts. "Art contains in itself the deepest principles of life, the truest guide to the greatest art, the Art of Living." Artistic revival required economic and political revival also – a thought that fitted perfectly with Gandhi's theory of the purusharthas. Swaraj was not just a political condition; it was also a moral and psychological condition of the consciousness of freedom from alien domination.[26]

It is true that according to Indian philosophy spiritual progress required some degree of asceticism. How would this affect the revival of interest in aesthetics? Properly understood, Coomaraswamy believed, aesthetics and spirituality should cause no problem for each other. Spiritual liberation, strictly speaking, lay outside the province of aesthetics; and aesthetics by itself could not bring about spiritual liberation. Nevertheless, art had a complementary role to play in the spiritual life. Indians, therefore, should know where the province of aesthetics ended and that of spirituality began. As spirituality would require restraint, they should appreciate the aesthetic value of restraint, but not to the point of embracing world-denying asceticism.[27] Art was compatible with the restraint, but not with asceticism. Gandhi could agree with Coomaraswamy on this; for his spirituality, though heroic, was not world-denying. Art could therefore mediate between material existence and the spiritual life, without in any way wanting to present itself as a substitute for spiritual life.

---

[24] Ibid., pp. 60–61.   [25] See for example CW, 6: 10, 155, 195, 235, passim.
[26] Coomaraswamy, *Essays in National Idealism*, pp. i–iii.   [27] Ibid., p. 29.

Coomaraswamy's chapters on Indian music made a deep impression on Gandhi. His interest in religious music deepened as a result. Folk music, agricultural music, and craft music were very important parts of national life in so far as they brought a degree of aesthetic pleasure into the otherwise drab lives of the toiling masses. Love of Indian music and comprehension of Indian art, Coomaraswamy concluded, were "tests unfailing" of India's regeneration.[28]

Gandhi recommended *Essays on National Idealism* to his colleagues as soon as it was published (1909). "Coomaraswamy's book is among Mr. Polak's books that are lying at Rustoomjee's Sheth's," he wrote to Maganlal Gandhi. "Please read it when you find time. It is worth reading. What the author has written about music and the harmonium seems to be right. The other things too, are worth perusal."[29] Again, in 1917 we find him recommending the same book for "serious study" to the Gujaratis in India.[30]

Gandhi an artist?

Even though he did not propound any original theory of art, he did integrate the ideas on art that he garnered from different sources. There is little doubt that this integration contributed to his evolution as a writer. The literary qualities of his Gujarati writings have been widely recognized. His autobiography stands out as a landmark in modern Gujarati literature. According to Professor C. N. Patel, his Gujarati writings had "the quality of true literature, a natural movement of thought not arranged by the logical intellect, but guided by spontaneous feeling and progressing from the right beginning to the true end according to an inner logic." His was a mind "alive to the beauty of nature and of the human figure, of fine emotion and noble character, of music expressing self-surrender in devotion, and of skilled craftsmanship."[31] It should not come as a surprise to anyone that he was the president of both the Gujarat Sahitya Parishad (Association of Gujarati Literature) and the Hindi Sahitya Sammelan (Association of Hindi Literature).

The aesthetic context of the writing of *Hind Swaraj*, his fundamental work, deserves mention here. There is no doubt that it met the Tolstoyan standards of a work of art. There was first of all the prior experience of intense inner feelings about its subject matter. There was also the burning

---

[28] Ibid., pp. 193–96.
[29] Gandhi to Maganlal Gandhi, 16 November 1910, CW, 10: 356.   [30] CW, 14: 30.
[31] C. N. Patel, *Mahatma Gandhi and His Gujarati Writings* (New Delhi: Sahitya Akademi, 1981), p. 10.

desire to communicate them to its readers. And the literary genre that he chose – dialogue – suited the author's talents. The ideas that went into the book were "brewing" in his mind for some time, he wrote to his friend Henry Polak. They had now (November 1909) taken "a violent possession of me," he informed him.[32] "I have written because I could not restrain myself," wrote the master of self-restraint in the Foreword.[33] Two decades later he recalled the experience with affection and quiet satisfaction: "Just as one cannot help speaking out when one's heart is full, so also I have been unable to restrain myself from writing the book since my heart was full."[34] And there was something of the heroic in the actual writing itself: it was written in ten days at such an uninterrupted pace that when the right hand got tired, the writing continued with the left – forty of the 275 manuscript pages being written in that remarkable way.

That is not all. The discovery of the meaning of the concept swaraj, central to the argument of the book, itself emerged from something akin to an aesthetic experience. He had first a personal experience of it, and once he experienced it, he felt the need to communicate it to others. Do not consider this swaraj to be like a dream, he tells the reader. "The swaraj that I wish to picture before you and me is such that, after we have once realized it, we will endeavour to the end of our life time to persuade others to do likewise. But such swaraj has to be experienced by each one for himself."[35] Swaraj for Gandhi was not merely a political concept, it was also a deep spiritual experience in the birth of which aesthetics had played its part.

In the same vein, the decision to adopt his famous loincloth as his regular attire also had something of an aesthetic experience prior to taking the decision. More about this shortly below. The point is that there are certain aspects of Gandhi's life that we can understand only from an aesthetic perspective. That was why, I think, he wanted the students of his thought to be familiar with art theory and art history.

There was no question, then, that he had some very settled views on the nature of art and its relationship to life in society. Everyone knows about the place that truth occupies in his philosophy. He was frequently asked how truth related to art and aesthetics. In his 1924 interview with G. Ramachandran he went into the subject in some detail. He said he saw "Beauty" in "Truth" or through "Truth." Art arose as the external expression of the internal striving for "Truth" or self-realization. "Whenever men begin to see Beauty in Truth, then true Art will arise."[36]

---

[32] CW, 9: 479–81.   [33] CW, 10: 6.   [34] CW, 32: 489.   [35] *Hind Swaraj*, p. 73.
[36] CW, 25: 249.

He returned to the question of truth and beauty in 1931 in Geneva, in his conversations with Romain Rolland. He could not see art "as a thing distinct from Truth." That was one of the reasons why he could not accept the formula "art for art's sake." His position, he explained, had its roots in Indian philosophy, according to which *sat* (Ultimate Reality), *chit* (consciousness) and *ananda* (joy) were aspects of Ultimate Reality.[37] The very first hymn of the *Ashram Hymnal* (drawn up under his direction) was a hymn celebrating this idea. "Early in the morning I call to mind that Being which is felt in the heart, which is *sat*, *chit*, and *sukham* [another word for *ananda*], which is the state reached by perfect men and which is the super-state."[38]

Gandhi was here pointing to the philosophic foundation of his aesthetics. Art had to be understood not only in terms of itself but also in terms of the other aspects of life, an essential point of the theory of the purusharthas. Obviously, the beauty in art that is being discussed here is created beauty. But created beauty had its source and ultimate explanation in uncreated Beauty, just as created or human truth had its source and ultimate explanation in uncreated Truth. The Sanskrit word *sat*, unlike the English word truth, easily lent itself to a metaphysical interpretation. With the general discredit of metaphysics in modern Western thought, Gandhi's position may not carry much weight in Western circles. But that is not the point: the point is that Gandhi did not think that a Western position was correct simply because it was a Western position. He might well have agreed with St. Thomas Aquinas that "the object of philosophy is not to find out what this or that philosopher may have said about this or that, but to discover what the truth of the matter is."[39] Similarly the question was not whether there was agreement between Indian philosophy and modern Western philosophy on the nature of aesthetics. The question was whether or not we can fully explain created beauty without reference to uncreated Beauty. In his view, the Western separation of goodness and beauty from uncreated Truth was a regrettable philosophical error, and Western art theories were paying heavily for it.

The relationship of art to religion was another question on which Gandhi had firm convictions. Here he was in full accord with Tolstoy. As he mentioned in his 1931 interview with Joseph Bard, editor of the British journal *The Island*, religion was "the proper and eternal ally" of art. This was not so much a matter of theory for him but one of history and

---

[37] *Romain Rolland and Gandhi Correspondence*, p. 209.   [38] CW, 44: 386.
[39] St. Thomas Aquinas, "Studium philosophiae non est ad hoc quod sciatur quid homines senserint sed qualiter se habeat veritas rerum," *Commentary on Aristotle's De caelo*, I, lectio 22 (Rome: Marietti, 1952), p. 109.

practice. In all cultures, except perhaps the contemporary modern Western culture, religious personages and religious themes had supplied not only the subject matter but also the inspiration for art. What religions taught, art brought near to the people on the plastic plane. The "central experience of life," he believed, was the relationship of humans to God; this would never be replaced or superseded by anything else.[40] This relationship is represented differently in different religions, and differently in different periods of time. But underneath the differences there lay a fundamental similarity of perception. The artist opting to be a "scoffer" (to use Gandhi's term) does more harm to himself or herself and to art than to religion: "he will frustrate his own vocation."[41]

Gandhi and music

The art form that appealed to him most was music, especially religious music. Music affected the whole person. There was the music of the mind, of the senses and of the heart. It introduced harmony into life.[42] The "triple accord of voice, the accompaniment and thought" created an atmosphere of sweetness and strength that no words could express.[43] It was also a means of spiritual development. To get the best out of music the worshipper had to become one with it.[44] Good music, he believed, had the power to transcend sectarian differences. That was one reason why he used music in his inter-religious prayer meetings.[45]

One of the first things he did upon establishing the Sabarmati Ashram in 1915 was to appoint a music teacher. Pandit Narayan Moreshwar Khare, a pupil of Pandit Vishnu Digambar Paluskar, the foremost music expert of Benares, was appointed on a monthly salary of Rs 20.[46] Training in music became part of the regular Ashram life. The Ashram also took a leading part in the music education of the entire region of Gujarat.[47] Gandhi, with the assistance of Paluskar and Khare, was responsible for organizing the first All India Music Conference held in Ahmedabad in 1921. The custom of holding music festivals at the time of the annual meeting of the Indian National Congress continued to be a tradition at least till 1938, the year Khare died of pneumonia while engaged in organizing a music camp at the Haripura Congress.[48] Holding art and handicraft exhibitions too at the time of the music festival became a tradition, and Gandhi was able to get such outstanding artists as

---

[40] CW, 48: 149.   [41] Ibid.   [42] CW, 83: 410–11.   [43] Ibid., p. 257.
[44] CW, 25: 223.   [45] CW, 79: 356.   [46] CW, 13: 176.   [47] CW, 37: 317–18.
[48] CW, 66: 356.

Nandalal Bose to decorate the Congress venues of Lucknow, Fazipur, and Haripura. As late as 1946, Gandhi used to give detailed directives on how such festivals should be conducted and what items should be included. They should include village music, village dramas, folk dances, and musical instruments. Experts should explain to the village people how to make village life more artistic.[49] Last but not least, Gandhi took an active part in the establishment of music schools, and got the support for them from such luminaries as S. Radhakrishnan and Pandit Madan Mohan Malaviya.[50]

Perhaps Gandhi's greatest contribution to religious music was the compilation, with the help of Khare, of the *Ashram Hymnal*, a collection of some 253 Indian hymns.[51] They were collected from different regions of India, and their primary aim, according to the Preface of the edition of 1947, was "to sustain right conduct."[52] These hymns were representative of both higher Hinduism and popular Hinduism – as many as thirty-five hymns were taken directly from the Upanishads. In 1930 he translated each one of them into English, and in 1934 John S. Hoyland published an edited version of it for the benefit of the British public.

Ramdhun and "Lead, Kindly Light"

Nothing illustrates better what religious music meant to him than his appreciation of *Ramdhun* and "Lead, Kindly Light." The first, also known as *Raghupati*, was his most favored hymn, being sung morning and evening daily, as part of the Ashram prayer schedule.[53] The second, based on Cardinal Newman's poem written in 1833, was his favorite Christian hymn.

The origin of *Ramdhun* is shrouded in legend. According to the legend that he preferred it was composed by the great Hindi poet Tulsidas (1532–1623). While on a pilgrimage visiting the Vishnu temple of Dakore, Northern India, Tulsidas was moved to bargain with Vishnu. Until Vishnu revealed himself as Rama he would not bow his head in prayer. His wish was promptly granted: Rama appeared in his mind with his wife Sita, and three of their devotees. Hence, explains Gandhi, "*Ramdhun*, meaning intoxication with God [Ram]."[54]

There were, and are, several versions of *Ramdhun* in vogue. The version that Gandhi used had an ecumenical flavor to it. The third line read that the Ishwar of the Hindus and the Allah of the Muslims were one and

[49] CW, 85: 3–4; 237.   [50] CW, 79: 356; CW, 80: 34.
[51] For the text of the *Hymnal* see CW, 44: 386–466.   [52] CW, 86: 444.
[53] CW, 50: 199.   [54] CW, 86: 222.

the same. It was to bear witness to this ecumenical fact that he used this hymn at the beginning of all his public prayer meetings. Even so, controversy sometimes marred its public singing. In 1947 the fundamentalist Muslims of Mashimpur, Bengal, objected to its being sung in their village. He insisted, however, that to him Allah, *Khuda* and God were the same, and that he would not stop singing it "at the bidding of any person or even if the kingdom of the world" was offered to him.[55] In another village, also in Bengal, the Muslims compromised: they had no objection provided the singing was not accompanied by the use of *tabla*, because the prayer meeting was conducted near a mosque. To which he gladly agreed.[56]

Turning to "Lead, Kindly Light," he admired it both for its aesthetic beauty and religious depth. We hear of it for the first time in 1908, when he was convalescing in the home of Joseph Doke, a British missionary in South Africa and also his first biographer. An irate Pathan had knocked him unconscious in the street because of some political differences that he had with Gandhi. Doke, who happened to be near the scene, took him to his home for medical treatment. When he regained consciousness he realized that he was being kept under very strict medical watch. As he was not allowed to talk for medical reasons, he asked his host in writing "that before and in order that [he] might lie down quietly" his young daughter Olive be allowed to sing "Lead, Kindly Light." The experience of hearing that music left an indelible mark on him. "Even today its message is the goal of my striving. Even now I pray every moment of my life for God's grace and inspiration," he wrote in 1920.[57] And in 1924, writing in *Satyagraha in South Africa*, he again referred to the experience of listening to it from his sick bed. "The whole scene passes before my eyes as I dictate this, and the melodious voice of little Olive reverberates in my ears."[58] In 1930 we notice him advising Prabhavati, the wife of Jai Prakash Narayan, to meditate on "Lead, Kindly Light."[59] "One step enough for me," the last line of its first stanza, remained something of a mantra for him.

He took a literary interest in its translation into Gujarati. He advised one translator how to capture the spirit of its key phrases such as "kindly light" and "one step enough for me."[60] In 1932 he arranged for Narasinhrao Divetia's translation under the title "Premal Jyoti" to be adopted as part of the Ashram prayers on every Friday.[61]

Why, one may ask, would a man who was busy with so many things take an interest in these matters in such a determined and systematic way? The

[55] CW, 94: 356.   [56] Ibid., p. 338.   [57] CW, 19: 177.
[58] M. K. Gandhi, *Satyagraha in South Africa* (Ahmedabad: Navajivan, 1972 [1928]), p. 157.
[59] CW, 44: 386.   [60] CW, 95: 17.   [61] CW, 49: 485–86.

answer is not difficult to find, once we take into account his theory of the purusharthas. Music was such an important part of human life that to leave it out of count and to focus solely on other things, however important they might be, would be to leave out of count something basic to the attainment of the joy of life. Just another example that illustrates our point that to understand Gandhi fully we have to understand his interest in the arts.

Gandhi and his clothes

The loincloth has given Gandhi his enduring public image. Perhaps it is to him what the contemplative pose is to the Buddha. Only, in his case the image was personally chosen to express his deep feeling for the sufferings of the poor. His clothes too could not be fully understood except in the context of symbolism and art.

Critics have often noted that he communicated his important messages through clothes.[62] According to Millie Graham Polak, wife of Henry Polak (the Grahams had lived for a time with the Gandhis), the clothes he wore gave an idea of the nature of the different phases of life.[63] In his own view, the loincloth represented the final phase in the evolution of his life.[64] As Ruskin had observed, the "great and subtle art of dress" performed both pedagogical and symbolic functions.[65] In Gandhi's case the pedagogy consisted in educating the nation about the relationship between art and the state of society; and the symbolic function consisted in making the people aware of the evils of mass poverty.

We have his own account of the circumstances that led to the choice of his new attire. It marked the transition from his middle-class life-style to the life-style of the poorest of the poor. The idea of the loincloth came to him, he remarked, "naturally, without effort, without premeditation."[66] He was touring the famine-stricken areas of Bengal and Madras. The experience "overpowered him."[67] It became painful for him to eat or dress, so long as the poor did not have "enough to eat or enough to cover their bodies with." He felt it to be our duty "to dress them first and then dress ourselves, to feed them first and then feed ourselves."[68] Several sleepless nights were spent mulling over what he should do. The idea of the loincloth came to him several times. The idea was taken up with his

---

[62] See Emma Tarlo's excellent *Clothing Matters: Dress and Identity in India* (Chicago: University of Chicago Press, 1996).

[63] M. G. Graham, *Mr. Gandhi the Man* (London: George Allen and Unwin, 1931), p. 174.

[64] CW, 47: 120.   [65] Ruskin, *"A Joy for Ever"*, pp. 55 and 60.

[66] CW, 47: 120.   [67] CW, 21: 225.   [68] CW, 24: 456–57.

colleagues such as Rajaji and Maulana Sobhani. They advised him against it, fearing that such radical change might make the people uneasy. Some might take him for a lunatic or an attention seeker.[69] Little did they know that he was having a Tolstoyan artistic moment. Finally, at the end of the debate and deliberation he decided to follow his inspiration and, on 23 September 1921, he decided to appear in his new attire before a mass meeting he was to address in Madura. His colleagues watched him in silence and the masses in bewilderment.[70]

As N. K. Bose, his secretary in the 1940s, had observed, he had a keen awareness of the fact that humankind thirsted for symbols.[71] The loin-cloth symbolized his love of the poor and his desire to put an end to mass poverty. It was not at all meant to glorify poverty, as some have thought. If anything, it was a subtle critique of the indifference of the Indian elite towards mass poverty. Nor was he encouraging sloppiness in dress and launching "a loincloth civilization."[72] Neither was he asking others to adopt his symbol.[73]

However, as befits a symbol, different people saw different things in it. Winston Churchill saw in it defiance of the empire, something that deeply disturbed him. It was "alarming, and also nauseating," he said, "to see Mr. Gandhi, a seditious Middle Temple lawyer, now posing as a fakir of a type well-known in the East, striding half-naked up the steps of the Viceregal palace ... to parley on equal terms with the representative of the King-Emperor."[74] Gandhi took the remark in good humor, thanking him for free, worldwide publicity.[75] J. C. Hill, a cartoonist of the *Auckland Star* (New Zealand), thought that the loincloth separated Gandhi morally from the rest of the world leaders of the day. Entitled "The Shirted and the Shirtless," the cartoon had seven of the world leaders standing in a single line, looking at a shirtless Gandhi sitting in a corner. Roosevelt was in a "thousand billion dollar shirt," Hitler in a brown shirt, Mussolini in a black shirt, Stalin in a red shirt, de Valera in a green shirt, Blum in a blue shirt, and the British prime minister in a "slump shirt." And they were saying in unison, "And he ain't wearin' any bloomin' shirt at all."

Beverley Nichols, a contemporary British writer, argued that Gandhi's shirtlessness itself was an ideology, especially in the light of his insistence on *khadi* (home-spun cloth). As an ideology, shirtlessness was not morally all that different from the choice of the shirts that the rest of the world

[69] CW, 21: 225.   [70] Ibid., p. 226.   [71] Bose, *My Days With Gandhi*, p. 141.
[72] CW, 46: 55.   [73] CW, 21: 226.
[74] M. Gilbert, *Winston S. Churchill*, vol. V (London: Heinemann, 1976), p. 390.
[75] CW, 46: 54.

leaders had made.[76] Still others read into it an ascetic meaning of renunciation. For Gandhi, however, it was the ultimate secular symbol of artha, which meant, in this case, the urgent need for plentiful supply of "food, clothing, and other necessities of life."[77]

The Gandhi–Tagore debate 1921–25

We conclude this chapter with a brief analysis of the celebrated debate between Gandhi and Tagore. It was one of the major events of modern Indian intellectual history. Initiated by Tagore, it covered two of Gandhi's key programmes – the non-cooperation movement and the introduction of the spinning wheel (the *charkha*) as a means to arouse public opinion regarding the plight of the poor. Its broader context was, of course, the relationship of art to society, or poetry to politics. It was between a poet (a Nobel laureate at that) and a statesman – Gandhi often referred to his friendly adversary as "the poet" or "the bard of Shantiniketan." Perhaps it is more accurate to say that it was a debate between two complementary visions of what the relationship of art to society should be.

Tagore had two complaints to make about the non-cooperation movement. The first was that it was a form of political asceticism. Students were asked to leave their books and lawyers their courtrooms. The merchants were to cancel their foreign contracts and those possessing foreign clothes were to make a bonfire of them. Secondly, it was widening the distance between East and West. What India needed was cooperation with the West, just as what the West needed was a deeper understanding of India. Truth led to unity among nations while delusion led to separateness. And separateness in this case was "spiritual suicide" too.[78]

Gandhi's reply, entitled "The Poet's Anxiety," sought to reassure Tagore that he was not trying to erect a Chinese wall between East and West. Non-cooperation was nothing but India's response to colonial "compulsory cooperation," "one-sided combination," and "armed imposition." Under colonial domination India had lost its capacity to say "no." Non-cooperation was the "nation's notice" that it was no longer satisfied to be in tutelage. Colonialism could last only as long as the colonized cooperated with the colonizer. The moment they withdrew their cooperation, it would begin to crumble.[79]

---

[76] For an analysis of Nichols' "fascist" interpretation of this cartoon, see Tarlo, *Clothing Matters*, pp. 79–80.
[77] CW, 81: 402.   [78] Ibid., p. 540.   [79] CW, 20: 162–64.

In an article entitled "The Call to Truth" Tagore attacked what he called "the cult" of the spinning wheel. Gandhi's insistence that it was the instrument for attaining swaraj and his demand that every Indian should engage in spinning were unacceptable. In Tagore's view, swaraj required a variety of economic activities, not just spinning and weaving. To focus solely on these was foolish, especially since their economic utility remained uncertain. Yet to one and all, the Mahatma was saying "spin and weave, spin and weave." Where was the argument, Tagore wanted to know. People were following the Mahatma not because of conviction but because of devotion. Such attitude only deepened the habit of blind obedience, which was in part one reason why the poor remained poor. What was needed was independence of thought and the freedom to engage in all kinds of economic activities, not just spinning.[80]

Gandhi conceded that blind faith in him did not help matters. But there was reason behind the spinning wheel – to make the Indian elite aware of the economic crisis in the nation. Poverty was due in part to the lack of work for the vast majority of the Indian people. In the absence of any work, spinning and weaving could give them something to do. If they engaged in it in an organized way they could acquire skills which they did not now possess, but which they could later transfer to other areas of economic life – self-discipline, economic motivation, the habit of saving, the ability to work with others, etc.

The elite had to spin in order to acquire an aesthetic experience of what poverty meant. A plea for the spinning wheel was a plea for raising the conscience of the nation. Gandhi was not suggesting that spinning and weaving were the only things needed for swaraj. They marked only a "transitional stage" before better economic opportunities would become available to the poor. In the meantime it filled an economic vacuum. Where was the argument for the spinning wheel, Tagore had asked. "Hunger" was the argument, was Gandhi's reply. What the hungry needed was not poetry but work. They had to earn their bread by the sweat of their brow. Only then would they regain their dignity as human beings. But in order for that to happen, they had to find work. Until better work became available they should spin and weave and produce home-spun cloth.

The elite, Gandhi conceded, did not need to spin for economic reason. But they needed to spin for aesthetic reason. Spinning daily for half an hour, he believed, would awaken them from their political slumber. Even

---

[80] For the text of Tagore's article see William T. de Bary (ed.), *Sources of Indian Tradition* (New York: Columbia University Press, 1958), pp. 792–98.

Tagore's poetry might improve, Gandhi was convinced, if he engaged in spinning as an aesthetic exercise.[81]

The debate helped clarify the complex issue of mass poverty. In addition, it enabled the two great figures to understand each other a little better. They understood each other's strengths and weaknesses. Tagore, Gandhi realized, was an inventor, whereas he was only an explorer. Tagore lived (and had to live) in a world of his own creation, whereas he remained a slave of someone else's creation – the spinning wheel. Tagore created new things day by day, whereas he could only show the hidden possibilities of old things. These differences were real but complementary, and not antagonistic.[82]

In the end Gandhi came to regard the spinning wheel as a poet would, as a symbol. Tagore came to see that poverty had to be experienced aesthetically by the economic elite that controlled the reins of economic power. Gandhi was implementing a Ruskinian norm according to which labor must be made available to all, and necessities should have priority over luxuries. Arts could not long flourish in an impoverished society. Gandhi's approach was critically examined, but not abandoned. It came out stronger for having been critically assessed. And it met with Tagore's final approval. He came to realize that there was an aesthetic element in Gandhi's seeming asceticism. "I have learnt to understand him as I would understand an artist," Tagore wrote in 1938.[83] Coming as it does from a great artist, this assessment is of great value to all those who want to understand Gandhi.

---

[81] CW, 21: 287–91; CW, 28: 427.   [82] Ibid., p. 426.
[83] Cited in Sumitra Roy-Chowdhury, *The Gurudev and the Mahatma* (Calcutta: Shubhada Saraswat, 1982), p. 152.

Part V

Spiritual liberation

Gandhi's thoughts on moksha or spiritual liberation are analyzed in chapter 10. Rather than make a philosophical analysis of liberation, as do the six systems of Indian philosophy, he took the indirect route to liberation through the *Bhagavad Gita*. For one thing, he was not in the least interested in metaphysical analysis. For another, he found in the *Gita* all that he needed to know about the pursuit of liberation.

10   The *Gita* and moksha

"The object of the *Gita* appears to me to be that of showing the most
excellent way to attain self-realization."[1]

The pursuit of moksha, it is by now almost trite to say, supplied the force
unifying all of Gandhi's different activities. It was also the unifying aim
of his practical philosophy. "What I have been striving and pining to
achieve," the famous Introduction to his autobiography runs, was self-
realization or moksha. He lived and moved and had his being in the
pursuit of that goal.[2] In this he was in full accord with the entire Hindu
tradition. "Self-knowledge" (*atma vidya*), as Sankara had pointed out,
was a "human good" (purushartha), and in realizing Brahman one realized "all the end of man" (purushartha).[3]

Though not a theologian, Gandhi's concept of moksha was fully
informed of its many theological nuances. Taken negatively, it was liberation from existence in time, from *samsara*, the cycle of birth, death, and
rebirth. Again, in the negative sense, it was freedom from the debt one
owed to karma. Taken positively, it was the attainment of either identity
with Brahman or union with *Ishwara*, depending on one's philosophic
orientation. The terminology that he used took these nuances into
account. To take just one of his writings, the autobiography, we find him
using at least eight different expressions for the same concept, which it is
useful to take note of here. In the English translation the philosophical-
theological flavor of the original Gujarati is lost. When the emphasis is
on Brahman, moksha is understood as the "realization of Brahman"
(*Brahma darsan*).[4] When the emphasis is on atman, it is referred to as
"self-realization" (*atma-darsan* or *atma-gyan*).[5] When the emphasis is on
Truth, it is called the "realization of Absolute Truth" (*satyano-sakshatkar*)
or "seeing the universal and all pervading spirit of Truth face to face"

[1] CW, 41: 94.   [2] CW, 39: 3.
[3] K. H. Potter (ed.), *Encyclopaedia of Indian Philosophies: Advaita up to Sankara and His
Pupils* (Princeton: Princeton University Press, 1981), p. 388 and p. 457.
[4] CW, 39: 168.   [5] Ibid., pp. 3, 130, 270.

(*satya narayana-praktyaksha-sakshatkar*).[6] When the emphasis is on God it is termed "seeing God face to face" (*ishwarno-sakshatkar*), or "God-realization" (*paramatmana-sakshatkar*) or "seeing the Highest" (*ishwar darsan*).[7] This is not to forget that he had his ecumenical moments too, as when he identified moksha with "the Kingdom of Heaven" familiar to Christians.[8]

One of his major concerns was to rescue the pursuit of moksha as a goal from the apathy with which the majority regarded it. As Kane, the great historian of *Dharmasastra*, had pointed out, the vast majority looked upon it as an ideal to be attained "in the most distant future," but not now, in the present life.[9] Julius Lipner shares Kane's realism. A great many did not actively expect or even seek some post-mortem salvation or liberation. They were most concerned "just to stay afloat" as they continued life's journey over the hazardous waters of *samsara*.[10] Duncan M. Derrett seemed to concur: there was a noticeable "decline of the desire for moksha" in modern India.[11]

Part of the explanation for the apathy lay in the "superstition" (Gandhi's word) that it could be attained only in the last stage of life, viz., *sannyasa*. Those who deferred it until then, he observed, would attain, not self-realization, but "a second and pitiable childhood, living as a burden on this earth."[12] This was yet another evidence that the *ashrama* system had outlived its usefulness. The *ashrama* system needed to be set aside and the pursuit of moksha made part of ordinary, day-to-day life. As he put it wryly, in order to pursue moksha, it was not necessary for him to seek the shelter of the cave; for he carried the cave about him.[13] As Margaret Chatterjee has noted, he "rethought" the philosophy of moksha.[14]

Moksha as a pursuit and as an achieved state of affairs

Part of the rethinking involved making a crucial distinction between moksha as an achieved state of affairs and moksha as a pursuit. Gandhi approached moksha not as an abstract or imagined goal, but as a goal to be realized in history, in and through action in time. He fought against the traditional otherworldly approach. Though moksha had its culmination

---

[6] Ibid., pp. 4, 401.   [7] Ibid., pp. 401, 171, 266.   [8] CW, 23: 349.
[9] Kane, *History of Dharmasastra*, vol. II, part 1, p. 8.   [10] Lipner, *Hindus*, p. 324.
[11] J. D. M. Derrett, "Social and Political Thought and Institutions," in A. L. Basham (ed.), *A Cultural History of India* (Delhi: Oxford University Press, 1998), p. 139.
[12] CW, 39: 270.   [13] CW, 23: 349.
[14] See Chatterjee, *Gandhi's Religious Thought*, ch. 9, "Moksha Rethought."

outside time, its actual pursuit took place gradually and in time. Yogis spent a good deal of time speculating on what the nature of moksha as an achieved state of affairs might be. He had no use for such speculations. He believed that those who indulged in them were only deceiving others (perhaps themselves too) – a strong condemnation, if ever there was one. The truth was, he claimed, that those whom the world knew as yogis were not really yogis. What they described as the four states of moksha – *salokya* (sharing the divine ambience), *samipya* (sharing the divine presence), *sarupya* (becoming an aspect of God), and *sayujya* (becoming conjoined with, or totally absorbed in, God) – were nothing but spiritual fantasies.[15] "These phrases are used merely to deceive the world."[16] Those who really lived a contemplative life paid no attention to them; they would outwardly seem "as people of the world." Their mind might be absorbed in God all the hours of the day, but they would move in the world "like other men."[17]

Even more radical was his rejection of the theory of *jivanmukta*, life in the world even after the attainment of liberation (*bodhisattva* in Buddhism). Preoccupation with this theory was yet another example of indulging in empty speculation. Major Hindu thinkers including Sankara, Ramanuja, and Madhva had given serious consideration to the possibility of living in the world after the attainment of liberation.[18] Two of Gandhi's contemporaries, Sri Aurobindo and Ramana Maharshi, were thought by many to have achieved the status of liberated souls. Liberated or not, they withdrew themselves from taking any active part in political life. Ramana Maharshi was on record as saying that Gandhi, though a good person, was sacrificing his "spiritual development" by taking too great burdens upon himself.[19] This was similar in spirit to the warning from Rajchandbhai that "for the good of his soul" he should not get too involved in the politics of Natal.[20]

The old notion that the pursuit of moksha, if it was to have any credibility, required the withdrawal from the world was alive and well even in Gandhi's time. No one gave greater currency to it than did Sri Aurobindo. He was so absorbed in his spiritual pursuits that he considered giving Gandhi a private interview an unwarranted distraction. The Mahatma had written "a long letter" requesting an interview.[21] Sri Aurobindo replied in "a short letter," in pencil, that the request could not

---

[15] CW, 32: 143. For the meaning of the four modes of moksha, see Lipner, *Hindus*, p. 323.
[16] CW, 32: 143.   [17] Ibid.
[18] For a recent survey of this idea in Hindu thought see A. O. Fort and P. Mumme (eds.), *Living Liberation in Hindu Thought* (Albany: State University of New York Press, 1996).
[19] B. R. Nanda, *Gandhi and His Critics*, p. 143.   [20] Ibid.
[21] This letter is not available, but it was written before 12 January 1934; see CW, 56: 500.

be granted.[22] He instructed one of his disciples to write that he was unable to see him because for a long time past he had made it an absolute rule not to have any interview with anyone. He would not even speak with his own disciples, giving them only silent blessings three times a year. All requests for an interview from others he had been obliged to refuse. The rule had been imposed on him by himself, or rather by the necessity of his *sadhana* (spiritual pursuit). The time had not come when he could depart from it.[23]

Gandhi took the refusal in his stride, stating that it was "courteous."[24] His personal respect for him remained undiminished. He recognized the cultural significance of mystics like him and Ramana Maharshi.[25] However, on philosophical grounds, he was dubious of the view that the pursuit of moksha required the sort of withdrawal from the world that Sri Aurobindo had adopted. He remained skeptical of the idea of *jivanmukta* too. As for himself he did not aspire to that condition, considering himself only as an aspirant after self-realization. Sri Aurobindo and Ramana Maharshi, he remarked, were "known to be," and perhaps were, realized souls. "Anyway their followers attributed to them full realization."[26]

The reason for Gandhi's skepticism was straightforward. He explained it in the following way. "[N]o one can be called a *mukta* [a liberated person] while he is still alive; one may be said at the most to have become fit for moksha … We must, therefore, say that the Dweller in the body cannot be free while He dwells in it … If it [moksha] is the most important thing in life, it should be clear to us that it cannot be attained while we live in this body. Till the gate of the body prison has opened, the fragrance of moksha is beyond our experience. Whether terrible or not, this is the truth."[27]

Throughout his life he fought against the otherworldly, esoteric approach to moksha. Indeed, finding an alternative route to it became one of his important life missions. In the *Bhagavad Gita*, he thought, he had found it. It was for him "the most excellent way," suited to the modern times.

Gandhi's competence in interpreting the *Gita*

The *Gita* was the single most important influence on his life. It was, as he said, the dictionary of daily spiritual life. His active interest in it began in

---

[22] This letter is not available, but it is referred to in ibid., n. 1.   [23] Cited in ibid.
[24] CW, 57: 113. However, we learn that he did give "a long interview" later in his life to K. M. Munshi. See R. R. Diwakar, *Mahayogi: Life, Sadhana and Teaching of Sri Aurobindo* (Bombay: Bharatiya Vidya Bhavan, 1954), p. ix.
[25] CW, 68: 298.   [26] Ibid., p. 40.   [27] CW, 32: 136–37.

1889, while he was still a law student in London. He read the whole of it for the first time in Sir Edwin Arnold's translation, *The Song Celestial*. From then on he began to recite the last nineteen verses of the second chapter as part of his daily prayer. And his "young mind," he tells us, began "to unify" the teachings of the *Gita*, the Buddha, and the Sermon on the Mount.[28] By 1903, he had taught himself enough Sanskrit to be able to read it in the original.

During his prison term of 1922–24, he spent part of his time preparing a *Concordance* (*Gita Padartha Kosha*) of the book, his first work on the *Gita*. Having never made a concordance of any work, he taught himself how to make one, spending twenty minutes daily for eighteen months. The outcome was that he now knew "where and how often" a particular word occurred in the work.[29] Though completed in 1924, it was not published until 1936.[30]

The *Concordance* prepared him to produce his second major work on the *Gita*, *Gandhijinu Gita-Shikshan*, known in its English translation under the title *Discourses on the Gita*. It was a commentary on each of the 700 verses of the work, given as homilies in 1926, to the inmates of the Sabarmati Ashram. It was published posthumously in 1955, based on the notes taken by Mahadev Desai, his secretary and Punjabhai, one of Desai's colleagues.[31]

This was followed in 1930 by the publication of his third, and by far his most important, work on the book – a translation from Sanskrit into Gujarati, entitled *Anasakti Yoga*. Significantly its publication on 12 March 1930 coincided with the commencement of the most famous satyagraha of his life, the Salt March. The timing underlined the political implications of the book.

Gandhi had a special reason for producing this Gujarati translation. This was to verify a principle dear to him, viz., the value of a translation of a book like the *Gita* would gain in authority and impact if the translator had implemented its teaching in his or her life. Due to the fact that he had spent more than forty years implementing its teaching in his personal life, he felt a special obligation to translate it. This did not mean any disrespect, he pointed out, for the other translations, each of which had its own unique value. He only wished that those Gujaratis who read his translation would be helped to shape their lives according to its teachings.[32]

There was another reason for producing a vernacular translation. It was to make the *Gita* available to those who were hitherto barred from reading

---

[28] CW, 39: 61.   [29] CW, 25: 155.   [30] For the Preface see CW, 63: 310–12.
[31] For the full text see CW, 32: 94–376.   [32] CW, 41: 92.

it – "women, the commercial class, the so-called Shudras and the like."
They had "little or no literary equipment," neither the desire nor the time
to read it in the original, and yet stood in need of its support. That was
why even his "unscholarly" Gujarati did not inhibit him from undertaking
the translation.[33]

Finally, he had a broader interest that went beyond Gujarat and
Gujaratis. For this reason he had Mahadev Desai, his secretary, translate
it into English. It was published under the title *The Gospel of Selfless Action
or Gita According to Gandhi.*[34] For he believed that its teachings transcended not only gender and caste differences, but also religious differences. It was a work "persons belonging to all faiths" could read. It did
not favor "any sectarian point of view." It taught "nothing but pure
ethics."[35]

Gandhi's fourth and final work on the *Gita*, entitled *Gita-bodh*, was also
a work done in prison. The English translation of it is known under the
title *Letters on the Gita*. Originally a series of eighteen letters, one on each
of the eighteen chapters of the book, written from Yeravda Prison,
between 1930 and 1932, they were to be read aloud to the members of
the Ashram.[36]

Gandhi charts his own course

His concordance, translations, and commentaries had given him sufficient credibility as a *Gita* interpreter. To add to this, he had also read all
the major classical commentaries on the work, as well as contemporary
commentaries such as those of B. G. Tilak and Sri Aurobindo. However,
he was not fully satisfied with any of them. Sankara, Ramanuja, Madhva,
and Vallabha, he wrote, were all dear to him. He had relished "delicacies
from all," but had not been able to satisfy his hunger through what he got
from "any of them."[37] They required withdrawal from the world as an
indispensable condition for any serious pursuit of moksha. The real world
of politics, economics, and social reform, the field of artha, did not
interest them. Besides, they presupposed the continued relevance of the
caste and the *ashrama* systems. These systems had by now lost their
ethical legitimacy. Any interpretation of the *Gita* for the present times
had to take these important changes into account. It was his "hunger" to
meet the present needs that the classical interpreters had failed to satisfy.

---

[33] Ibid.
[34] The text of the English translation and its Introduction are found in ibid., pp. 90–133.
[35] CW, 32: 350.   [36] CW, 49: 111–49.   [37] CW, 34: 93.

Sri Aurobindo's commentaries fared no better.[38] He had no intention of "going spiritual" the way the yogi of Pondicherry had gone.[39] The latter's alleged experience of moksha on 24 November 1926 had made him withdraw completely from the real world of politics, economics, and social reform.[40] Even meeting a person such as Gandhi, as we saw, was thought by him to be an obstacle to life divine. There was no question of someone like Sri Aurobindo visiting a poor village around Pondicherry or parleying with a viceroy, or a Jinnah, or an Ambedkar. All this would have been deemed inconsistent with the spiritual life. Gandhi could not accept such an esoteric mode of seeking self-realization. For him in the embodied state, i.e., in historical time, the quest was the real thing. "An ideal ceases to be an ideal if it is realized. One can contemplate it, come ever closer to it, but never reach it," was his position.[41]

Gandhi's difficulty with Tilak's interpretation of the *Gita* was of a different kind.[42] For the latter also believed that taking part in politics was consistent with the teachings of the *Gita*. Unfortunately by politics he meant modern politics, the politics of violence and "tit for tat," politics as "a game of worldly people," and not of spiritual people.[43] Spirituality therefore had no place in the practice of modern politics.

Gandhi took exception to Tilak's political theory, accusing him of defending the doctrine that everything was fair in politics.[44] If this doctrine were accepted, he insisted, politics would become "thoroughly corrupt." It was his view that only "the strictest adherence to honesty, fair play and charity" could advance "the true interests" of politics.[45] And the true interests of politics required that it be treated as a mode of achieving purushartha and, therefore, as being compatible with the spiritual ends of the practitioner of politics.

In charting his own course in the interpretation of the *Gita*, Gandhi wanted to avoid the Scylla of doctrinaire secularism and the Charybdis of traditional asceticism. He wanted a course that would affirm the values of the world and the purusharthas on the one hand and those of a world-transcending spirituality open to every human being on the other. To accomplish this he had to reaffirm the dynamic nature of the relationship

---

[38] Gandhi had read Sri Aurobindo's *Essays on the Gita* in Purani's translation known under the title *Gita-nishkarsha* (CW, 23: 179).

[39] CW, 52: 37.

[40] The following is Diwakar's description of what happened to Sri Aurobindo on 24 November 1926, called "the date of victory." "The coming down of the Overmind leading to the descent of the Supermind to the earth-consciousness. Observed since then as the day of victory." Diwakar, *Mahayogi*, p. 258.

[41] CW, 88: 70.   [42] Gandhi had read Tilak's *Gita-Rahasya*. See CW, 41: 91.

[43] CW, 16: 490–91.   [44] Ibid., p. 484.   [45] Ibid.

of the four purusharthas among themselves. As mentioned in chapter 1, that was exactly what he did in the Introduction to his Gujarati translation of the *Gita*. There he rejected the "common opinion" that the pursuit of moksha had nothing to do with that of artha. In his opinion, there was no evidence in the *Gita* of any opposition between these two pursuits. On the contrary it taught that in performing one's duties rightly – whatever they might be, whether political or economic or any other – one could attain the goal of moksha.[46]

From a historical perspective Gandhi's project of attempting to bring the four purusharthas closer together was of the greatest significance. It put an end to the historic estrangement between the political and the spiritual. The separation of artha from dharma and moksha – politics from ethics and spirituality – was at the root of India's political and economic stagnation. As Daya Krishna has pointed out, there was the longstanding tradition, going back to the beginning of *sramanic* (ascetic) tradition, of seeing moksha as the negation, not the fulfillment, of the other three purusharthas. The family, society, the nation, and the state had to suffer as a consequence. The spiritual life was seen as a "male-centric" and "self-centric" pursuit. The Advaita doctrine of moksha, in Daya Krishna's view, went so far as to deny the ultimate reality of the "other." Even in the non-Advaita doctrines reality was attributed to the self "primarily" in relation to the Lord, and only "secondarily" in relation to other selves. Basically the relationship of one self to another self, Daya Krishna explained, was "mediated through the relation of each to the Lord."[47]

Gandhi modified the traditional approach to moksha. According to him the fact that human beings had a soul – a spark of the divine – in them, placed on them the natural obligation to love and serve one another. It also provided the foundation for their inalienable right to be free, respected, and not violated by others. In linking their spiritual nature to their political rights Gandhi went beyond all the great figures of modern India. In this regard, he went beyond even Swami Vivekananda. The latter had urged Indians to get involved in social action, philanthropic work, care for the poor, etc., but not politics, especially if it involved acting against the colonial state. "Let no political significance be ever attached falsely to any of my writing or sayings," was his injunction.[48]

---

[46] CW, 41: 98.

[47] See Krishna, *Indian Philosophy: A Counter Perspective*, pp. 7, 43, 197–98. Also Dumont, *Homo Hierarchicus*, p. 274.

[48] R. Rolland, *The Life of Vivekananda and Universal Gospel*, translated by E. F. Malcolm-Smith (Almora, India: Advaita Ashram, 1965), p. 103, n. 1.

India would remain immortal if she persisted in her search for God. But if she went in "for politics and social conflict" she would die.[49] We witness here, once again, the paralyzing fear of the political on the part of those who pursue the spiritual. It was Gandhi who found a way of overcoming this fear, and he found the inspiration for it in the *Gita*.

To understand his approach to the *Gita*, it is important to know his rules of interpretation. It was for him not a historical work.[50] Neither was it an "aphoristic work," like the *Brahmasutra*; it was basically a poetic work.[51] The poet put across his vision of reality with the aid of concepts available to his time. However, the meaning of concepts changed with time, and to this extent a poet's meaning would be open to reinterpretation. This was not a theological issue, but a socio-linguistic one. The poet could not foresee how the meaning of concepts that he or she used would change with time. In the case of the *Gita*, for example, the meanings of certain key concepts such as "sacrifice" (*yagna*), "work," and "warfare" have changed with time. At one time sacrifice meant human sacrifice; later it meant animal sacrifice. In the *Gita* it meant action dedicated to the Lord. Similarly, at one time, work was forbidden to those who pursued moksha. That was how the pursuit of moksha came to be associated with *sannyasa* (the last stage of life). In the *Gita* work does not mean abstention from work, but only from selfish motives. Likewise, the war between members of a feuding royal family might have been the background of the original story in the *Gita*. Its central teaching was not about the legitimacy or illegitimacy of war, but about how to perform one's duties without the tinge of egoism. A present-day interpreter of the *Gita* must take into account the history of the ideas contained in it, and interpret them the way he or she thinks fit, provided the fundamental teaching is preserved and communicated. The *Gita* was a work meant for "the people at large," and not for specialists, such as yogis and academics. That was why there were plenty of what Gandhi called "pleasing repetitions" in it. But "the seeker" was at liberty to extract from this treasure any meaning he liked so as to enable him to enforce in his life its central teaching.[52]

There was another interpretative issue that had to be taken into account, and that was the role that Krishna played in the *Gita*. Arjuna had to find his way to moksha by himself, by acting according to *his* calling, *svadharma*. Krishna was only his guide. His guidance would be helpful because He was an avatar of Vishnu. But then what was an avatar? The question was of critical importance to Gandhi.

---

[49] Ibid., p. 168.   [50] CW, 15: 288.   [51] CW, 41: 100.   [52] Ibid.

He had been mulling over this question from at least 1894. The nature of Rama and Krishna as avatars was among the questions he had raised in his famous letter to Rajchandbhai that he wrote that year. "Rama and Krishna are described as incarnations of God. What does that mean? Were they God Himself or only part of Him? Can we attain moksha through faith in them?"[53] Rajchandbhai replied that they could be considered God in so far as they had realized the atman in them, i.e., in so far as they had attained moksha. But faith in them could not produce moksha. It had to be achieved by each person by himself or herself.[54]

The notion that an avatar was really a self-realized human, one who had attained a divine status by attaining moksha, stayed with Gandhi throughout his life. Avatar, therefore, did not mean any descent of God into human form; it meant, instead, the ascent of humans to divine status. In as much as avatar was related to the successful achievement of moksha, it was open to every human being to become an avatar. In attributing it to specific human beings, such as Rama or Krishna, human imagination played a key role. Whenever society found itself in morally and spiritually desperate times, "belief in avatar [came] to prevail." Those who stood against the prevailing wickedness and immorality were looked upon as avatars – normally after their death.[55]

Regarding Krishna specifically, the Introduction to the Gujarati translation described him as "perfection and right knowledge personified." "The perfection," however, was "imagined." The idea of a perfect incarnation was "an after growth." The status of an avatar was ascribed to him because of the extraordinary achievements of his life, and, of course, because of his successful attainment of moksha. That was why Krishna enjoyed, and still enjoys, "the status of the most perfect incarnation."[56] In *Gita* IV: 6 this was how Krishna revealed himself as an avatar: "Though unborn and inexhaustible in My essence, though Lord of all beings, yet assuming control over My nature, I come into being by My mysterious power [*maya*]."

Gandhi's comments on this were as follows. "It is not as if God comes down from above. It would be right to say, if we can say it without egotism, that each one of us is an avatar."[57] The atman in each human being seeks moksha, i.e., yearns to become divine. "When Krishna says that He incarnates Himself as a human being, he only uses the idiom of common speech. God never incarnates Himself as an atman and is never born as a human being. He is ever the same. When from our human point of view, we see special excellence in some individual we look upon him as

[53] For the letter of Gandhi to Rajchandbhai of 20 October 1894, see CW, 32: 601.
[54] Ibid., p. 601.   [55] CW, 12: 126.   [56] CW, 41: 94.   [57] CW, 32: 189.

an avatar. In God's language there is no such word as avatar; it exists only in the language of human beings."[58]

Even as late as 1947 he held on to the same view. To say that "God incarnated in the form of a man only means that that man has more godliness in him than other men ... We call Rama and Krishna incarnations of God because people saw divinity in them. In truth Krishna and others exist in man's imagination – they are creations of his imagination. Whether they were historical figures or not, has nothing to do with man's imagination."[59]

The role that imagination plays in understanding the status of Krishna in the *Gita* accords well with his basic claim that it is more a work of religious poetry than religious philosophy. It is obviously true that its teachings gain in authority and validity in the eyes of popular readers because they are seen as coming from Krishna, the eighth avatar of Vishnu. Devotion to him rests on the belief that he attained the divine status by successfully attaining moksha, and devotion to him is helpful to Arjuna, who is seeking to attain moksha. But devotion to Krishna by itself would not produce moksha, it could be produced only by Arjuna's own effort or purushartha. Krishna is not a savior, but a divine counsellor. Arjuna's liberation has to be achieved by Arjuna, for Arjuna, and the key to this is selfless action. In order to act selflessly, Arjuna – any human being – must acquire certain moral and spiritual qualities, comprehensively termed as "stable wisdom." Arjuna – and every aspirant after moksha – therefore, must become "a person of stable wisdom" a *sthitha-prajana*, famously described in *Gita* II: 54–72.

The person of stable wisdom (*sthitha-prajna*)

Striving for stable wisdom, propelled by a combination of self-discipline and daily spiritual exercises, is the *conditio sine qua non* of the pursuit of moksha. The last nineteen verses of *Gita* II draw the portrait of the person who strives in this fashion. They occupy a unique place in Gandhi's interpretation of the *Gita*. For him they constitute the book's *mahavakya*, "great saying."[60] As mentioned, from 1889 onward, when he first came across them, until the day of his death in 1948, he had recited them every day, as part of his daily evening prayers. They remained, he said, "engraved" in his heart. For him they embodied "the essence of dharma," and the principles enunciated by them were "immutable."[61] They prepared the moral and spiritual conditions necessary

---

[58] Ibid.   [59] CW, 88: 148.   [60] Jordens, *Gandhi's Religion*, p. 139.   [61] CW, 28: 316.

for the pursuit of moksha, viz., achievement of the enlightenment of the intellect (*buddhi*) brought about by self-discipline and divine assistance. Throughout his life he regarded the *sthitha-prajna* as his model of life.

To understand the process of self-discipline that the *sthitha-prajna* is engaged in – and all aspirants after moksha are invited to engage in – it is necessary to bear in mind the basics of the underlying psychology. There is, first of all, the matter–spirit, body–soul duality of human nature. The inner human world is made up of the senses, the mind, the ego, the intellect, and the Self, "a minute part of God" (*Gita* XV: 7) that dwells within humans. All except the Self are parts of nature. There is a struggle between matter and spirit, body and soul. Success in this struggle depends on the influence that the Self radiates over the senses, the mind, the ego, and the intellect. For this "radiation" to take place, the senses, which are the seats of the passions, must be brought under control of the mind, which is the seat of discursive reason. For the mind to be able to influence the senses, it must be open to the influence of the intellect, the faculty nearest to the Self. If the intellect becomes enlightened, the passions become rightly ordered, the ego becomes pliable, and self-discipline becomes a possibility. Otherwise, the passions remain disorderly and harmful to the interests of the Self. The ego will remain the attention-seeking centre of human existence. Without a spiritual enlightenment humans cannot cease to be egotists, and self-discipline is out of the reach of the egotist. Self-discipline maintains the basic condition necessary for spiritual enlightenment and the pursuit of moksha. The combination of self-discipline and self-enlightenment produces stable wisdom. Stability in this wisdom is what the *sthitha-prajna* achieves. As long as one lived one was not sure of maintaining the stability, which was the reason why Gandhi had to pray daily for the grace to remain stable.

The contents of those famous nineteen verses may now be briefly analyzed. A person of stable wisdom is one who, knowing what the ultimate purpose in life (moksha) is, takes all the necessary means to attain it. In choosing the means, such a person remains highly self-disciplined, taking only those means that are conducive to the end, regardless of personal likes or dislikes of a given means. The major obstacles to the choice of right means are internal to the individual – the disorderly state of the passions. The following passions are specifically mentioned – lust (*kama*), anger (*krodha*), bewilderment (*moha*), delusion (vv. 62–63), possessive individualism (the feeling of "this is mine") and radical egotism (the feeling of "this I am") (v. 71).

One way of overcoming these obstacles is to acquire an evenness of temper or equanimity in choosing the most apt means to the end. In choosing them such a person would not be swayed by considerations of pleasure or pain, sorrow or joy, success or failure, appetites or aversions (vv. 56, 57, 64).

A second way of overcoming the internal obstacle is to engage in the practice of daily spiritual exercises – prayer, meditation, and the like – by which the intellect (*buddhi*) is brought into close contact with the Self that dwells within. The outcome is that the seeker gradually becomes content with the Self (v. 55). This contentment removes even the residual remnants of the disorderly passions. Self-discipline or self-effort by itself cannot bring about this contentment, only "the vision of the Supreme" can do it (v. 59).

There is yet a third means necessary to put order in our passions, and that is to become "intent on God" (*mat-parah*) – in this case, on Krishna, the divine avatar (v. 61). Contentment with the divine within has to be supplemented with communion with God, who is distinct from the seeker.

Assuming that these three steps are taken – self-discipline, contentment with the divine Self within, and love for God – the person of stable wisdom must be realistic and fully aware of the difficulties lurking on the path to spiritual progress. He or she should proceed, says the *Gita*, like a tortoise – with caution. Just as the tortoise withdraws its limbs inward when it senses danger, so the wise person should periodically withdraw inwards and seek self-analysis (v. 58).

Even all the caution in the world would sometimes fail. The passions have the power to tear the mind violently or to seduce it subtly (v. 60). Even the wisest person could be tossed about by the passions, like a ship on a stormy sea (v. 67). Hence the emphasis in these verses on stability in wisdom. It is not enough to be self-disciplined for a day or two. One has to be self-disciplined habitually.

The marks of a person of stable wisdom are easily recognized. As mentioned, he or she is content with the atman within (vv. 55, 57, 65) and is indifferent to the hardships of the means to be taken. As all the disorderly passions have disappeared (v. 56), such a person will remain peaceful and serene in adversity (vv. 64, 66). Such a person has truly undergone a spiritual enlightenment and, therefore, sees the world in a new light (v. 69). Such a person does not flee the world with all its turbulence. He or she is like the ocean whose depths remain calm, even though waters from turbulent rivers flow into it (v. 70). The passions are not suppressed but "sublimated into tranquillity," and integrated into a transformed personality.[62] The desires are not so much destroyed as

---

[62] Zaehner, *The Bhagavad-Gita*, p. 157.

purified.[63] Everything that contributes to the realization of purushartha of the seeker is preserved and enhanced.

The end result of stable wisdom is the attainment of the *brahmi-state*, the state of enlightenment of the *buddhi* (intellect). But this cannot take place until death (*anta kale*), as v. 72 explicitly states. As far as Gandhi is concerned, there is no hint here that the *sthitha-prajna* is the *jivanmukta* (one who has attained liberation while still living in time). The emphasis on stability contains a warning that he takes into account. The warning is that it would be highly foolish of a person to think that he or she is beyond failure. The metaphors of the tortoise and the ship caught in a storm suggest the distinct possibility of a fall, no matter how advanced one is in wisdom. As Gandhi wryly adds, "call no man good until he is dead."[64]

Three things come together in the notion of "stable wisdom." First, there is the desire to attain the ultimate end of existence, a desire that can sublimate all the other desires. This requires self-discipline and the subsequent enlightenment of the intellect (*buddhi*). Second, there is the spiritual transformation of the seeker achieved by the contentment with the higher Self. Third, there is the love (*bhakti*) that relates the wise person to the avatar. Surprisingly, Gandhi's favorite avatar is not Krishna, the ninth avatar and the charioteer of the *Gita*, but Rama, the seventh avatar, and the hero of the *Ramayana*.

Karma yoga: the path of action

Karma yoga or action is the real test of whether one is pursuing stable wisdom. Of the three paths mentioned in the *Gita* – those of action, knowledge, and devotion – Gandhi favored the path of action. Not that the others were ignored, but that he gave primacy to action. The reason was that the other two, if given undue emphasis, had a tendency to promote a world-abandoning sort of spirituality. Such spirituality did not do justice to the needs of human existence in time. It did not encourage work – socially and politically necessary work. It was a challenge that Indian spirituality had posed since the days of the Buddha, hence, as we saw in chapter 4, Gandhi's wonderment at why the Buddha did not ask his followers to devote more time to work than to prayer. The more he studied the *Gita*, the more he realized that it supported a world-affirming spirituality.

---

[63] On the idea of purification present in the *Gita* see Julius Lipner (ed.), *The Fruits of Our Desiring, An Enquiry into the Ethics of The Bhagavad Gita for Our Times* (Calgary: Bayeux Arts Inc., 1997).

[64] CW, 32: 146.

According to him, the obligation to engage in some socially useful work was universal. However, with this obligation came the question of the debt that karma brought with it. How to work, and yet not incur this debt, was the question. The answer was to work in such a way that karma would not extend its dark shadow on those who work. This was possible if work was done in the spirit of detachment, as selfless service. Work as selfless service did not mean work done for free. It only meant that work would be free of the harmful effects of karma. One would work, not to benefit the ego to the exclusion of others, but to benefit oneself as well as others, and society in general. This was Gandhi's new work ethic, one that would benefit everyone materially as well as spiritually. He raised ordinary work – whatever it was that one had to do to earn a livelihood – to a high level of spiritual efficiency.

In preferring work to contemplation and devotion, Gandhi was not undermining the importance of these other paths that the *Gita* also recognized. The metaphor that he used to expresses his thought brought this out very well: work was the sun, and contemplation and devotion were its satellites.[65] The spiritual "solar" system constituted a system – for contemplation and piety had their due share to contribute to the pursuit of the spiritual life.

For work to meet the standards of karma yoga several conditions had to be met. In the first place, it had to be done in a spirit of detachment: "work alone is your proper business, never the fruits thereof; let not your motive be the fruit of works," was the injunction of *Gita* II: 47. And according to *Gita* II: 51, "those who have renounced the fruit that is born of works, these will be freed from the bondage of re-birth."

Secondly, the work in question had to be in conformity with what was required (*niyatam*) of the worker, whether the requirements arose from the demands of universal ethics or those of the holy books (*Gita* 3: 8). That is, good intention alone was not enough. Work that was inherently evil could not be made good by appeal to good intention, as Nathuram Godse, Gandhi's assassin, attempted to do.

Thirdly, work had to contribute to the general welfare of the world (*lokasamgraha* – the welfare of all – *Gita* III: 20, 25). Action in the field of artha that did not meet some practical need, Gandhi implied, lacked in morality; it was an *a-dharma*.[66] *Lokasamgraha* included works done in the service of the nation.[67] The linking of karma yoga to political action, artha to moksha, was indeed an original contribution to political philosophy.

---

[65] CW, 41: 95.   [66] CW, 32: 152.   [67] CW, 49: 137.

Fourthly, the desire for moksha had to be present in whatever work humans engaged in. It would of course not be the immediate goal of the activities taking place in the field of artha. All the same, the human agent as a pursuer of purushartha could not afford to forget that moksha was the ultimate goal of life. That is, nothing that humans did may deliberately exclude the intention to attain moksha. In this sense, the fourth purushartha acted as an integrating force.

Fifthly, work had to be dedicated to God as an offering, as a sacrifice (*yagna*). As the *Gita* says everything that humans did incurred the debt of karma save those done in the spirit of sacrifice (III: 9 ff.). The idea was not unique to the *Gita*: one could find it in the Benedictine notion of "work as prayer" – *laborare est orare* – a notion with which Gandhi was quite familiar since his South African days.

The new work ethic rejected the hierarchical conception of work, for long the bane of the Indian social order. Thus it put paid to the caste concept of *svadharma* alluded to in *Gita* III: 35. One is no longer obliged to work in a job determined by one's caste. Gandhi often spoke of scavenging, perhaps the most despised work in the Indian scheme of things, and other "lowly" work as being honorable.[68] Everyone was encouraged to engage in these so-called menial jobs as a means of breaking down social barriers. The idle life of yogis who lived by begging was a form of anti-social behavior, hardly worthy of being considered an "offering" to God.

Sixthly, the new work ethic had to be conducive to promoting non-violence. Even though the *Gita* was not written specifically to teach non-violence – and Gandhi conceded this – its karma yoga as it was applied today had to promote non-violence.[69]

Finally, the success of the new work ethic would depend on the practice of daily contemplation and devotion to God (*bhakti*). The role of devotion, in particular, was indispensable. The idea was fully developed in chapter XII of the *Gita*, which, according to Gandhi, was worthy of being learned by heart.[70] The love of God complemented the self-discipline of the enlightened. In this way the new work ethic became more than a work ethic: it became a full-blown spirituality. The karma yogi was no ordinary worker: he or she was also a spiritually enlightened and devout worshipper. The self-disciplined *sthitha-prajna* was also a *bhakta* (devotee of God).

Gita XII: 6–20 gives a vivid description of devotion, paralleling that of stable wisdom in II: 54–72. Gandhi's commentary on these verses forms a fine synthesis of thought concerning action, contemplation, and

---

[68] CW, 32: 152, 184.   [69] CW, 41: 98; CW, 45: 96–97.   [70] Ibid., p. 125.

devotion. The enlightened and self-disciplined human agent is also a compassionate citizen who translates his or her love for God into the active service of fellow citizens.[71] The new work ethic has elements of secular ethic in it – in many instances its immediate object is the attainment of material well-being. At the same time, it is more than a secular ethic, for with the right motivation, it can lead to spiritual liberation as well.

Gandhi's interpretation of the *Gita* has achieved two important things. First, it has demystified the process of the pursuit of moksha without secularizing it. He did not see political liberation as a substitute for spiritual liberation. He has put an end to the historic stand-off between ordinary, everyday life and world-abandoning asceticism. The ordinary life for most people meant earning a livelihood, living in a political community, engaging in economic, political, and civic activities. The new work ethic would improve the quality of the ordinary life by introducing into it elements of duty and selfless service. Just as spirituality was demystified, so political and economic life was rescued from the path of selfish consumerism. The starting point of the successful pursuit of moksha, as Gandhi's interpretation of the *Gita* would have it, is self-enlightenment – however slight – brought about by self-discipline. It is then maintained by the daily practice of prayer, and love of God translated into selfless service.

Gandhi had hoped that this new work ethic would become part not only of a spiritual life, but also of the public philosophy of India, if not of all of humanity. For it was meant to be a form of praxis that cut across religious, national, and political lines. It is true that modern India has not formally accepted it as part of its public philosophy. However, there are many voluntary organizations that have adopted elements of it in their corporate activities. There are also many thoughtful Indians who have accepted it in their personal lives. The example of a very distinguished Indian Muslim Muhamad Currim Chagla – jurist, diplomat, cabinet minister, and statesman – comes to mind. He found in the ethic of the *Gita* the minimum basis for a public philosophy. This was how he concluded his autobiography: "I have, therefore, never empathized with the *sannyasi* [ascetic] ideal ... The better and more satisfying philosophy is the one that the *Bhagavad Gita* teaches – the philosophy of non-attachment. One must not give up anything, one must do one's duty in whatever stations of life one is placed; and having done one's duty one must remain indifferent to the results. The doing of the duty is in one's

---

[71] CW, 49: 137–38.

own hands – the achievement of results one must leave to Providence or whatever power it may be that guides our destinies."[72]

Nothing better reflects Gandhi's theory of karma yoga than does Chagla's statement. As he himself stated in his Introduction to the *Gita*, "Purushartha alone is within man's control, not the fruit thereof."[73] And, when exercised with the right disposition, it paves the path to human development in the comprehensive sense.

[72] M. C. Chagla, *Roses in December: An Autobiography* (Bombay: Bharatiya Vidya Bhavan, 1990), p. 475.

[73] CW, 41: 101. In Gujarati, "manushya keval purusharthano adhikari chche, parinamano nathi" (Mahadev Desai [ed.], *Anasakti Yoga* [Ahmedabad: Navajivan, 1930], p. 11).

11 Conclusion: the political and the spiritual

Gandhi's revaluation of the purusharthas had a special impact on his conception of the relationship of the political to the spiritual. This was not because he was a saintly man who chose to give his politics a spiritual orientation. More profoundly, this was because he had understood that their relationship had its grounding in truth – independently of any personal preferences. To understand Gandhi on this, however, we have first to understand his notions of truth (*satya*).

Truth (*satya*)

Anyone who reads his autobiography, *The Story of My Experiments with Truth*, will be struck by the role that the concepts of truth play in his life and thought. Participation in politics was for him one way of realizing truth. He used the term truth (*satya*) in different senses, which it is useful to review briefly. The term truth (*satya*) is derived from the Sanskrit *sat*, meaning Ultimate Reality, the ground of being. This is the sense in which it is used, for example, in a famous verse in the Brihad-Aranyaka Upanishad:

> From the unreal [*asat*] lead to the real [*sat*],
> From darkness lead me to light,
> From death lead me to immortality.[1]

Here truth is thought of as being the light that enlightens every mind and the life that leads to immortality. The attainment of truth understood in this sense is the goal towards which all human strivings are oriented. This verse was very important to him; it was included in the *Ashram Hymnal*,[2] and it was part of his daily prayer.

In a theological sense, truth was identified with God. In order to accommodate the secularists, the unbelievers, the Buddhists, and others he revised the standard formula "God is Truth" to read "Truth is God."

---

[1] Brihad-Aranyaka Upanishad, I, 3: 28.   [2] CW, 44: 399.

In simple terms, the end result of the soul's movement towards truth was nothing short of its union with the divine.

In an epistemic sense, truth was what humans sought in every act of knowing. This was especially true of philosophic knowledge.

Truth also meant truthfulness in communication between humans. In this sense it was one of the eleven virtues of his ethical system.

Then there was "relative truth" or practical truth, truth realized in action. The truth sought in politics, especially satyagraha, was relative truth.

Finally, linking all the above meanings, there was the notion of "truth realization," the undercurrent that gave human strivings their dynamism and final destination. In historical time, in *samsara*, what was crucial was the pursuit of truth; its full realization lay outside time, outside *samsara*.

The spiritual

We are now in a position to appreciate Gandhi's notion of the "spiritual." In general, it is that which concerns the pursuit of truth in all its diversity. More specifically, spirituality is concerned with the eternal in us as distinct from the temporal that surrounds us.

In another sense, the pursuit of the spiritual is concerned with the desire for communion with God. This meaning was consistent with his Vaishnava theism.

In still another sense, the spiritual is what concerns the welfare of the immortal "spirit" – purusha, or atman – that dwells within. In Gandhi's ordinary language the term used for spirit was soul. This concern expressed itself in many ways: for example, in the exercise of soul-force, as in satyagraha. All that contributed to and maintained the welfare of the soul was part of the spiritual life.

Gandhi's spirituality had a special affinity with the aesthetic elements in the human experience. He found in music a powerful means of expressing his spirituality. The perfection of the spiritual life could not be reached without the aid of the arts.

Very typically, the spiritual life for Gandhi was inseparable from action in the world, from the active life in the fields of politics, economics, and social reform. In this respect his spirituality differed radically from the spirituality of the yogis and ascetics of the past and the present. Social and political action informed by true spirituality was able to take the true measure of wealth, power and pleasure. In this sense the spiritual life facilitated the practice of justice and non-violence.

Finally, true spirituality for him was an indispensable means of overcoming the most evil of all hatreds – hatred based on religion. That was why in his spiritual life respect for all religions was counted as one of the eleven virtues. Gandhi's humanism had a very deep spiritual content.

In affirming the intrinsic connection between the spiritual life and the political life, he stands almost alone among the great teachers of India, including the Buddha.⟩

The political

The political too has several meanings in Gandhi. In the first place, being a purushartha, politics belongs to the field of artha. As such it is the pursuit of legitimate self-interest, both individual and collective, attained through the exercise of constitutionally permitted use of force. Politics is both a mode of life and a mode of activity. As a mode of life, it is life lived in the political community, which today, in most cases, is the civic nation. As a mode of activity, it is the striving for power and wealth within the bounds of ethics (dharma) and within the requirements of a healthy spiritual life (the pursuit of moksha). Because politics is a purushartha, it is necessary for full human development. Again, because it is a purushartha, it is by definition, compatible with the other basic ends of life – dharma, kama, and moksha. The practice of sound politics should therefore be mindful of the need to cultivate the relationship between all the purusharthas. Such cultivation should take place in the realm of civil society, however. It therefore forbids the use of the coercive power of the law or other means of coercion to promote spirituality. That is to say, the maintenance of the relationship between the spiritual and the political may not lead to the establishment of a state-religion, persecution, tyranny, or theocracy of any kind. On the contrary, the harmony between the political and the spiritual is possible only in a free society – a civic nation presided over by a secular constitutional state. The spirituality that Gandhi has in mind has nothing to do with sectarianism coming from any quarter. Any spirituality that promotes justice, non-violence, and peace is compatible with Gandhian politics.

Being part of the system of the purusharthas also means that politics may not claim any radical autonomy for itself from other goals of human life.

In a second sense, politics means the free exercise of citizenship in terms of rights and duties. This conception of politics brings Gandhi's politics closer to liberal politics than to any other type of politics. Fortunately Gandhi found an Indian term that admirably suited this aspect of politics: swaraj. Literally, it meant self-rule. Elsewhere I have unpacked this concept and have identified its four modes – political independence of the country from foreign domination or hegemony, the political liberties of citizens, the economic liberty of citizens, and the pursuit of spiritual liberty or self-realization. I have also argued that what is original in Gandhi is the claim that these should be taken as one package – because of their interconnectedness.[3]

Because politics is a purushartha, Gandhi rejects the modern definition of politics *solely* as the struggle for power. Such a conception of politics favors the principle that "the end justifies the means." For him the ethics of the means had to be as legitimate as the ethic of the end itself. The modern conception of politics also posits a radical opposition between the political and the spiritual, as in the case of Machiavellian politics. The latter goes even further and claims that spiritual salvation (in our terminology, moksha) may be sacrificed for the sake of the salvation of the state (artha). It accepts reason of state (*prajana-swarth*),[4] as "the State's first Law of Motion" – to use Friedrich Meinecke's famous phrase.[5] Such views of politics, Gandhi fears, would lead to its corruption. The simile he uses here is that of the snake and its coil: corrupt politics "encircles" citizens like the coil of a snake from which they may not be able to escape. That is why the *telos* of his politics is to wrestle with this snake.[6]

Not surprisingly, Gandhi's concept of the political and the spiritual offers a solution to a problem that has plagued modern politics, at least since Machiavelli – the problem of the relationship between the ethic of responsibility and the ethic of ultimate end.[7] According to modern politics, one cannot choose both; instead one must choose between the two. Gandhi's position, based on the *Bhagavad Gita*, is that both can be chosen. Arjuna manages to choose both. He reconciles the perceived conflicts between his duties as a soldier, as a member of a conflicted royal family, and as a pursuer of spiritual liberation. He is able to reconcile the two ethics by moderating his egoism. Only when the use of violence or the pursuit of wealth and power is for the exclusive interest of the ego does it become incompatible with the spiritual life. Training the ego to become attentive to the needs of the atman (spirit) is the key. Arjuna has to become both a *sthitha-prajna* (a person of stable wisdom) and a *bhakta* (a devotee of God) before he can reconcile the political and the spiritual. The modern citizen is in the position of Arjuna, and is called upon to engage in political pursuits the way he did – through self-discipline and sound piety.

Unfortunately, modern politics sees no need to reconcile the political and the spiritual. Politics as a vocation for the modern politician means

---

[3] See Parel, *Gandhi, Freedom and Self-Rule*, pp. 1–25.   [4] *Hind Swaraj*, p. 87.

[5] F. Meinecke, *Machiavellism: The Doctrine of Raison D'Etat and Its Place in Modern History* (New Haven: Yale University Press, 1957), p. 1.

[6] Gandhi, "Neither a Saint nor a Politician," *Young India*, 2 (12 May 1920), pp. 2–3, at p. 2.

[7] See Max Weber's essay "Politics as a Vocation," in H. H. Gerth and C. Wright Mills (eds.), *From Max Weber: Essays in Sociology* (New York: Oxford University Press, 1946).

the attainment of domination and power over others. This is as true of the liberals as the socialists. The soft liberals, as distinct from the hard ones, may look upon the need for reconciliation between the political and the spiritual as one option among many available to citizens. Even they do not recognize any obligation to bring about the reconciliation between the two. This is the error that Gandhi's liberalism is not prepared to make. It does not say that every citizen should be coerced to lead a spiritual life. To say that would, of course, be inconsistent with the idea of swaraj. What it does say, however, is that there is a moral obligation on every citizen to reconcile the political and the spiritual. This obligation arises from the truth about politics being a part of artha, a purushartha.

Finally, politics for Gandhi sometimes means "protest politics" or "politics of resistance" to injustice, oppression, and tyranny. His satya-graha movement developed protest politics into an art and a science.[8] It was similar to, but also different from, civil disobedience already well known in the West. They were similar in that both presupposed the reserved right of the individual to disobey unjust laws. They were also similar in their acceptance of the state as a positive institution. They also shared the view that even the best available forms of government, being human inventions, were not perfect. They represented, to use John Rawls' words, only "nearly just" societies, not perfectly just ones.[9] Therefore, *ex hypothesi*, there was always room for protests and improvement.

However, Gandhian civil disobedience differed in several respects from Western civil disobedience. First, it was grounded in truth (*satya*) and was part of a broader programme of the reform of civil society. Western civil disobedience did not require any such grounding or the reform of civil society, being just another technique of conflict resolution, serving the political interests of the protesters. Secondly, it was different in its attitude towards violence. It adhered to non-violence in principle, a principle that was flexibly applied. Western civil disobedience approached non-violence out of expediency, being open to the condi-tional use of violence. Thirdly, it required a minimum degree of moral fitness, involving the practice of certain virtues. Western civil disobe-dience did not require virtue as a condition for its practice. Fourthly, it accepted the punishment consequent upon disobedience without com-plaint, whereas Western civil disobedience normally considered punish-ment an undeserved imposition. Finally, Gandhian civil disobedience

---

[8] For a discussion of Gandhi's politics as protest politics, see Hardiman, *Gandhi in His Time and Ours*.
[9] Rawls, *A Theory of Justice*, p. 363.

had to be complemented by the reform of civil society. As he remarked in *Constructive Programme*, civil disobedience without the reform of civil society would be like a paralyzed hand attempting to lift a spoon.[10] Legislation and voluntary reform had to work hand in hand.

Gandhi faces challenges

Gandhi is fortunate to have many positive interpreters in the twenty-first century. The names of Judith Brown, Margaret Chatterjee, Antony Copley, Dennis Dalton, B. R. Nanda, Thomas Pantham, Bhikhu Parekh, Susanne and Lloyd Rudolph, Ronald Terchek, Thomas Weber, and Stanley Wolpert come easily to mind. If one may generalize here, they in their own way see him as bridging the divide between India and the West, tradition and modernity, freedom and coercion, freedom and equality, rights and duties. But he still faces challenges from a number of quarters. Those from separatist Islam and *Hindutva* nationalism have already been dealt with in chapter 2. Those coming from Indian Marxism and Neo-Marxism, Navayana Buddhism, and secular humanism may now be briefly discussed.

Indians who are committed to realizing the vision of Marx have splintered into different groups. There are now orthodox Marxists, disillusioned Marxists, embarrassed Marxists, Marxist politicians at the federal and state levels, Neo-Marxist academics of the Subaltern school, and Maoists (known also as Naxalites) who combine guerilla terrorism with peasant manipulation. They agree on their rejection of the Gandhian paradigm. The purusharthas mean nothing to them. They do not see themselves as even inheriting the mantle of the materialist Lokayata tradition. They do not seem to believe that there can be an independent Indian canon of political thought – which is in keeping with Marx's own belief. The latter believed that Marxism was the new universal canon, replacing all pre-Marxian political canons, whether Indian or Chinese or Islamic or Western. As such Indian Marxists and Neo-Marxists look outside the Indian canon for the means to understand and change India. Because of this they do not have an authentically Indian framework into which they can integrate what they take from Marx and his successors. This lack of rootedness in the Indian ethos explains why they seem more at home with Marx, Mao, or Gramsci than with Gandhi, and why they have more in common with the European Left than with anything

---

[10] CW, 75: 166.

Indian. If Indian Marxism is not exactly "Marxism on stilts," it appears to be able to walk in India only with the help of European crutches.[11]

According to Ranajit Guha, the leader of the Subaltern historians, Gandhi was "the most important" bourgeois politician,[12] but no more than that. What he did was to stifle the revolutionary enthusiasm of the subalterns – peasants and the working class – in the interest of the Indian bourgeoisie. But he did so in his own way – not by the use of force but by the use of self-discipline. Self-discipline here meant crowd control through self-control.[13] Self-control, a spiritual technique, was used to smother the force of violent revolution.

The Indian Maoists, adding insult to injury to Gandhi, still believe in the power of class war to bring about social change. Whether the change it hopes to produce will lead to a better society or a worse one is the question. And because they have no intellectual anchor in India, their revolution does not succeed but only ends up in frustration and disillusionment, when it does not lead to further mindless violence – a predicament described by Sir V. S. Naipaul in his *Magic Seeds*.

Gandhi did not have a theory of history – history as a movement towards a predetermined goal. He did not believe in historical inevitability. But he did have a notion of social change. The motor of change was artha. Artha can be an agent of change for the better when it operates in conjunction with the other three purusharthas; but when it operates in isolation from them, it becomes constricting like the coil of a snake. That is to say, the limited constitutional state can be an agent of change. If it acts in conjunction with organizations of civil society, the change can be timely, non-violent, and beneficial.

Gandhi was committed to social change, but, unlike the Marxists and the Neo-Marxists, he was able to integrate the idea of social change within the framework of an independent Indian canon. If Indian Marxists and Neo-Marxists can follow Gandhi's example here, they will have a chance of integrating what is still viable in Marx within an independent Indian canon. They can then take Marx on Indian terms instead of taking India on Marxist terms.

Navayana Buddhism, also called "engaged" or "political" Buddhism, is a sect founded in India in the mid-twentieth century by B. R. Ambedkar (1891–1956), the celebrated constitutional expert and the chief draftsman of modern India's secular constitution. Its challenge to Gandhi comes

---

[11] For an overview of the Marxist and Neo-Marxist critique of Gandhi, see Thomas Pantham, *Political Theories and Social Reconstruction: A Critical Survey of the Literature in India* (New Delhi: Sage, 1995).

[12] Guha, *Dominance Without Hegemony*, pp. 143–44.   [13] Ibid., pp. 143–51.

from the resentment the Dalits still feel against the stand that he took in 1932 against separate electorates for them. Even today the Dalits tend to regard him as no more than a Hindu leader who wanted to keep them within the Hindu fold. They believe that the ultimate solution to their plight lies in mass conversion to Buddhism. Ambedkar set the example by converting to Navayana Buddhism. As far as Gandhi was concerned, "the Gandhi age" was part of India's dark age.[14]

But the political philosophy of Navayana, in so far as it can be said to have one, is not free of problems. Ambedkar had made the Buddhist *dhamma* its theoretical basis. But *dhamma* is an ethical, not a political, theory. Classical Buddhism saw no positive value in artha, and had rejected it from its philosophy. Navayana, on the other hand, has accepted the politics of modernity as its brand of politics. But the latter is hostile to religion, even Buddhism. How or whether *dhamma* can co-exist with modernity is anybody's guess. How can one practice the politics of modernity (which is hostile to all religions) and live by the ethics of Buddhism, especially since the latter sees no positive value in artha?

Gandhi solved the problem of the relationship of artha, dharma, and moksha thanks to his theory of the purusharthas. Artha has positive value and is compatible with the pursuit of moksha. If Navayana can find a way of integrating satisfactorily the anti-religious modernity with itself, it can have a political philosophy that can do justice to both politics and religion. And if it chooses to do that, it will find in Gandhi a sympathetic model. As for the past resentment felt against his stand on the separate electorates, it is a stand that the Dalits themselves have now endorsed in practice. Dalits are in power in certain states and they do not need separate electorates to stay in power. Perhaps *karuna* (compassion) can help them to go beyond the stage of resentment and see in Gandhi a friend rather than a foe.

The challenge from secular humanism is of a still different sort. For it is both philosophic and cultural in nature. It wants to oust God and the soul from modern politics, philosophy, and culture, and to locate values solely in the human will and desires. Several intellectual currents contributed to this development. The notion that only truth established by the method of natural sciences counted as truth, even in the spiritual life, was one of them. As Ernest Renan had argued, all truth henceforth had to be scientific. The suprasensory could not be verified. Therefore, it did not exist.[15] Marxism dismissed religion "as the sigh of the oppressed creature, the feeling of a heartless world, the soul of soulless circumstances ... the

---

[14] Gail Omvedt, *Buddhism in India Challenging Brahmanism and Caste* (New Delhi: Sage, 2003), p. 253.
[15] Chadwick, *The Secularization of the European Mind*, p. 217.

opium of the people."[16] Darwinism, atheistically interpreted, put paid to the transcendental basis of religious beliefs and ethics. Freud debunked religion as a "universal neurosis," and religious ideas as "illusions, fulfillment of the oldest, strongest, and most urgent wishes of mankind," and God as nothing more than "an exalted father figure."[17] As Isaiah Berlin has noted, and noted with approval, secular humanism brought about a twofold displacement. The displacement of God by "the conception of the rational life," and the displacement of the soul seeking union with Him, by the individual who wanted to be guided by reason, and reason alone.[18] As Nietzsche declared God dead in the consciousness of a section of the Western elite, secularism attempted to resurrect "Man as the measure of all things."[19] And, if Pankaj Mishra is to be believed, the secularism of the modern West had its counterpart in the ancient East as well. For, "Like Nietzsche, the Buddha too had attempted to reaffirm the natural dignity of human beings without recourse to the ambitious scheme of metaphysics, theology, reason, or political idealism."[20] And as Berlin argued, negative liberty alone would be compatible with the secular life, positive liberty being liable to promote all sorts of dangerous things ranging from paternalism to despotism.[21]

Gandhi was sympathetic to the plight of the secular humanist as he had a deep understanding of the nature of its philosophic and cultural roots. He had addressed this issue to some extent in *Hind Swaraj*; but nowhere did he address it more directly and honestly than he did in his lecture to a European, largely skeptical, audience in Lausanne, in 1931. "What is Truth?" he was asked, and why did he hold that "Truth is God?"[22]

He was sympathetic, he said, to the problem that "God language," used in ordinary religious discourse and liturgy, had created for the rationalists. Reason pursuing scientific knowledge – knowledge of physical universe confined to time and space – was "a limited thing," as it had to labor under the limitations of time and space. Truth that lay outside time and space was thought to be "beyond the power of man to grasp."[23] He would have agreed with Frederick Copleston that the human "conceptual web" was ill equipped to catch the Absolute.[24] At the same time, reason in the sense of *buddhi*, being the closest human faculty to atman,

---

[16] D. McLellan (ed.), *Karl Marx: Selected Writings* (Oxford: Oxford University Press, 1987), p. 64.
[17] Cited in P. Ricœur, *Freud and Philosophy*, pp. 232, 252, 539.
[18] I. Berlin, *Four Essays on Liberty* (Oxford: Oxford University Press, 1969), p. 138.
[19] Plato, *Theaetetus*, 160d.   [20] Mishra, *An End to Suffering*, p. 378; also pp. 111–52.
[21] Berlin, *Four Essays on Liberty*, p. 144.   [22] CW, 48: 403–9.   [23] Ibid., p. 405.
[24] F. Copleston, *Religion and the One: Philosophies of East and West*, (London: Continuum, 1982), p. 3.

had a natural affinity for *satya* (truth). The capacity of *buddhi* was not limited to just scientific truth. It was capable of experiencing religious truths that lay outside time and space.

Besides, there was the conscience and its "voice" within. The latter was not a subjective trap, for its prompting was open to empirical experiments. The eleven virtues of his moral philosophy provided the laboratories for such experiments. That was why he called his life, "experiments with truth." He discovered as a result of his experiments that the major obstacle to the discovery of religious truth was, apart from scientific rationalism, the ego, and the notion that Man was the measure of all things. Unless the role of the ego was reduced to zero, there was no chance of discovering religious truths of any real value. It was the relentless search for truth through his experiments that led him to the conclusion that "Truth is God." What he was telling his largely skeptical audience was that religious truth from the Indian point of view had the status of truth.

Secular humanism poses yet another challenge to him. It is the assertion that positive values are not all compatible with one another or entailed one another.[25] Berlin had asserted that "the ends of men [were] many, and not all of them [were] in principle compatible with each other."[26] They were not "commensurable" and were "in perpetual rivalry with one another:" to say that it was otherwise, was to throw a "metaphysical blanket" over self-deception or hypocrisy.[27] The desire for an objective basis for harmony between ultimate values, in Berlin's view, was a residue left behind by childhood craving or primitive mentality.[28]

This is tantamount to admitting that secular humanism lacks a principle of harmony that can reconcile in theory if not in practice diverse human strivings. In attributing the desire for harmony to childhood fantasy, Berlin comes close to Freud's position. He may not be far off from Marx's position either, when he claims that human goals are "in perpetual rivalry" with one another. Though pessimism is not the rule of secular humanism, there is, underneath, a strong current of it, resembling fatalism, a point conceded by Nietzsche.

The solution that Berlin proposes with approval is to realize "the relative validity of one's convictions" and to stand for them "unflinchingly."[29] But why unflinchingly? What is the difference between those who hold absolute values unflinchingly and those who hold relative values unflinchingly? The relativity or the absoluteness of values, in this instance, does not seem to affect the degree of unflinchingness. What if

---

[25] Berlin, *Four Essays on Liberty*, p. 167.   [26] Ibid., p. 169.   [27] Ibid., p. 171.
[28] Ibid., p. 172.   [29] Ibid.

the two parties discover that their differences can be resolved only by fight to the death? Where, then, is the advantage of holding on to the relative validity of one's convictions?

What is implicit in Berlin's position is that secular humanist value system lacks an internal arbiter. This is because it has its basis in individual wills and desires, between which an impartial mediator is not given, reason being but the servant of the passions.

This is where Gandhi's concept of values grounded in truth becomes significant. Conflicts between values, of course, exist and Gandhi readily admits this. Satyagraha would not make sense if conflicts did not exist. Indeed the recognition of their factual existence is its starting point. But in his philosophy conflicts have a common reference point in truth. This provides his philosophy with a basis for optimism. The purusha is open to truth, and each purushartha contains within itself a capacity for ultimate harmony with truth. Life is a quest for truth, which in turn is a quest for harmony. He is able to claim this precisely because his truth is not entirely time-bound, i.e., it is not entirely secular. Whereas secular truth has no access to what lies outside time, his has. A passage from E. M. Forster illuminates the point aptly. "He [Gandhi] is likely to be the greatest of our century. Lenin is sometimes bracketed with him, but Lenin's kingdom was of this world, and we do not know yet what the world will do with it. Gandhi's was not. Though he impinged upon events and influenced politics, he had his roots outside time, and drew strength thence."[30]

Forster had it right. The Gandhian paradigm was concerned with not only the temporal but also the eternal. Because of this, no one could be content with the possession of truth at any moment in time; truth had always to be pursued as long as one lived. The emphasis had to be on the quest for truth, rather than on its possession in time. As long as one lived, movement was more important than any sense of having arrived.

A final question arises: is the Gandhian paradigm still relevant, given India's emergence as a major political and economic power in the world? The answer is plain: it is more relevant now than ever before. For it teaches Indians how to pursue artha without sacrificing the pursuit of moksha. Indeed if they do not follow this paradigm they may well lose their identity as a polity and as a civilization. If they follow it, however, they can not only develop properly, but also give encouragement to those who are also seeking political and economic power. For the Gandhian paradigm teaches everyone, not just Indians, how to seek wealth and power without sacrificing ethics, beauty, and transcendence.

---

[30] Forster, "Mahatma Gandhi," p. 315.

Bibliography

Ahmed, Akbar S., *Jinnah, Pakistan and Islamic Identity: The Search for Saladin*, London: Routledge, 1997.

Alberuni, Abu Rihan Muhammad, see Sachau, E. C.

Allen, C., *The Buddha and the Sahibs: The Men who Discovered India's Lost Religion*, London: John Murray, 2003.

Alter, J. S., *Gandhi's Body: Sex, Diet and the Politics of Nationalism*, Philadelphia: University of Pennsylvania Press, 2000.

Ambedkar, B. R., *What the Congress and Gandhi Have Done to the Untouchables*, 2nd edn, Bombay: Thackar, 1946.

"A Vindication of Caste by 'Mahatma' Gandhi," in *Dr. Ambedkar Birth Centenary Souvenir*, London: Ambedkar Centenary Celebration Committee, vol. III 1991, 52–6.

The Buddha and His Dhamma: Dr. Babasahib Ambedkar, Writings and Speeches, vol. XI, Bombay: Education Department, Government of Maharashtra, 1992.

Arnold, D., *Gandhi*, London: Longman, 2001.

Aurobindo, Sri, *On Himself: Compiled from Notes and Letters*, Pondicherry: Sri Aurobindo Ashram, 1989.

Austin, G., *The Indian Constitution: Cornerstone of a Nation*, Delhi: Oxford University Press, 1966.

Azad, M. A. K., *India Wins Freedom: An Autobiographical Narrative*, New Delhi: Orient Longman, 1959.

Barker, E., "Gandhi, as Bridge and Reconciler," in S. Radhakrishnan (ed.), *Mahatma Gandhi: Essays and Reflections on His Life and Work*, Bombay: Jaico, 1995, 39–42.

Basham, A. L., *The Wonder That Was India*, London: Sidgwick and Jackson, 1956.

Bayly, S., *Caste, Society and Politics in India from the Eighteenth Century to the Modern Age*, The New Cambridge History of India, IV. 3, Cambridge: Cambridge University Press, 1999.

Belloc, H., *Europe and the Faith*, London: Constable, 1920.

Berlin, I., *Four Essays on Liberty*, Oxford: Oxford University Press, 1969.

Bhargava, R. (ed.), *Secularism and Its Critics*, Delhi: Oxford University Press, 1998.

Blount, G., *A New Crusade: An Appeal*, London: The Simple Life Press, 1903.

Bondurant, J., *Conquest of Violence: The Gandhian Philosophy of Conflict*, rev. edn, Berkeley: University of California Press, 1967.

Borman, W., *Gandhi and Non-Violence*, Albany: State University of New York Press, 1986.

Bose, N. K., *Selections from Gandhi*, Ahmedabad: Navajivan, 1957.

My Days With Gandhi, New Delhi: Orient Longman, 1987.

Brown, J. M., *Gandhi: Prisoner of Hope*, New Haven: Yale University Press, 1989.

and M. Prozesky (eds.), *Gandhi and South Africa: Principles and Politics*, Pietermaritzburg: University of Natal Press, 1996.

Buber, M. and J. L. Magnes, "Two Letters to Gandhi," *The Bond, Pamphlets of the Group "The Bond"*, Jerusalem: Rubin Mass, 1939.

Chadwick, O., *The Secularization of the European Mind in the 19th Century*, Cambridge: Cambridge University Press, 1993.

Chagla, M. C., *Roses in December: An Autobiography*, Bombay: Bharatiya Vidya Bhavan, 1990.

Chapple, C., *The Concept of Will (Paurusa) in Yogavasishta*, Ph.D. thesis, Fordham University, 1980.

Chatterjee, M., *Gandhi's Religious Thought*, London: Macmillan, 1983.

Gandhi and His Jewish Friends, London: Macmillan, 1992.

Hinterlands and Horizons: Excursions in Search of Amity, Lanham, MD: Lexington Books, 2002.

Chatterjee, P., *Nationalist Thought and the Colonial World: A Derivative Discourse?*, London: Zed Books, 1986.

Conrad, D., "Gandhi as Mahatma: Political Semantics in an Age of Cultural Ambiguity," in V. Dalmia, A. Malinar, and M. Christof (eds.), *Charisma and Canon: Essays in the Religious History of the Indian Subcontinent*, New Delhi: Oxford University Press, 2001.

Constituent Assembly Debates, Official Report, vol. I, 2nd reprint, New Delhi: Lok Sabha Secretariat, 1989.

Coomaraswamy, A. K., *Essays in National Idealism*, Campden, 1909.

Copleston, F., *Religion and the One: Philosophies of East and West*, London: Continuum, 1982.

Copley, A., *Gandhi: Against the Tide*, Delhi: Oxford University Press, 1997.

Religions in Conflict: Ideology, Cultural Contact and Conversion in Late Colonial India, Delhi: Oxford University Press, 1997.

(ed.), *Hinduism in Public and Private: Reform, Hindutva, Gender and Sampraday*, Delhi: Oxford University Press, 2003.

and G. Paxton, *Gandhi and the Contemporary World*, Chennai: Indo-British Historical Society, 1997.

Coward, H. (ed.), *Indian Critiques of Gandhi*, Albany: State University of New York Press, 2003.

Dallmayr, F., *Border Crossings: Toward a Comparative Political Theory*, Lanham, MD: Lexington Books, 1999.

and G. N. Devy (eds.), *Between Tradition and Modernity: India's Search for Identity*, New Delhi: Sage, 1998.

Dalton, D., *Mahatma Gandhi: Non-violent Power in Action*, New York: Columbia University Press, 1993.

Das, A., *Foundations of Gandhian Economics*, New Delhi: Allied Publishers, 1979.

Das, V., "Kama in the Scheme of *Purusharthas*: The Story of Rama," in Madan, T. N. (ed.), *Way of Life: King, Householder, Renouncer*, Delhi: Vikas, 1982, 183–203.

Dasgupta, S. N., *A History of Indian Philosophy*, vol. II, Delhi: Motilal Banarsidass, 1988.

Dear, J., S. J. (ed.), *Mohandas Gandhi: Essential Writings*, Maryknoll, NY: Orbis Books, 2002.

De Bary, W. T. (ed.), *Sources of Indian Tradition*, New York: Columbia University Press, 1958.

Derrett, J. D. M., "Social and Political Thought and Institutions," in A. L. Basham, (ed.), *A Cultural History of India*, Delhi: Oxford University Press, 1998, 124–40.

Desai, M., *Day-to-Day with Gandhi: Secretary's Diary*, vol. I, Varanasi: Sarva Seva Sangh Prakashan, 1968.

(ed.), *Anasakti Yoga*, Ahmedabad: Navajivan, 1930.

Dhupelia-Mestrie, U., *Gandhi's Prisoner?: The Life of Gandhi's Son Manilal*, Delhi: Permanent Black, 2005.

Diwakar, R. R., *Mahayogi: Life, Sadhana and Teachings of Aurobindo*, Bombay: Bharatiya Vidya Bhavan, 1954.

Diwan, R. and M. Lutz (eds.), *Essays on Gandhian Economics*, New Delhi: Gandhi Peace Foundation, 1985.

Doke, J. J., *M. K. Gandhi: An Indian Patriot in South Africa*, Varanasi: Sarva Seva Sangh Prakashan, 1959.

Doniger, W., *Asceticism and Eroticism in the Mythology of Siva*, London: Oxford University Press, 1973.

and S. Kakar (trans.), *Vatsyayana Kamasutra*, Oxford: Oxford University Press, 2002.

and B. K. Smith (trans.), *The Laws of Manu*, London: Penguin, 1991.

Douglas, I. H., *Abul Kalam Azad: An Intellectual and Religious Biography*, edited by Gail Minault and C. W. Troll, Delhi: Oxford University Press, 1988.

Dumont, L., *Homo Hierarchicus: The Caste System and Its Implications*, translated by M. Sansbury, L. Dumont, and B. Gulati, rev. edn, Chicago: University of Chicago Press, 1980.

Dupuis, J., S. J., *Toward a Christian Theology of Religious Pluralism*, Maryknoll, NY: Orbis Books, 1997.

Edgerton, F. (trans.), *The Bhagavad Gita*, Cambridge, MA: Harvard University Press, 1972.

Eliade, M., "Purusharthas," *Encyclopedia of Religion*, 16 vols., New York: Macmillan, 1987.

Emerson, R., *From Empire to Nation*, Cambridge, MA: Harvard University Press, 1960.

Engineer, A. A., *The Islamic State*, 2nd edn, New Delhi: Vikas, 1994.

Erikson, E. H., *Gandhi's Truth: On the Origins of Militant Nonviolence*, New York: W. W. Norton, 1969.

Flood, G., "The Meaning and Context of the *Purusharthas*," in J. Lipner (ed.), *The Fruit of Our Desiring: An Enquiry into the Ethics of the Bhagavad Gita for Our Times*, Calgary: Bayeux Arts, 1997, 11–28.

Forster, E. M., "Mahatma Gandhi," in S. Radhakrishnan (ed.), *Mahatma Gandhi: Essays and Reflections on His Life and Work*, Bombay: Jaico, 1995, 313–15.

Fort, A., and P. Mumme (eds.), *Living Liberation in Hindu Thought*, Albany: State University of New York Press, 1996.

Freud, S., *An Outline of Psycho-Analysis*, translated and edited by James Strachey, New York: W. W. Norton, 1969.

Galtung, J., *The Way is the Goal: Gandhi Today*, Ahmedabad: Gujarat Vidyapith Peace Research Centre, 1992.

Gandhi, M. K., *The Collected Works of Mahatma Gandhi*, 100 vols., New Delhi: Publications Division, Ministry of Information and Broadcasting, Government of India, 1958–1994.

Satyagraha in South Africa, Ahmedabad: Navajivan, 1972 [1928].

Anasakti Yoga, Ahmedabad: Navajivan, 1975.

Gandhi, R., *Understanding the Muslim Mind*, Delhi: Penguin, 1986.

The Good Boatman, Delhi: Viking, 1995.

Gilbert, M., *Winston S. Churchill*, vol. V, London: Heinmann, 1976.

Gilson, E. (ed.), *René Descartes: Discours de la méthode*, Paris: Vrin, 1976.

Gerth, H. H., and Mills, C. W. (eds.), *From Max Weber: Essays in Sociology*, New York: Oxford University Press, 1946.

Golwalkar, M. S., *We or Our Nationhood Defined*, 4th edn, Nagpur: Bharat Prakashan, 1947.

Bunch of Thoughts, 2nd edn, Bangalore: Jagarna Prakashan, 1980.

Gopal, S., *Jawaharlal Nehru: A Biography*, vol. I, *1889–1947*, Delhi: Oxford University Press, 1975.

Radhakrishnan: A Biography, Delhi: Oxford University Press, 1989.

Graham, M. G., *Mr. Gandhi the Man*, London: George Allen and Unwin, 1931.

Green, M., *Gandhi: The Voice of New Age Revolution*, New York: Continuum, 1993.

Griffiths, B., *The Cosmic Revelation: The Hindu Way to God*, London: Collins, 1983.

Gruzalski, B., *On Gandhi*, Belmont, CA: Wadsworth, 2001.

Guha, R., *Dominance Without Hegemony: History and Power in Colonial India*, Cambridge, MA: Harvard University Press, 1997.

Haksar, V., *Rights, Communities and Disobedience: Liberalism and Gandhi*, Delhi: Oxford University Press, 2001.

Hardiman, D., *Gandhi in His Time and Ours: The Global Legacy of His Ideas*, Pietermaritzburg: University of Natal Press, 2003.

Hasan, M., *Legacy of a Divided Nation: India's Muslims Since Independence*, London: Hurst and Company, 1977.

Hayes, C. J. H., *The Historical Evolution of Modern Nationalism*, New York: Macmillan, 1951.

Heehs, P., "Shades of Orientalism: Paradoxes and Problems in Indian Historiography," *History and Theory*, 42 (2003), 169–95.

" 'The Centre of the Religious Life in the World': Spiritual Universalism and Cultural Nationalism in the Work of Sri Aurobindo," in A. Copley (ed.), *Hinduism in Public and Private: Reform, Hindutva, Gender, and Sampraday*, Delhi: Oxford University Press, 2003.

Herrenschmidt, O., "Ambedkar and the Hindu Social Order," in S. Jondhale and J. Betz (eds.), *Restructuring the World: B. R. Ambedkar and Buddhism in India*, Delhi: Oxford University Press, 2004.

Hume, R. E. (trans.), *The Thirteen Principal Upanishads*, 2nd rev. edn, Madras: Oxford University Press, 1954.

Hunt, James, D., *Gandhi and the Nonconformists: Encounters in South Africa*, New Delhi: Promila, 1986.

Ignatieff, M., *Blood and Belonging: Journeys into the New Nationalism*, Toronto: Penguin, 1993.

Ingalls, D. H. H., "Dharma and Moksha," *Philosophy East and West*, 7 (1957), 41–8.

Iyer, R., *The Moral and Political Thought of Mahatma Gandhi*, Santa Barbara, CA: Concorde Grove Press, 1983.
    The Moral and Political Writings of Mahatma Gandhi, 3 vols., Oxford: Oxford University Press, 1986–87.

Jaffrelot, C., *The Hindu Nationalist Movement and Indian Politics 1925 to the 1990s*, New Delhi: Viking, 1993.
    Dr. Ambedkar and Untouchability: Fighting the Indian Caste System, New York: Columbia University Press, 2005.

Jalal, Ayesha, *The Sole Spokesman: Jinnah, the Muslim League and the Demand for Pakistan*, Cambridge: Cambridge University Press, 1985.
    Self and Sovereignty: Individual and Community in South Asian Islam since 1850, London: Routledge, 2000.

James, William, *The Varieties of Religious Experience: A Study of Human Nature*, London: Fontana, 1960.

Johnson, R. L., "Of Modern-Day *Karmayogis* and *Bodhisattvas*: Gandhi's Spiritual Politics and Engaged Buddhism," *Gandhi Marg*, 23 (2001), 29–45.

Jordens, J. T. F., *Gandhi's Religion: A Homespun Shawl*, London: Macmillan, 1998.

Juergensmeyer, M., *Gandhi's Way: A Handbook of Conflict Resolution*, Berkeley: University of California Press, 1984.

Kakar, S., *Intimate Relations*, Chicago: University of Chicago Press, 1989.
    Mira and the Mahatma, Delhi: Viking, 2004.

Kane, P. V., *History of Dharmasastra: Ancient and Medieval Religious and Civil Law in India*, 5 vols., Poona: Bhandarkar Oriental Research Institute, 1968–77.

Kangle, R. P. (trans.), *The Kautiliya Arthasastra*, 2nd edn, Delhi: Motilal Banarsidass, 1997.

Kapur, S., *Raising Up a Prophet: The African-American Encounter with Gandhi*, Boston: Beacon Press, 1992.

Khilnani, S., *The Idea of India*, London: Hamish Hamilton, 1997.

Kishwar, M., "Gandhi on Women," *Economic and Political Weekly*, 20 (1985), 1691–1702, 1753–58.

Klostermaier, K., "Moksha and Critical Theory," *Philosophy East and West*, 35 (1985), 61–72.
    A Survey of Hinduism, 2nd edn, Albany: State University of New York Press, 1994.

Koelman, G., *Patanjala Yoga*, Poona: Athaneum, 1970.

Kohn, H. (ed.), *The Idea of Nationalism: A Study of Its Origins and Background*, New York: Van Nostrand, 1955.

Nationalism: Its Meaning and History, New York: Van Nostrand, 1955.

Krishna D., *Indian Philosophy: A Counter Perspective*, Delhi: Oxford University Press, 1991.

Kumar, R. (ed.), *Essays on Gandhian Politics*, Oxford: Clarendon Press, 1971.

Lal, V., "Nakedness, Nonviolence, and *Brahmacharya*: Gandhi's Experiments in Celibate Sexuality," *Journal of the History of Sexuality*, 9 (2000), 119–27.

Lanza del Vasto, J. J., *Return to the Sources*, New York: Schocken Books, 1972.

Gandhi to Vinoba: The New Pilgrimage, New York: Schocken Books, 1974.

Make Straight the Way of the Lord, New York: Knopf, 1974.

Principles and Precepts of the Return to the Obvious, New York: Schocken Books, 1974.

Warriors of Peace: Writings on the Techniques of Non-violence, New York: Knopf, 1974.

Lingat, R., *The Classical Law of India*, translated by J. D. M. Derrett, Berkeley: University of California Press, 1973.

Lipner, J., *Hindus: Their Religious Beliefs and Practices*, London: Routledge, 1994.

Brahmabandhab Upadhyay: The Life and Thought of a Revolutionary, Delhi: Oxford University Press, 1999.

(ed.), *The Fruits of Our Desiring, An Enquiry into the Ethics of The Bhagavad Gita for Our Times*, Calgary: Bayeux Arts Inc., 1997.

Livy Titus, *The Early History of Rome*, bks. I–IV, translated by Aubery de Selincourt, London: Penguin, 1976.

Ludden, D. (ed.), *Making India Hindu: Religion, Community, and the Politics of Democracy in India*, Delhi: Oxford University Press, 1996.

Macpherson, C. B., *The Political Theory of Possessive Individualism: Hobbes to Locke*, Oxford: Clarendon Press, 1962.

Madan, T. N. (ed.), *Way of Life: King, Householder, Renouncer*, Delhi: Vikas, 1982.

Modern Myth, Locked Minds: Secularism and Fundamentalism in India, Delhi: Oxford University Press, 1997.

Maritain, J., *Man and the State*, Chicago: University of Chicago Press, 1951.

Mathai, M. P., M. S. John, and S. K. Joseph (eds.), *Meditations on Gandhi: A Ravidra Varma Festschrift*, New Delhi: Concept Publishing, 2002.

Mattilal, B. K. (ed.), *Moral Dilemmas in the Mahabharata*, Delhi: Motilal Banarsidass, 1989.

Maude, Aylmer, *The Life of Tolstoy: The Later Years*, London: Oxford University Press, 1910.

Maududi, S. A. A., *Political Theory of Islam*, edited and translated by Khurshid Ahmad, Lahore: Islamic Publications, 1960.

Jihad in Islam, Damascus: The Holy Koran Publishing House, 1977.

Mazzini, G., *The Duties of Man*, London: J. M. Dent, 1907.

McLellan, D. (ed.), *Karl Marx: Selected Writings*, Oxford: Oxford University Press, 1987.

Meinecke, F., *Machiavellism: The Doctrine of Raison D'Etat and Its Place in Modern History*, New Haven: Yale University Press, 1957.

Meissner, W. W., *Ignatius of Loyola: The Psychology of a Saint*, New Haven: Yale University Press, 1992.

Minor, R. M., *Bhagavad-Gita: An Exegetical Commentary*, New Delhi: Heritage Publishers, 1982.

(ed.), *Modern Indian Interpreters of the Bhagavad-Gita*, Albany: State University of New York Press, 1986.

Mishra, P., *An End to Suffering: The Buddha in the World*, London: Picador, 2004.

Mitter, P., *Art and Nationalism in Colonial India 1850–1922: Occidental Orientations*, Cambridge: Cambridge University Press, 1994.

Mirza, H., *From Plassey to Pakistan*, rev. edn, Lanham, MD: University Press of America, 2002.

Monier-Williams, Sir M., *A Sanskrit-English Dictionary*, Oxford: Oxford University Press, 1899.

Muggeridge, M., "Nationalism and Christianity," *Young India*, 8 (1926), 258–59.

Munshi, K. M., *Indian Constitutional Documents*, Bombay: Bharatiya Vidya Bhavan, 1967.

Nadvi, A. H. A., *Islam and the World*, 7th English edn, Lucknow: Academy of Islamic Research Publication, 1982.

Nanda, B. R., *Mahatma Gandhi: A Biography*, Delhi: Oxford University Press, 1958.

Gokhale: The Indian Moderates and the British Raj, Princeton: Princeton University Press, 1977.

Gandhi and His Critics, Delhi: Oxford University Press, 1993.

(ed.), *Mahatma Gandhi: 125 Years*, New Delhi: Indian Council of Cultural Relations, 1995.

Nandy, A., *At the Edge of Psychology: Essays in Politics and Culture*, Delhi: Oxford University Press, 1990.

The Illegitimacy of Nationalism: Rabindranath Tagore and the Politics of Self, Delhi: Oxford University Press, 1996.

Nasr, S. V. R., *The Vanguard of Islamic Revolution: The Jamaat-e-Islami of Pakistan*, Berkeley: University of California Press, 1994.

Mawdudi and the Making of Islamic Revivalism, New York: Oxford University Press, 1996.

Nehru, J., *The Discovery of India*, London: Meridian Books, 1956.

An Autobiography, new edn, London: The Bodley Head, 1958.

Olivelle, P., *The Asrama System: The History and Hermeneutics of a Religious Institution*, New York: Oxford University Press, 1993.

(trans.), *The Pancatantra: The Book of Indian Folk Wisdom*, Oxford: Oxford University Press, 1997.

Omvedt, G., *Buddhism in India: Challenging Brahmanism and Caste*, Delhi: Sage, 2003.

Orwell, G., "Reflections on Gandhi," *Partisan Review*, 16 (1949), 85–92.

Paniskar, V. L. S. (ed.), *The Yogavasishta of Valimiki*, Delhi: Motilal Banarsidass, 1984.

Pantham, T., *Political Theories and Social Reconstruction: A Critical Survey of the Literature in India*, New Delhi: Sage, 1995.

Paranjape, M., *Decolonization and Development: Hind Swaraj Revisioned*, New Delhi: Sage, 1993.

Parekh, B., *Gandhi's Political Philosophy*, Notre Dame, IN: Notre Dame University Press, 1989.

Gandhi, Oxford University Press, 1997.

Colonialism, Tradition and Reform: An Analysis of Gandhi's Political Discourse, rev. edn, New Delhi: Sage, 1999.

Rethinking Multiculturalism: Cultural Diversity and Political Theory, London: Macmillan, 2000.

Parel, A. J., *The Machiavellian Cosmos*, New Haven: Yale University Press, 1992.

"Gandhi as a Man of Prayer," *ReVision: A Journal of Consciousness and Transformation*, 24 (2001), 39–44.

"Gandhi on the Dynamics of Civilizations," *Human Rights Review*, 4 (2003), 11–27.

"Gandhi, War and Peace," *Gandhi Marg*, 26 (2004), 5–19.

(ed.), *Gandhi: Hind Swaraj and Other Writings*, Cambridge: Cambridge University Press, 1997.

(ed.), *Gandhi: Freedom and Self-Rule*, Lanham, MD: Lexington Books, 2000.

and R. C. Keith (eds.), *Comparative Political Philosophy: Studies Under the Upas Tree*, 2nd edn, Lanham, MD: Lexington Books, 2003.

Patel, C. N., *Mahatma Gandhi and His Gujarati Writings*, New Delhi: Sahitya Akademi, 1981.

Patnaik, T., "*Purusharthas* in Aesthetics," *Indian Philosophical Quarterly*, 22 (1995), 55–67.

Paz, O., *In Light of India*, translated by Eliot Weinberger, New York: A Harvest Book, 1997.

Pelican, J. (ed.), *The Rig Veda: Sacred Writings, Hinduism*, translated by R. T. H. Griffith, New York: Book-of-the-Month Club, 1992.

Philips, C. H. (ed.), *The Evolution of India and Pakistan 1858–1947*, London: Oxford University Press, 1962.

Potter, K. (ed.), *Encyclopedia of Indian Philosophy: Advaita up to Sankara and His Pupils*, Princeton: Princeton University Press, 1981.

Prabhu, R. K., and R. Kelkar (eds.), *Truth Called Them Differently: Tagore-Gandhi Controversy*, Ahmedabad: Navajivan, 1961.

Prasad, N. (ed.), *Hind Swaraj: A Fresh Look*, New Delhi: Gandhi Peace Foundation, 1985.

Puri, B. (ed.), *Mahatma Gandhi and His Contemporaries*, Shimla: Indian Institute of Advanced Studies, 2001.

Radhakrishnan, S., *Religion and Society*, 2nd edn, London: Allen and Unwin, 1956.

(trans.) *The Bhagavad Gita*, 2nd edn, London: George Allen and Unwin, 1976.

(ed.), *Mahatma Gandhi: Essays and Reflections on His Life and Work*, Bombay: Jaico, 1995.

Ramanujan, A. K., "Is There an Indian Way of Thinking? in M. Marriott (ed.), *India Through Hindu Categories*, New Delhi: Sage, 1990, 41–59.

Rawls, J., *A Theory of Justice*, Cambridge, MA: Harvard University Press, 1973.

Ricœur, P., *Freud and Philosophy: An Essay on Interpretation*, translated by Dennis Savage, New Haven: Yale University Press, 1970.

Robinson, F., *Islam and Muslim History in South Asia*, New Delhi: Oxford University Press, 2000.

Rolland, R., *The Life of Vivekananda and the Universal Gospel*, translated by E. F. Malcolm Smith, Almora, India: Advita Ashram, 1965.

Romain Rolland and Gandhi Correspondence, Delhi: Government of India Publications Division, 1976.

Roy-Chowdhury, S., *The Gurudev and the Mahatma*, Calcutta: Shubhada Saraswat, 1982.

Rudolph, S. H., and L. I. Rudolph, *Gandhi: The Traditional Roots of Charisma*, University of Chicago Press, 1983.

Ruskin, J., *"A Joy for Ever": And Its Place in the Market*, London: George Allen, 1900.

Unto This Last and Other Writings, edited by C. Wilmer, London: Penguin, 1985.

Sachau, E. C. (ed.), *Alberuni's India: An Account of the Religion, Philosophy, Literature, Geography, Chronology, Astronomy, Customs, Laws and Astrology of India about A.D. 1030*, 2 vols. in one, Delhi: S. Chand and Co., 1964.

Sankaran Nair, C., *Gandhi and Anarchy*, Delhi: Mittal Publications, 1995.

Savarkar, V. D., *Hindutva: Who Is a Hindu?*, 6th edn, New Delhi: Bharti Sahitya Sadan, 1989.

Schumacher, E. F., *A Guide for the Perplexed*, London: Abacus, 1978.

Small Is Beautiful: A Study of Economics as if People Mattered, London: Abacus, 1978.

Seeley, J. R., *The Expansion of England*, London: Macmillan, 1883.

Sen, A. K., "Tagore and His India," *The New York Review of Books*, 44 (1997), 55–63.

Development as Freedom, New York: Knopf, 1999.

Shah, K. J., "*Purushartha* and Gandhi," in R. Roy (ed.), *Gandhi and the Present Global Crisis*, Shimla: Indian Institute of Advanced Study, 1996, 155–61.

"Of *Artha* and the *Arthsastra*," in A. J. Parel and R. C. Keith (eds.), *Comparative Political Philosophy*, 2nd edn, Lanham, MD: Lexington Books, 2003, 140–62.

Sharma, A., *The Purusharthas: A Study in Hindu Axiology*, East Lansing, MI: Asian Studies Center, Michigan State University, 1982.

Sharp, G., *Gandhi as a Political Strategist*, Boston: Porter Sargent, 1979.

Singh, G. B., *Gandhi: Behind the Mask of Divinity*, Amherst, NY: Prometheus Books, 2004.

Slade, M., *The Spirit's Pilgrimage*, New York: Coward-McCann, 1960.

Sooryamoorthy, R. and K. D. Gangrade, *NGOs in India*, Westport, CT: Greenwood Press, 2001.

Strauss, L., *Natural Rights and History*, Chicago: University of Chicago Press, 1971.

"Comments on Carl Schmitt's *Der Begriff des Politischen*," in G. Schwab (ed. and trans.), *Carl Schmitt: The Concept of the Political*, New Brunswick, NJ: Rutgers University Press, 1976, 81–105.

Sundara Rajan, R., "The *Purusharthas* in the Light of Critical Theory," *Indian Philosophical Quarterly*, 7 (1979–80), 339–50.

"Approaches to the Theory of the *Purusharthas*: Husserl, Heidegger and Ricœur," *Journal of the Indian Council of Philosophical Research*, 6 (1988–89), 129–47.

Tagore, R., *Nationalism*, Delhi: Rupa and Co., 1994.

Tarlo, E., *Clothing Matters: Dress and Identity in India*, University of Chicago Press, 1996.

Taylor, Charles, "What is Wrong with Negative Liberty," in A. Ryan (ed.), *The Idea of Freedom: Essays in Honor of Isaiah Berlin*, Oxford University Press, 1979, 175–95.

Terchek, R., *Gandhi: Struggling for Autonomy*, Lanham, MD: Rowman and Littlefield, 1998.

Thomson, M., *Gandhi and His Ashrams*, Bombay: Popular Prakashan, 1993.

Tolstoy, L., *What is Art? and Essays on Art*, translated by Aylmer Maude, London: Oxford University Press, 1929.

The Kingdom of God and Peace Essays, translated by Aylmer Maude, London: Oxford University Press, 1935.

"Letter to a Hindu," in B. S. Murthy (ed.), *Mahatma Gandhi and Leo Tolstoy Letters*, Long Beach, CA: Long Beach Publications, 1987; 40–61.

Van Buitenen, J., "Dharma and Moksha," *Philosophy East and West*, 7 (1957), 33–40.

van der Veer, P., *Religious Nationalism: Hindus and Muslims in India*, Delhi: Oxford University Press, 1996.

Imperial Encounters: Religion and Modernity in India and Britain, Princeton: Princeton University Press, 2001.

Watson, F., *The Trial of Mr. Gandhi*, London: Macmillan, 1969.

Weber, M., "Politics as a Vocation," in H. H. Gerth and C. Wright Mills (eds.), *From Max Weber: Essays in Sociology*, New York: Oxford University Press, 1946.

Weber, T., *Gandhi as Disciple and Mentor*, Cambridge: Cambridge University Press, 2004.

Weil, S., *The Need for Roots: Prelude to a Declaration of Duties Towards Mankind*, London: Routledge, 1997.

Wolpert, S., *Tilak and Gokhale*, Berkeley: University of California Press, 1962.

Jinnah of Pakistan, New York: Oxford University Press, 1984.

Nehru: A Tryst With Destiny, New York: Oxford University Press, 1996.

Gandhi's Passion: The Life and Legacy of Mahatma Gandhi, New York: Oxford University Press, 2001.

Woodroffe, J., *Shakti and Shakta: Essays and Addresses*, 7th edn, Madras: Ganesh, 1969.

Zaehner, R. C., *At Sundry Times: An Essay in the Comparison of Religions*, London: Faber and Faber, 1958.

Mysticism Sacred and Profane: An Inquiry into Some Varieties of Praeternatural Experience, New York: Galaxy Books, 1961.

Hinduism, Oxford: Oxford University Press, 1966.

(trans.), *The Bhagavad-Gita*, Oxford: Oxford University Press, 1973.

Zimmer, H., *Philosophies of India*, New York: Meridian Books, 1961.

Glossary

acharyas	philosopher-saints
adharma	irreligion, immorality
ahimsa	non-violence
aparigraha	freedom from possessiveness; one of the eleven Gandhian virtues
artha	wealth, power (economics and politics), one of the four purusharthas
ashrama	one of the four stages of life according to traditional Hinduism
astea	non-stealing, one of the eleven Gandhian virtues
atma-darshan	self-realization
atman	the immortal spirit, the spiritual foundation of human personality
bhagya	destiny, fate
bhakta	a devotee of God
bhakti	devotion to God, one of the three ways of attaining moksha
bhikhu	a Buddhist mendicant
brahmachari	a celibate
brahmacharya	celibacy
Brahman	the ultimate principle of reality
brahmin	the highest of the four castes
buddhi	intelligence and will
charkha	the spinning wheel, made famous by Gandhi
chit	consciousness
Dalit(s)	the "oppressed," a member of a low caste
dharma	duty, religion, ethics, one of the four purusharthas
himsa	violence
Hindutva	Hinduness, the ideology of contemporary extremist Hindu nationalism
Ishwar	God, as distinct from the impersonal Brahman

jivanmukta	one who has attained moksha but who still lives in time
kaivalyam	aloneness, the final state of those who have attained moksha
kama	pleasure, sexual desire, one of the four purusharthas
karma yoga	the path of action; one of the three ways of attaining moksha
khadi	homespun cloth, made famous by Gandhi
kshatria	the second highest of the four castes
lokasamgraha	the welfare of the world, mentioned in the *Gita*
moksha	spiritual liberation from samsara, one of the four purusharthas
praja	nation, according to *Hind Swaraj*
prarthana	prayer
purna swaraj	full national independence
purusha	the immortal spirit, the spiritual foundation of the human person
purushartha(s)	human effort; a goal or aim of life; the four aims of life
Ramarajya	the reign of Rama, the ideal state, the golden age
sadhana	spiritual exercises directed towards attaining moksha
sadharana dharma	universally valid dharma
sadhu	a holy man
sakshatkar	direct vision or experience of Brahman or God
samsara	the temporal cycle of birth, death, and rebirth
sanatana dharma	eternal religion, orthodox religion
sannyasa	the fourth stage of life, life of renunciation
sannyasi	one who is at the stage of sannyasa
sarvodaya	the welfare of all; Gandhi's economic philosophy
sat	Ultimate Reality
satya	truth
satyagraha	firm adherence to truth; Gandhian civil disobedience
satyagrahi	one who practices satyagraha
Shastra	scientific treatise; sacred text
shastri	an expert in shastra
shudra (sudra)	the lowest of the four castes
sramana	an ascetic, a renouncer, an ancient ascetic movement
sramanic	that which pertains to the life of a sramana
sthitha-prajna	a person of stable wisdom, described in the *Gita*
su-rajya	the good state
svadharma	one's own dharma, traditionally based on one's caste

swadeshi	economic self-reliance; one of the eleven Gandhian virtues
swaraj	self-rule, national independence
swarajya	one's own country
vaisya	the third highest of the four castes
varna	"caste" according to traditional Hindu sociology
varnashrama	ethics based on varna and ashrama
vasana	latent psychological residue active in the psyche
vikar	the passions that disturb the soul
virya	semen
vishay	poison; a metaphor for sexual desire
yagna	sacrifice

Index